Understanding Mass Higher Education

In recent decades most developed nations have experienced a shift from elite to mass higher education, with the United States leading the way. This book compares the experience of this very important social change within different nation states. Whilst recognising the critical global economic forces that appear to explain the international nature of the change, it sees the issues as rooted within different national traditions.

There is a particular focus upon the discourse of access, especially the political discourse. The book addresses questions such as:

- How has expansion been explained?
- Has expansion been generated by state intervention or by a combination of economic and social forces?
- What are the forms of political intervention?
- What points of agreement and conflict are generated within the wider society by expanding access?

Leading academics explore the ways in which different systems of higher education have accommodated mass access, constructing comparative pictures and comparative interpretations and lessons in an accessible and informative style. This book should be critical reading for students in education, sociology and politics, as well as policy-makers and academics.

Ted Tapper is Emeritus Professor of Politics at the University of Sussex, Brighton, and a Fellow of the Oxford Centre for Higher Education Policy Studies. **David Palfreyman** is Bursar at New College, Oxford, and Director of the Oxford Centre for Higher Education Policy Studies (oxcheps.new.ox.ac.uk).

Understanding Mass Higher Education

Comparative perspectives on access

Edited by Ted Tapper and David Palfreyman

RoutledgeFalmer
Taylor & Francis Group

LONDON AND NEW YORK

Woburn Education Series

First published 2005 by
RoutledgeFalmer
2 Park Square, Milton Park, Abingdon, Oxon OX14 4RN

Simultaneously published in the USA and Canada
by RoutledgeFalmer
270 Madison Ave, New York, NY 10016

RoutledgeFalmer is an imprint of the Taylor & Francis Group

Typeset in Times by Wearset Ltd, Boldon, Tyne and Wear
Printed and bound in Great Britain by MPG Books Ltd, Bodmin

British Library Cataloguing in Publication Data
A catalogue record for this book is available from the British Library

Library of Congress Cataloging in Publication Data
A catalog record for this book has been requested

ISBN 0-415-35491-9

Contents

Preface

The genesis of this book lay in the interest of the editors in watching the debate unfold in the past five years or so within the UK over expanding access to, and widening participation in, higher education; what, indeed, we may term a row over 'the politics of access'. The debate, whilst usually framed in the language of social equity, institutional autonomy and educational standards, occasionally degenerates into cheap political jibes founded in the tendency of the British to take any opportunity to fight yet another battle in their centuries-old class war. The current conflict passed through a critical stage as the Higher Education Bill 2004 wound it way through parliament, a process which furnishes us with some of the quotations set out below from the ensuing endless stream of articles in the press and from the Bill's lengthy second reading session in the Commons.

The essence of the cause for concern is whether higher education, as a quasi-public good substantially financed by the state through general taxation, is being disproportionately consumed by the children of the middle classes. In particular, do the more privileged socio-economic groups dominate access to the prestigious universities, and more especially Oxford and Cambridge. To what extent do the children from less privileged social backgrounds become undergraduates at 'elite' universities, or in fact even participate in higher education? Seemingly, the answer to the first part of the question is 'Hardly at all', and to the second, 'Not nearly to the extent of children from better off families'. Has the picture changed over the decades as higher education in the UK 'massified' (belatedly by US and European norms)? Apparently there has been some improvement, but the doubling of the size of the UK system of higher education since the mid-1980s has meant that going to university has become almost universal for middle-class children, while still leaving the age participation index (API) of the lowest two of the five socio-economic groups (essentially those from working-class families) significantly trailing even if it has more than doubled over the past twenty years.

Was this issue, we wondered, of social equity in access to higher education also alive, and if so as lively debated, in other countries? We were aware that for many decades access had been a political issue in the USA in terms of the opportunity for racial and ethnic minorities to go to college and of the resultant affirmative action policies pursued by many universities, and litigated over at the highest level of the US court hierarchy. But did the Americans worry whether poor whites went to the local public university or even community college, let alone to the private, high-tuition-fee Ivy League universities? Do the French, we asked, keep access data, as do the British, by way of recording parental occupations and analysing the postcode of the family homes of the incoming student cohorts so as to determine their socio-economic backgrounds? Do the French know, or care, about the class origins of students at the Sorbonne or at the Grandes Ecoles as opposed to those at the provincial universities? Are equity issues even on the Italian policy agenda given the scale of the problems generated by the rapid, but underfunded, access to higher education in Italy?

Is a German senior government minister likely to enter the access debate, assuming it is even an issue on the political radar as to who goes to which university, as did Chancellor of the Exchequer Gordon Brown in publicly challenging Oxford's decision not to offer an undergraduate place to study medicine to Ms Laura Spence? She was an academically talented schoolgirl with top A-level grades, but allegedly burdened with the twin disadvantage of coming from the unfashionable north of England and also attending a state school (as opposed to an independent, private school) – and even worse it was a school of the type that, in another political context, a senior government adviser called 'a bog standard comprehensive school' (a local high school in contrast to those few remaining state schools that select their pupils according to academic ability at age 11). The protestations of Oxford that almost all its applicants possess such top A-level grades and that, inevitably, some have to be rejected was not an easy message to communicate in the midst of a media furore. And the fact that Ms Spence subsequently accepted a scholarship to study instead at Harvard simply added fuel to the fire.

Is any other country, we mused, about to create a regulatory authority (as proposed in the Higher Education Bill 2004) charged with ensuring that universities unable to comply with their social equity access targets should have their public funding reduced? This new regulator, the 'Office for Fair Access', is symbolic of the access discourse in the UK, but, as far as we knew, unknown elsewhere. Perhaps in other countries with well-established mass systems of higher education, we thought, access is seen to have long since been adequately addressed by a fairly open and easy entry route. But do such countries then concern themselves, as the British do, with recording and analysing non-completion/retention (once known as 'drop out') rates and asking whether students from poorer family backgrounds are more likely to leave or be failed before graduating? Or has the focus been on a broader set of questions? Who pays for expanded access? And, what is its impact upon the meaning and experience of higher education?

So, it was this range of questions that we had in mind as we sought to put together a team of colleagues each willing to write an essay on the politics of access to higher education in his or her country. We have tried to achieve a reasonable spread of other nations besides the UK, and also allow for the very different historical experiences of the accessibility debate even within the UK (hence two separate chapters, first on England, and then essentially on Scotland and Wales). Space constraints, however, mean that not even all major OECD nations have been covered, and the limits of 'networking' for two UK-based editors also means that, regrettably, the coverage is narrower than ideally we would have wished. However, our case studies represent important examples of interacting traditions of higher education: notably the American, the British and the continental European, and with a recognition of the importance of national variations within those traditions.

We remain, of course, deeply grateful to those colleagues who have been willing to contribute a chapter; we have not, as editors, wielded a heavy editorial red pen and hence the chapter styles do vary, but they in their interestingly different ways address the themes set and any shortfall overall in the book's attempt at a comparative approach to the politics of access to HE is the responsibility of the editors. We also want to thank Kate Hunter and Andy Tapper for their varied inputs into the completion of the manuscript. We hope that this volume will be the first of a comparative series on various aspects of mass higher education covering funding, teaching, research, academic freedom, governance, and the current meaning of higher education.

Finally, we now present a range of quotes from the recent UK debate on the politics of access which illustrates the depth of feeling that, in the UK at least, this issue engenders. Those readers who are not British may well wish to begin by asking themselves whether they can recall any similar expressions of such vehemence in relation to their own national system. And, if not, to ask further why this is so. Is there no need for such heated discussion in that the system is widely accepted as socially fair? Or are those social groups disproportionately benefiting from any shortfall in the social equity of access able to block its emergence as a political issue? Or, do those social groups not gaining equity of access really not see it as a significant political issue? Or, are they simply too weak politically to make it one, and/or lack powerful supportive allies who could put it on the political agenda?

> The student fees argument has become a bundle of nonsense wrapped in humbug enveloped in class prejudice.
>
> Simon Jenkins, *The Times*, 28 January 2004

> [T]he massive, vicious class differential in our higher education system has remained consistent ... the appalling obscenity of the deep class difference that affects people who go to our universities ... That is what the Office for Fair Access is about.
>
> The Secretary of State for Education and Skills, *Hansard*, 27 January 2004

I passionately believe that the 'marketisation' of higher education is wrong – for me it is a matter of not only economics and funding but social justice and social cohesion.

Nicholas Brown, *Hansard*, 27 January 2004

Mention of debt aversion really irritates me. It is old fashioned, patronizing and condescending: the assumption seems to be, 'Working class people don't really know how to handle money. That's why they've got so little.' They know how to handle money all right. And they know a bargain when they see one. Higher education is a bargain.

Jim Dowd, *Hansard*, 27 January 2004

[T]he Bill ... creates a new regulatory structure which removes, for the first time, the freedom of universities to decide which students to admit ... The Bill gives Ministers the power to decide who goes to which university and to take money away from a university that does not do what it is told ... It brings all universities under tighter political control than ever before.

Tim Yeo, *Hansard*, 27 January 2004

[T]the director of fair access is not to be an independent person, but must follow the guidance issued by the Secretary of State ... He will be a creature of Ministers.

Michael Fallon, *Hansard*, 27 January 2004

This extraordinary control-freakery in pursuit of a social, rather than an academic agenda has never been seen in this country before.

Gillian Shephard, *Hansard*, 27 January 2004

The social class gap among those entering university remains too wide ... [and] cannot be tolerated in a civilized society ... [it] is inherently socially unjust ... [that] young people from professional [family] backgrounds are over five times more likely to enter higher education than those from unskilled backgrounds.

The 2003 Higher Education White Paper

If all the above quotations are highly political, a more measured assessment can be found elsewhere, noting especially Halsey's comment which takes us beyond the parochialism of UK HE and into the comparative dimensions of this book:

The problem of under-representation [of lower socio-economic groups in HE is] a reasonable cause for public concern ... [and such students also cluster] in lower status courses at lower status institutions.

Report 6 of 'The Dearing Report', 1997

[T]two broad messages are plain. First, although the number of students has tripled during the past three decades, there has been only a limited shift in the composition of the student body. British higher education has become a mass system because participation rates among the spreading middle class are now 'universal' (in Trow's terminology) while among the working class access to higher education has remained an 'elite' experience ... Second, working class students are heavily concentrated in less prestigious institutions. The student mix in elite universities has changed remarkably little since the 'golden time' of the 1960s.

Peter Scott in *The State of UK Higher Education*,
edited by Warner and Palfreyman, 2001

[UK HE is] disproportionately consumed by people from better off backgrounds ... [for whom the substantial] taxpayer subsidies are regressive: the taxes of truck-drivers pay for the degrees of old Etonians.

Nicholas Barr, *The Welfare State as Piggy Bank*, 2001

An important cross-national hypothesis which awaits rigorous test – that [HE] expansion in the post-war period has been accommodated by a pattern of institutional development ... such that the most prestigious universities (the Harvards and Stanfords in the USA, the Grandes Ecoles in France, the ex-Imperial universities in Japan) have actually narrowed their recruitment on to the upper echelons of the professional, managerial, and bourgeois classes.

A.H. Halsey, *Decline of Donnish Dominion*, 1992

The perspectives, partisan and reflective, manifested in the above quotes form the core concerns of this book: access by whom, to what and with what purposes and outcomes? And, increasingly coming into focus, at whose expense?

Contributors

Per Olaf Aamodt is currently a Special Adviser at the Norwegian Institute for Studies in Research and Higher Education (NIFU) in Oslo. By training he is a sociologist and has conducted research on a broad range of topics in higher education but focusing particularly on questions of access, learning environments and student retention rates. He is currently working on an evaluation of the recent reforms in Norwegian higher education designed to enhance its quality with a specific focus on how changes in the structure of degree programmes and modes of teaching and assessment have affected learning outcomes and student retention rates.

Cécile Deer researches at the Department of Economics, Oxford University where she is a Research Fellow of SKOPE (Research Centre on Skills, Knowledge and Organisational Performance). Her main research interest is in comparative education policy. Her publications include *Higher Education in England and France since the 1980s* (Symposium, 2002) which complements a range of articles on issues relating to higher education that have been written from a multi-disciplinary perspective. She is particularly interested in the European dimension in educational policy which she pursues both through her research and writing as well as her membership of the Board of the Paris-based European Institute for the Promotion of Innovation and Culture in Education.

John Douglass is a Senior Research Fellow at the Center for Studies in Higher Education at the University of California-Berkeley. He is currently Director of the University of California's History Digital Archives Project and co-directs a longitudinal on-line survey on the academic experience and engagement of undergraduates. His book *The California Idea and American Higher Education* analyses how California developed its pioneering higher education system whilst his forthcoming *The Social Contract of Universities* discusses the historical purpose of public universities in the United States with particular reference to issues of access. His future research, will comparatively explore issues in science policy, the role of universities in regional and national economic development, and the globalisation of higher education.

Chris Duke is a part-time Professor at the Royal Melbourne Institute of Technology and holds an honorary Chair at the University of Leicester. He has worked across the full spectrum of universities in Australia, New Zealand and the United Kingdom including serving as Pro-Vice-Chancellor at the University of Warwick and President of the University of Western Sydney Nepean. Therefore, by good fortune his interest in higher education policy and its implementation has allowed him to live in his laboratory throughout his working life. He considers universities to be a vital estate of the realm and within this context he is especially interested in how institutions of higher education relate to their societies and regions to achieve common purposes.

Frans Kaiser is a Senior Research Associate of the University of Twente's Centre for Higher Education Policy Studies. He is Co-Ordinator of the ongoing project International Higher Education Monitor in which trends and issues in eleven higher education systems are monitored. A major focus of his research is the use of higher education indicators in the formation of national policy. This interest is coupled with the quest to unravel the complex knot of factors that have created the perceived shortage of engineers.

Svein Kyvik is a Senior Researcher at the Norwegian Institute for Studies in Research and Higher Education (NIFU) in Olso. By training he is a sociologist and political scientist and has undertaken research in both the sociology of science and higher education policy. His current research interests fall into two fields: change and continuity over the past twenty-five years in the roles of academic researchers in Norwegian universities, and analysing the processes of change over the past forty years in the non-university sector of higher education in Norway.

Simonetta Michelotti is a Researcher in the Department of Historical, Political, Juridical and Social Sciences of Italy's University of Siena. She has a longstanding interest in various European higher education initiatives. In 1989 she was involved in the ERAMUS Programme and is currently co-ordinating research, within the context of a transnational Leonardo project, on the European Union's policy on education and training. She has developed a particular interest in the emergence of the 'new' University in Italy, relating it to the wider developments in European higher education. She has published, taught post-graduate courses, acted as a consultant and been a member of various research projects in the fields of quality control, planning and accreditation in higher education.

Clare McManus-Czubińska has been a Lecturer in the Department of Central and East European Studies at the University of Glasgow since

1999. Her doctoral dissertation analysed the reform of the Polish higher education system since the collapse of communism. Her expertise also incorporates relationships between state and society in Poland as well as Polish relations with the EU. She has published extensively on these topics. She was also the overall co-ordinator of the ESRC project 'Poland's Third Transition: Beyond 2001'. She is the Reviews Editor, and a member of the Editorial Board, of *Europe-Asia Studies* and for the past three years has been Secretary for the Committee of the Study Group on Education in Russia, the Independent States and Eastern Europe (SGERISEE).

Hanna Ostermann is a Senior Lecturer at Northumbria University where she teaches German language and area studies concentrating on the economic, and more particularly, the business environment of Germany. Her research interests focus on the challenges facing higher education in Germany today as well as the pattern of economic development in Germany, with special reference to the *Standort*-debate – Germany's attractiveness as a location for investment. Naturally, the main intellectual focus of her research is how the economic developments interact with those in higher education.

David Palfreyman is Bursar and Fellow of New College, Oxford having previously worked at the Universities of Liverpool and Warwick. He is (Joint) Director of the Warwick/Oxford Higher Education Management Programme and of the Universities UK Management Development Course for Higher Education Administrators. Besides being a member of the Editorial Board of the AUA's journal *Perspectives* he is Joint Editor of the journal, *Education and Law*. He has written numerous articles, as well as editing several books, on a wide range of issues in higher education management. With David Warner, he established the Oxford Centre for Higher Education Policy Studies (http://oxcheps.ox.ac.uk/), which pursues a range wide of activities designed to assist our understanding of contemporary developments in higher education internationally.

Gareth Parry is Professor of Education at the University of Sheffield. He began his academic career in further education and prior to his current appointment he held positions at the Warwick, City and Surrey Universities as well as the Institute of Education, University of London. He is a Fellow of the Society for Research in Higher Education and Co-editor of the Higher Education Quarterly. He was a consultant to the National Inquiry into Higher Education in the United Kingdom (the Dearing Committee, 1996–97). His current research is focused on the policy history of both higher and post-secondary education in the United Kingdom.

Ted Tapper is Emeritus Professor of Politics of the University of Sussex's International Relations and Politics Department and Visiting Fellow at the Oxford Centre for Higher Education Policy Studies. Most of his research on higher education has been concerned with issues of governance with a particular focus on the changing relationship between the state and the universities in the British context. His current research continues in this vein and focuses upon the decline of institutional autonomy, the fragmentation of the state's attempts to control the university system, and the increasing influence of the market accompanied by greater diversification and stratification within British higher education.

Hans Vossensteyn is a Senior Research Associate of the University of Twente's Centre for Higher Education Policy Studies. He has worked on a wide-array of topics including: globalisation pressures in higher education, the creation and use of performance indicators, and comparative quantitative and qualitative analyses of international tends. But his major research interest is in the economics of higher education incorporating the development of national allocation models, patterns of student financial support, and the impact of pricing upon access to higher education.

1 The rise of mass higher education

Ted Tapper and David Palfreyman

This introductory chapter underlines the universality of the rise of mass higher education in the second half of the twentieth century as a shift from an elite system and as a significant element of wider social change in advanced capitalist economies with liberal democratic political systems. And, moreover, as one generally recognised as a positive social development. Concentrating on mass higher education as the growth in undergraduate student numbers, the USA led the way with the GI Bill and the expansion in the late 1940s. But is social equity in access still in the early twenty-first century an important part of the political agenda in all such countries? If so, why? If not, why in some countries and not in others? If higher education is an increasingly desirable social good, and possession of a degree is seen as an ever-more important credential in the job market, one might expect that, within a liberal democratic context, individuals will attempt to utilise their political rights to enhance their chances of accessing the best of what is on offer. Hence, access to higher education would almost inevitably, sooner or later, become a public policy issue to which political parties will need to respond.

Moreover, access to higher education, or at least to the better parts of the system, may also be a function of the deployment of non-political resources by students and their families: most notably personal wealth in purchasing appropriate schooling which is more likely to lead on to places at elite universities or in meeting the higher tuition fees levied by private universities as an alternative to public institutions. To what extent, across a range of countries, is it possible to gain access to their 'top universities' by employing personal economic resources in this way? Furthermore, just how viable is it to use such purchasing power to create alternative private institutions of credible and worthwhile status, to develop new models for the delivery of higher education if the public sector near-monopoly is seen as failing to meet the needs of a significant section of society? Or is such purchasing power used simply to escape Galbraithian 'public squalor' by seeking 'private affluence' abroad?

Thus, the decision-making about the provision of higher education and its expansion to meet demands for wider access has historically been a complex process, in which a combination of personal preferences, economic pressures and political variables is interwoven. This combination of forces will differ in its exact mix from country to country, and indeed will differ over time within the same country. Nor is it merely a matter of access to a quantity of provision. There is also the issue of the quality: is quality in the student educational experience achieved, sustained and enhanced better by political intervention and regulation, by the application of student/ family spending power through the payment of higher tuition fees, or by some combination of external accountability, if not actual state control of universities, and the creation of the empowered student-consumer?

While there may be global economic forces which explain the international nature of the rise of mass higher education, this broad contextual analysis needs to be rooted within different national traditions; for example, the French perspective on access as a citizenship right, the British preoccupation with educational opportunity and individual social mobility, and the American emphasis on diversity and choice. The political discourse on access to higher education will vary in its intensity and complexity from country to country depending on these national traditions and the relative balance of agreement or conflict that they engender. In the context of an aging population in most Western democracies, and hence increased pressure on the taxpayer to fund pensions and health/social care for the elderly – not to mention the general reluctance to see tax rates rise – higher education is caught in the weak position of not having political priority against spending on health, schools, policing, transport and defence, and especially so in times of fiscal constraint. The issue then becomes the means of funding a mass system of higher education, and particularly any growth in it to further widen access, by balancing the relative contributions of the state/taxpayer seeking a social return on public expenditure and of the student/family achieving a private rate of return from gaining a degree.

How then do different nations finance expansion and increased social diversity within higher education? What balance do they strike between the public share of the cost met from general taxation and that borne by the student as tuition fees? In fact, there may be a third contributor to the cost of achieving expansion and diversity, in that the universities themselves might have to meet at least part of the burden of expanded student numbers without proportional extra resources (as in the UK where the number of students has doubled since *c*.1985 while the annual government funding per student has almost halved!).

Are we seeing divergence or convergence in terms of this balance of funding? If the USA is broadly a mixed-economy, public–private model for the delivery of a national system, and continental Europe a virtual state monopoly with higher education as a public service, is the UK drifting towards one rather than the other, towards Americanisation (marketisation) or towards Europeanisation (as indeed in theory it should be as a member of the EU and given Europe's trajectory towards a degree of harmonisation by 2010 begun with the Bologna Declaration)? Or might the USA come under political pressure to move away from a free market model as its private universities and colleges repeatedly increase tuition fees well above consumer price inflation and even salary inflation? And might at least parts of Europe be tempted to shift some of the financial burden from the hard-pressed taxpayer to the student/family by introducing tuition fees, just as, amidst much political acrimony, the current British government will triple tuition fees at English universities from 2006? If, thereby, the English model is drifting across the Atlantic, might the USA anyway be moving towards it as American universities demonstrate greater accountability as they attempt to justify large fee increases? Moreover, might the UK also be towing in its wake the European HE model (Palfreyman, 2004)?

In this book we have space to explore the HE model of only the following nations against the issues and the pressures for change outlined above: England, and, to complete the UK, the Celtic fringe of Scotland, Wales and Northern Ireland; France; Germany; Italy; Poland; the Netherlands; Nordic countries; Australia; and the USA. The authors of the chapters have been asked to think in terms of common themes, while not being required to fit their chapter to a mould. The prompts to their thinking that they were given by the editors are set out below:

- What were the pressures that led to the transition from elite to mass in HE provision? Clearly definitional complexity can make comparison of student numbers across different HE systems somewhat haphazard but the general expansionist trend is there for all to see.
- To what extent was the expansion encouraged by purposeful political action? In particular, has the shift to a mass system been seen politically as leading to desirable social benefits (for example, an enhancement of social justice) and as constituting a national economic necessity (the need to enhance the nation's competitive edge in the global economy)? Alternatively, is expansion an issue that has failed to penetrate the political agenda and hence has not been a topic for national debate? In our case studies the shift to a mass system seems to have happened without widespread political discussion, but contemporarily how to pay for the new model is on the political agendas of most nations.
- What are the central themes that have justified expansion? Have such themes been consistent over time? In short, what has been the discourse of expansion?
- Has expansion generated scepticism? For example, are doubts emerging: whether mass HE can really achieve desired social and economic goals; whether it generates an undue emphasis on 'vocationalism' and 'credentialism' at the expense of the liberal arts; that it leads to higher

drop-out rates; and whether quality can be sustained within a mass system ('more means worse' and mass leads to 'dumbing down')? In short, access to what and for how long?

- How has expansion been funded? If there has been a political consensus over the relative share of the financial burden between the taxpayer and the student/family, is that consensus now being challenged? Is there any feeling that there has been 'expansion on the cheap' leading to an unacceptable decline in quality?
- Has expansion involved the delivery of higher education through new kinds of institutions (perhaps, say, private business schools), through new models of delivery (for example, the US two-year Associate Degree, matched in the UK by recent talk of Foundation degrees taken over two years in colleges of further/higher education and in continental Europe of the emerging $3+2$ BA/MA programmes), or through the disproportional growth of one particular kind of HE institution (concentrating US expansion in the community colleges or in the vocational higher education institutions of continental Europe)?
- Has expansion involved the sacrifice of institutional autonomy and a shift towards greater accountability and bureaucratic intervention (or even outright regulation) as public funding has increased and the political drive for social equity has intensified?
- To what degree has expansion been completed, or are there unincorporated groups? If so, is this seen as a political problem and what strategies have been considered or devised to ensure their inclusion?
- Does 'massification' change the purpose of a university beyond the roles of transmission of knowledge (teaching) and the expansion of knowledge (research)? Are other missions for HE institutions coming to the fore, such as 'regionalisation', intellectual property exploitation and links with industry?

In the chapters that follow each of our contributors will explore expansion along many of the lines suggested above. In the concluding chapter we will bring together the major trends and reconsider the degree to which national systems are peculiarly a product of their own historical circumstances. Or are we witnessing the emergence of transnational pressures that will lead to the dominance of one model for the delivery of higher education? Consequently, will we see the globalisation of higher education, with any clinging to national distinctiveness risking marginalisation and increasing irrelevance? Most critically, how will individual nation states balance the input of public and private resources in the funding of access? If the commitment to open access at the expense of the state is to be retained, does the political will exist to ensure a level of public funding that sustains the overall quality of the system of higher education? Alternatively, if private funding is to increase, how can the access of the gifted but economically deprived, especially to prestigious institutions, be ensured? Finally, whether funded basically by private or public means, does a mass system of higher education inevitably lead to institutional differentiation and hierarchy? And, in that context, will there be sufficient institutional links to sustain the idea of higher education as a system?

Reference

Palfreyman, D., *The Economics of Higher Education* (Oxford: Oxford Centre for Higher Education Policy Studies, 2004).

2 Values, discourse and politics

An Australian comparative perspective

Chris Duke

The question of what a university stands for – what central values it ought to embody – is seldom addressed directly and in depth, although it is really the most fundamental question in this crisis. It is gestured at in mission statements, strategic plans and other attempts to mimic the corporate world, but few can find the time or inclination to address the challenge.

(Fraser, 2000)

Introduction

The language of policy-makers, politicians and bureaucrats moves through evolving codes.[1] Writing about adult education, including the access of young and older aspirants to higher education, varies between the technical and apolitical through the sociologically informed to the committed, heuristic, politically alert and frankly polemical. Access to mass higher education is infused with equity values. The extent varies to which these values have informed and continue to inform the drive to widen access, as the once elite higher education system becomes universal.[2] Australia and New Zealand share a belief in equity and opportunity, values expressed colloquially as *mateship* and *a fair go*.

The political contexts of these two countries differ from each other and one from the other over time. Australia's federal political system differs more from the UK system than does that of unitary New Zealand. Current political alignments are, however, closer between Helen Clark and Tony Blair than with John Howard; yet currently all Australian states have Labour administrations, some of distinctly New Labour complexion. The Australian states cannot be directly compared with either the emergent 'four-nations' tendency in Britain, or the attempted regionalism within England. Yet there is value in comparing and contrasting what takes place in these different modes of decentralisation, old and new. New Zealand has recoiled from extreme test-to-destruction free market neo-liberalism to a more steered and planned system, its new Tertiary Education Commission set up in 2003 superficially resembling in some respects the UK Higher Education Funding Councils. Australia's 'Crossroads Inquiry' (in the name of the federal Minister for Education, Brendan Nelson) followed the UK review of higher education leading to the January 2003 White Paper on *The future of higher education* (Department for Education and Skills, 2003).

Picking its way through parallels, analogies and contrasts, this chapter teases out trends, forces and assumptions behind access to higher education in Australia. It speculates about the deeper historical and cultural forces which facilitate or inhibit developments, and the way that Access with a capital A – widening participation, pathways, stair-casing – advanced in different political climates.

Australia became a federal nation in 1901. Today it comprises six states, the Australian Capital Territory and the Northern Territory. The quarter century since the reforming Whitlam Administration of the early 1970s provides the time-frame, corresponding with a widely recognised shift in mood globally, and subsequent bipartisan adoption of economic rationalism Down Under.

Australian mass higher education

Higher education became a national rather than a state responsibility under Whitlam. Other tertiary education, known as TAFE – technical and further education – remained a states matter. Federal partnership funding for TAFE was politically fraught at the end of 2000 when the federal administration failed to spend $220 million allocated to TAFE and handed it back to the treasury. In practice the 'clever country' suffers from divided administrative responsibilities across all tertiary including higher education, while a federal small government ideology holds down public expenditure. There is near paralysis between refusal to increase public expenditure on higher education for a 'knowledge society' and sensitivity about driving more private funds into the sector. But these are relatively short-term and trivial factors to explain the condition of Australian higher education. We need also to dig into national history and character formation.

'A nation rich and rare'[3]

The idea of a university is a creature of time and place. It is in no valid sense a disembodied abstraction (see Barnett's discussion of essentialism for a contrasting view; Barnett, 2000). The university migrated from England and Scotland to these fatal shores, as Blake described them, cursed with Blainey's 'tyranny of distance' yet enfolding Donald Horne's ironic 'lucky country', later for Craig McGregor the 'poor little rich country'. Australia has long sought, with less than total success, to forget about 'Mother Country' and the 'old country'. Paul Keating has called, also unsuccessfully, for it to become 'the clever country'.

The western university is deeply rooted in different histories of nation-hood (compare this perspective with Readings, 1996). Australia and its universities owe much to British models and traditions, but look also, especially from the eastern coastal cities, to the USA. Aspects of the British higher education system are still embedded in the evolving Australian system, which blends the British and the American. But Australia has also struggled for over a quarter century, from the time of the 1972–75 Whitlam Administration, to come to terms with and be part of Asia as a good regional partner and citizen. It is also a Pacific nation seeking to lead Oceania but finding the backyard Pacific pond no longer peaceful.

Facing in these four directions, Australia finds its identity other than as a sporting nation troubling and potentially divisive. The former Labour Prime Minister, Paul Keating, who sought to make Australia the clever country and looked to Singapore and elsewhere in neighbouring Asia, castigates subsequent political leadership for failure of direction and purpose. The role and predicament of the university in Australia is comprehensible in the context of this dilemma.

A *land of short poppies*

'Mateship' or 'fair go' equity is a culture of the practical, pragmatic and unpretentious. A celebration of ordinariness can be emancipatory and democratic in recognising the wit and talent of 'ordinary people'. Every ignorant phone-in listener's opinion is as good as any other – and probably better than any expert's or academic's. Invigorating egalitarianism can be hostile to ideas, levelling, opposed to taking oneself seriously to the point of being actively anti-intellectual.

The tension between the Australian City and the countryside, now called the Bush, reflects this as well. The Bush is mythical home of the Australian dream of the self-reliant pioneer, a suburban block in a sprawling metropolis (known as Gloria Soame in satirical celebration of the Australian accent) the dominant reality. It is also the scourge of the political parties, the home of One Nation and a national divide that cuts across the historical accident of state boundaries. The City is home to over 90 per cent of Australians. It is caricatured with hostility – the 'chattering classes', the 'cappuchino and chardonnay set'. In with this negative stereotype goes the academic, the intellectual and, perhaps, the dream of the 'clever country' and hope for a knowledge society.

Australia was a set of states and a convict settlement (bureaucracy, soldiers and police) before becoming a set of (white) societies divided by distance. Even today bureaucratic authoritarianism runs wide and deep, manifesting itself in motor registries and road signs, government regulation of public and some private behaviour in and beyond the workplace. By comparison Britain feels libertarian and France borders on the anarchic. For all the celebration of larrikin humour, ingenuity and mateship,

Australia is a regulated, self-distrusting society. It does not take easily to intellectually founded creativity and innovation. The cultural cringe towards attainment abroad, officially dead, lives on in self-doubt, shallow aggressiveness in being Australian and a dislike of tall poppies. Universities have been slow to grow roots and gain confidence, as expressions of such a society.

Today Australian universities are uncertain about their identity and destiny, buffeted by political and economic forces and by rapidly changing demographic demands. Many are riven internally, unsure of their academic standing and resentful that resources are scarce, even less equipped to hold to a strong sense of purpose than the also stressed systems in the Northern Hemisphere.

Market forces have enjoyed a loose but not unfettered rein over the past generation. At one level of consciousness Australia sees the need to become a knowledge society, as work for the national Innovation Summit showed: an 'innovative economy' scenario contrasted with a 'business-as-usual' scenario, for example (Department of Industry, Science and Resources, 1999). Lack of positive and supportive purpose for universities has limited their systematic involvement in the nation's 'core business', denying affirmation of identity in this or any other firm sense.

Comparison with New Zealand is interesting. That country followed a path similar to but more rocky than Australia's in recent times. The period of rampant economic liberalism from 1984 to 1999 was bruising (Boshier, 2000). Yet New Zealand may prove more self-confidently self-critical and robust in confronting its reality.[4] For the universities this may be assisted because its unitary administration has a record of more decisive action than Australia's federal one. It is now purposefully addressing the condition and planning of higher education, whereas Australia suffers from a vacuum in policy and leadership (Tertiary Education Advisory Commission, 2000).

The Unified National System – 1989 and after

The creation of a Unified National System (UNS) in 1989 transformed Australian higher education. The number of universities was increased as a result of merging the former two higher education sectors (Dawkins, 1988). Most former colleges of advanced education merged with others, or with established universities, to produce today's thirty-six public universities, all members of the Australian Vice-Chancellors' Committee (AVCC, 1999).

There was vision in this rationalisation. The government held that the arts, humanities and social sciences should not be jeopardised and that individuals and the community as a whole should benefit. 'Equally, it affirms its view that our higher education institutions should not be isolated from the major changes occurring in Australian society and the economy. Rather, they should be one of the prime agents in the process of change.' Higher education also 'promotes greater understanding of our culture, often at odds with majority attitudes and, in so doing, supports the development of a more just and tolerant society ... We do not want a higher education system that fails to analyse and, where necessary, criticise the society in which it operates' (Dawkins, 1988: 5–7). This was generous for the economically dry late 1980s. A decade later it sounded utopian.

Easy and significant growth in student numbers and public funding (Coaldrake and Stedman, 1998) changed from the mid-1990s. A review of higher education management (Hoare, 1995) criticised university gover-nance and administration, recommending changes, which were attacked within the sector but have been implemented in part. A change of govern-ment in 1996 brought in a conservative coalition administration and an unwelcome budget. The Minister for Education, Amanda Vanstone, was confrontational (Vanstone, 1996, 1996a). When her style cost her the posi-tion, the equally unpopular successor, David Kemp, a former academic, continued a similar vein of criticism from a more ideological stance.

The new administration appointed a retired private school headmaster, Roderick West, to lead a transparently right-rationalist review of higher education (West, 1998). The report took late and controversial advice from an aggressively right-wing consultative group, Global Alliance Ltd (West, 1998: Appendix 11). It recommended substantial deregulation and partial privatisation of higher education.

Meanwhile the level of public funds to higher education dropped in absolute terms, and more significantly as a proportion of national revenue and as grant per student. Universities were permitted to recruit full-fee domestic as well as international students. The issue divided campus communities, sometimes in bitter and even violent confrontation. It was seen as favouring 'thick rich kids', reneging on equity in the interest of income. Access it was said could be bought with cash, rather than earned on merit and with social justice. The Higher Education Contribution Scheme, widely admired as an Australian innovation to fund growth and widen access at manageable cost to the student, was adjusted upwards, transferring more of the costs of teaching from the state to students or parents.

Universities were at first allowed to over-enrol, in other words to take more students than their fully funded 'student load', and encouraged by means of a marginal per-student grant of about a quarter the normal level for this. By the end of the decade however, they were being castigated by Minister Kemp for taking additional students, access mission notwith-standing. Over-enrolment was now held to demonstrate two things. Uni-versities must be working below capacity at a higher than necessary per capita payment, rather than attempting to widen access in spite of a short-age of funds. They must also or alternatively be failing in terms of stand-ards and quality, since they were willing to expand at marginal cost, and worsen the staff–student ratio.[5]

A critical turning point might have been a paper prepared by Minister Kemp for the federal Cabinet in late 1999, following the West review, but it was leaked before Cabinet considered it and abandoned by the Prime Minister, leaving a policy vacuum (Kemp, 1999; Coaldrake, 2000). The page one banner headline of the *Sydney Morning Herald* on 15 October was 'Uni war engulfs Howard' [the Prime Minister]; and on 19 October 'PM and Kemp routed over uni plans'. Kemp's paper would have traded a slightly more benevolent funding regime for sharper movement towards free-market competition and partial privatisation.

In the resulting vacuum speculation and lobbying flourished. Some called for out-and-out free-market deregulation, with differential fees charged at each institution's discretion, a scenario familiar in New Zealand but not yet implemented in the UK. Non-government (enterprise or earned) income rose sharply at most universities. Its proportion of total income became a key performance indicator, joining research perform-ance and the employment of graduates as measures of success. After the 2001 general election Kemp was succeeded by Brendan Nelson. The 'Crossroads' consultation followed, leading to further deregulation through legislation at the end of 2003. Throughout these coalition years, and in the vigorous debate which ensued, for example in the weekly *Campus Review*, access barely surfaced, such was the change from the 1970s to mid-1990s period.

During these years increasing financial pressure posed the question whether some universities might not become bankrupt and close. Pork-barrel politics, however, provided protection in the form of 'bale-out', with diminution of institutional autonomy. Divisions widened between differ-ent groups of universities. In 1999 the elite 'Sandstone' group (or Gang) of Eight universities withdrew from the employers' federation which negoti-ated nationally with the two main staff unions. The Eight set up a separate body with a presence in the federal capital, Canberra, to represent elite interests and lobby government, while remaining dominant in the Aus-tralian Vice-Chancellors' Committee (Group of Eight, 2000). By the end of 2000 they had adopted the practice of commenting on AVCC state-ments of which they were part-authors and owners; for example, the AVCC discussion paper *Our Universities, Our Future* (AVCC, 2000).

The universities share a view that Australia needs to be internationally competitive and that, especially in respect of research, more public funds are needed. More divisive is the proposition that the nation can afford very few truly international, some say simply 'real', universities. Research funds, according to the Eight, had to be much more concentrated if Aus-tralia was to be internationally competitive. Despite the absence of a sys-tematic research assessment exercise (RAE), research funding became almost as divisive as in the UK. This raises fears of return to a *de facto* binary system in which lower status institutions receive no funds for research and become teaching-only institutions, with a responsibility to the local community and for wider access from which privileged universities are exempt.

The fumbling of diversity and the diminution of access

Pragmatism left little room for vision as expansion took place. The surviving outreach or extramural tradition with its political and civic overtones – what we now call education for active citizenship – was already squeezed in the 1960s. Even the social and educational philosopher P.H. Partridge in the mid-1960s barely considered mission.[6] All was system, including diversity. What Australia needed was an 'integrated system of diverse institutions' each with its own function.

Forty years later – *plus ça change*. A diverse system could accommodate growth and meet needs: 'we will do best if we bring about a radical diversification in our pattern of higher education, by creating a number of new institutions with their own character and with specialized functions' (Partridge, 1965). Partridge also argued for protecting disinterested study in the face of increasing vocational demand and for the progressive democratisation of society. He noted that diversity of mission (protecting disinterested study from vocational demands) 'collides with a powerful Australian sentiment – the belief that all universities should be similar and equal' (Partridge, 1965: 9, 17). Belief in equity drifts into sameness. Since Partridge wrote, political rectitude has been eclipsed by the triumph of economic rationalism applied to higher education as an industry.

Though never about access and equity, the post-war foundation of the only national university, the ANU, was based on an ideal of serving the nation, as a powerhouse of Australian society. Despite its uniquely generous funding and founding purpose, ANU quickly found its place among the elite 'Sandstone' group, as a privileged premier division team player.

Vision was less explicit for the older universities, state institutions in each capital city that became the prestigious 'Sandstones'. Some of these, old universities, notably Melbourne and Western Australia, and two new Group of Eight members, 1960s-foundation Monash and the former 'Kenso-tech' University of New South Wales, have enjoyed vigorous leadership in the exercise of proper ambition and won enviable stature internationally. In a utilitarian and generally hedonistic society, however, universities old and new were seen to be there mainly to provide professional and vocational training and meet labour market needs.

No strong sense of access through purposeful diversity is visible here; rather, a competitive quest for survival by groups of look-alikes, as automatic funding of continuous growth ceased but school-leaver and adult demand and participation rates continued to rise. An Organisation for Economic Co-operation and Development (OECD) seminar on tertiary education in Sydney in 1998 saw the Australian system not just as mass rather than elite, but moving towards universal. It was already approaching 90 per cent rather than Trow's 40 per cent participation in tertiary if not higher education, with half or more of the population in universities at one time or another.[7]

An OECD country review of the first years of tertiary education in 1997 saw Australia's university system as vital and dynamic, with 'a remarkable ebullience' within the institutions. The review called for further innovation and policy development initiatives (OECD, 1997), but by then the government was on the way to abolishing the independent and developmental Higher Education Council despite a 1996 discussion paper on how to develop it (Vanstone, 1996).

There was rhetorical commitment after, as there was before system unification in 1989, to diversity among universities to meet different needs. The government's own higher education reports display this, notably 1994, Report No. 22, 'the first to focus on sector-wide diversity' and 1996, Report No. 26 'diversity is an important feature of Australia's higher education sector' (Department of Employment, Education and Training, 1994, 1996). The late 1990s saw more discussion of the need for diversity. A study by four authors on enhancing diversity in 1999 examined the roots of unease about being different, the main inhibitors to diversity, and the policy and institutional changes needed to secure it (Kemmis *et al.*, 1999; Marginson, 1999).

Debate in Australia echoed a sporadic debate in Britain in which Roger Brown, formerly Chief Executive of the Higher Education Quality Council, has been a lead contributor (Brown, 1999). It revealed the same natural dynamic towards convergence, assisted by benchmarking and performance indicators that compare across the whole system. It was becoming evident that the idea of an independent university needed reconciling with the fact of a higher education *system* of which universities are sub-systems, and with diversity of mission and identity for each particular institution. The idea of a university in Australia is inevitably compromised by the fact and functions of a tertiary or higher education *system*.

Diversity has been consistently fumbled, resulting in herd-like behaviour. Greater 'freedom' under a nominally deregulating but audit-hungry administration drives institutions towards homogeneity. Government benchmarking and auditing tendencies encourage this, as does informal how-to-do-it support and mentoring within the Vice-Chancellors' (AVCC) club. Neither the cultural legacy of distrustful bureaucratic control nor the newer demand for enterprise and diversity of income sources has helped the cause of access.

Late in the 1990s risk management became daily discourse. Often this came to mean being risk-averse, missing opportunities by being similar to others, although some enterprising universities carved bold and distinctive business paths. In practice, without the political will and purpose shown for example in South Africa (Council on Higher Education, 2000) and even in New Zealand at this time, diversity remains rhetorical. Still missing is a clear and authoritative view of what is required to be a public university in the early twenty-first century. Clarifying this could rehabilitate access and mark out a field within which diversity is both legitimate and rewarded.

Instead universities' behaviours approximate one another, especially in respect of research strategies, international and offshore business, and a new wave of managerialism. A small cadre of scholars critique these tendencies academically and in the media (Coady 2000, 2000a; Marginson and Considine, 2000). Universities cluster into affinity groups – the eight 'sandstones', the former institutes of technology, sometimes the 'regionals'. Regionality holds prospect for diversity in engaging diverse local needs and settings. However, the meaning and number of 'regional' universities changed remarkably in the second Kemp research paper (Kemp, 1999), and 'regional' is often seen as meaning weak and of low status, useful only for promoting sectarian financial interests.[8]

The result at the beginning of the twenty-first century is a club of the most wealthy and prestigious universities seeking to enhance their resource base and interests by kicking away the ladder. The other universities, huddled in groups for security, are united in a wish to be like and if possible part of the top Eight. As in Britain, where the Russell Group takes the part of the 'Sandstones', some thirty universities aspire to be among the top ten.

Influences and ideals, utility and enterprise – no time for access?

Relative and absolute contraction of public funds has driven universities to do ever more with less, and to strip away the non-essential. The public university has become the *entrepreneurial* (Clark, 1998) or at least the *enterprise* university of Australians (Marginson and Considine, 2000). There are two problems here. First, few academic and often few of the administrative staff feel passionate about institutional money-making, necessary as they may concede it to be. In Australia, perhaps more than in the United Kingdom, staff tend to care very much about teaching, though some are no less passionate about research. Analysis of the columns of *Campus Review* reveals the high salience of university teaching, an impression borne out by conversations in the Australian universities I know best. With this common passion to teach well there frequently goes a wish to make a social contribution by reaching the more disadvantaged and excluded.

Second, long-formed habits of dependence on state-funded growth, a bureaucratic instinct to control and micro-manage, and enhanced risk-aversion, militate against entrepreneurialism. There is cultural dissonance between the external drivers of HE and the commonly shared values of those who constitute the university, and who continue in the main to hold older social equity values.

Another non-benign general cultural influence is the popular stereotypes of a media-fed culture that militates against becoming enthusiastic about big, noble ideas. Academics who speak out, unless they are 'glamorous' and preferably also larrikin, are cut down to size and advised not to take themselves too seriously. It would be fanciful to discern much high principle in the public and political arena. Notions of the good society, social amelioration and social justice have a better chance if presented in the fair-go mateship tradition, but even there they struggle. Events extraneous to higher education where students, staff and institutions have 'given comfort to the enemy' of government exacerbate hard–soft polarities. Tampa 'refugees overboard', asylum-seekers and the war on Iraq have been divisive. The indirect effect palpably harms the soft-left cause of widening participation, through guilt by association, or requires that access masquerades only in hard-nosed human capital and labour market terms.

At institutional level, in the quest for competitive advantage and reputation, each university tries to recruit the best-scoring students who bring status, rather than the socially excluded. It can no more afford to be generously soft to the special cases of non-traditional students in a wider public interest than it would feel that it can harbour asylum-seekers, now known as illegals.

The Business Higher Education Round Table (BHERT) on the other hand is a club of corporate chief executives meeting with vice-chancellors that gently lobbies government for university resources, and gently seeks to align universities with industry's needs. BHERT also promotes other concepts about universities and their contribution to society, including lifelong learning, that are often broader than those vaunted by the universities themselves.[9] Compared with the reputations of some vice-chancellors within their own institutions in difficult times, the BHERT influence is more supportive and benign towards wider public values and purposes. Few university staff would be aware of the existence of BHERT, but here the voice of the enlightened private sector offers a relatively broad, and in an older sense liberal, notion of the university and its place in society.

The dominant ideology invading the space of the university, however, is free-market economic liberalism. Added to the older functional and pragmatic utilitarianism that always oriented Australian universities vocationally, this converts easily into hostility to ideas and ideals which ignore the familiar single bottom line.[10] Self-interested protectionism by cappuccino-set academics is suspect in a world of rorting politicians and corruptible police forces. The worst rather than the best is thought of academics. Universities are fair game for the rationalist right. Managements in turn are tempted to distrust their own staff, seeing academic freedom as precious, or a shield for the work-shy. Assertive exercise of 'management prerogative' (instead of administrative service to 'internal clients') betrays a managerialist ideology. The new Vice-Chancellors as Presidents (an increasingly favoured title) emulate presidential change in the United

States by bringing in their own management teams. At first glance how the university runs appears to have nothing to do with its access mission. In reality there is a powerful connection: hard management instinctually distrusts soft goals and soft measures.

Some journalists are consistently hostile, echoing the ideology frequently expressed by former Minister David Kemp, who sought to impose 'voluntary unionism' on universities and to break the influence of the National Union of Students. Student politics echo society's conflicting ideologies but are generally hostile to the conservative government that has been in power since 1996, as are the great majority of university staff. In these circumstances a countervailing ideology and value system to that of the competitive free market is less confidently expressed by those trying to liberalise within the system. A number of recent broadsheet articles express concern for the erosion of traditional political and intellectual as distinct from economic liberal values, and the erosion of the freedoms of academe to exercise these, internally and for the broader society. Hesitancy may reflect a wish not to appear self-seeking. The Coady essays (Coady, 2000) were criticised by self-critical academics not wishing to appear protectionist in resisting change and accountability. As a result, arguments for a broad and humane rather than a narrowly instrumental curriculum, and for a stronger social equity agenda, may be expressed more forcefully outside than within the university.

Not only is socially altruistic and purposeful *community* among scholars eroded, but each individual university also becomes less visible to government other than through individual and local interest group lobbying. It merges into the activities, efficiencies, costs and productivities of the higher education *system* or, as West insisted quite aggressively in the opening paragraphs of his report, the higher education *industry*. It is the same for research as for teaching-as-human-resource-skill-development: the particular university is subsumed within the *higher education-system-as-industry*. The success of each particular university increasingly approximates the bottom line of a successful business corporation.[11] None of this brings wider participation or social equity up management's priority list of key performance indicators.

Ideals are not dead, but their expression is muted among those managing the sector. Perhaps the last of the grand old men of Australian liberal humane scholarship, Max Charlesworth, reflecting in 1998 on fifty-four years in academic life, found himself still moderately optimistic. However, he found the debate about the future of the universities being held in the context of a very powerful ideology. He called it 'a curious amalgam of Adam Smith capitalism but where the market is now defined in global terms, allied with a form of utilitarianism where all values are seen as instrumental values, and ... basic community goods such as education are no longer the concern of the government'. *Economic rationalism* was a poor attempt to describe this powerful amalgam. Charlesworth concluded that 'the university is one of the finest flowers of ... Western civilisation and that we must defend it, and the values it embraces, with all our hearts and minds' (Charlesworth, 1998).

More typical is another grand old man, Peter Karmel, thrice Vice-Chancellor as well as Chair until its abolition of the Tertiary Education Advisory Commission. Karmel writes of the system and its funding as ideally an efficient meritocracy, with effective arrangements to give opportunity for the poor (equity scholarships) and make the system function well to help build an open and meritocratic society. The best of thinkers and writers concentrate on the national interest and on (funding) mechanisms that might enable the system to meet those objectives. It is less clear how 'the system' should behave at institutional level to achieve these goals. Does it make sense for research output so to dominate the prestige stakes, or to garner all the highest higher school certificate achievers, as the second most important measure of success for every university?

Government demand is for utility, efficiency, productivity and economy. The criteria are tightly economic, with barely token reference to social purposes, although the state administrations incline to broader purposes. Universities should function like corporations, contributing to the national economic good through a strong export industry (international students) and through skill-formation needed in the labour market. As presented to the public and the media (Gallagher, 2000), universities are models of poor industrial practice. Government criticism is a tricky matter, muted by recognition that higher education as an export industry requires the protection of a strong Australian brand.

In this climate and world of discourse purposes other than the economic fall off the agenda. Access and equity policy and strategy take a back seat in terms of government influence. Communities, however, especially new ethnic communities, continue to place high value on access and opportunity. At election time this may matter. University staff and their unions also incline, often strongly, in the direction of social equity and a community service mission. For academic staff universities have been more or less congenial places of intellectual and social employment. Job satisfaction and self-valuing through work deemed to be worthwhile have been eroded by 'proletarianisation' in recent years. The values base is, however, still very evident in the conversations and meetings of staff and in the policies of the still strong higher education unions. Generally these take a longer, more socially purposeful, critical and high-minded view of the role of the sector than in the main does its management.

In one area 'access' has had a revival. Australia is well known for its outreach to remote rural communities, in education as well as in health matters. The threat posed by One Nation rekindled political interest in 'the Bush'. It brought rural disadvantage and relatively low participation up the agenda, first in terms of studies of the impact of remoteness or proximity to a campus on participation rates (Stevenson *et al.*, 1999;

Stevenson *et al.*, 2000). At the end of 2003 there was included in the post-Crossroads legislation a very modest *per capita* premium to compensate institutions for the higher cost of teaching in remote locations. This access initiative resonated with lasting concern about the tyranny of distance, now made urgent by party politics. A larger context, however, is growing interest in universities' engagement with their communities, especially in the Crossroads inquiry into the regional or 'modern' universities. The discovery of *engagement* as a metaphor for community service and outreach in stronger partnership form is certain to carry with it a requirement to revisit individuals' access as well as to stimulate local economies and involve more diverse local classes, groups and communities.

Access to the credit society

By contrast with the dominant discourse about access, and by way of relief from it, little is said here about paying for higher education. In Australia, as in the UK, it is the aspect of policy that attracts by far the most attention. The issues and arguments that are essentially similar, as is the trend towards increasing the student or parental[12] contribution to the cost of study for a degree. Australia was a leader in allowing deferral by means of what is called the Higher Education Contribution Scheme (HECS). The principle has been widely accepted and generally welcomed. The differences are less about the principle of HECS than about the level of fees themselves, the tendency towards deregulation away from a national fixed tariff, and the income point at which, and how rapidly, repayment is made out of income.

Free initial higher education was introduced by Whitlam in the early 1970s. Assertion about the impact on the participation of the poor of the fees and HECS regime that replaced it is commoner than clear evidence about its impact. The New Zealand experience is likewise often cited both to prove and to disprove that high fees militate against access and equity. New Zealand has a variable and quite high-fee free-market regime which leaves some students with very large debts. While the system there has been very open, and the main (Maori and Pasifika) low participation communities are widely targeted, the result can be frequent unsuccessful repetition of courses and a very large debt with little or nothing to show for it at the end. The more socially oriented and less free-market government of Helen Clark has now stepped in to cap fee rises, using grant increase as a lever on universities to check unfettered rises. Australia's high participation levels, and particularly their rapid rise in the 1980s and 1990s, suggest that HECS has not been a serious deterrent, although, as in the UK, there is belief and evidence that working-class communities tend to be debt averse. The high levels of participation by OECD standards, and the relative ease of access, may owe much to the facts that students with few exceptions go to a local university, earn income throughout their degree years, and enjoy flexibility and variability of pacing not usually found in the UK.

The long-established Australian HECS arrangement is essentially similar to that to which England is now moving. Moreover, both governments are now permitting institutions to set their own variable fee levels, in a wave of anti-cartelisation. In Australia the overseas student fee regime has become a large and vital income stream for many institutions.[13] The difference is that the conservative government of the late 1990s controversially also allowed universities to charge full fees for up to 25 per cent of domestic places on certain conditions. That limit is now being raised. Initially only a few institutions took this unpopular income-making option, but the number has increased, and will probably rise further

Different universities have different strategies for widening access and providing financial assistance by means of fee remission or scholarships. Some target bright youngsters from disadvantaged schools or work with such schools to encourage working-class and minority ethnic group students to consider university. Some make partnerships with Tertiary and Further Education (TAFE). In Victoria the several dual sector institutions have the opportunity to maintain pathways between their own TAFE and HE departments, sectors or divisions. Many of these arrangements have only a minor financial dimension, but the hidden and opportunity costs of making special arrangements may be significant, and are now more consciously factored in. An extra premium announced by the government in 2003 was referred to earlier, for teaching students in remote locations. It illustrates greater awareness about higher costs falling on institutions that adopt this aspect of an access mission by teaching on satellite campuses to compensate for remoteness, in recognition that travelling and studying away from home is impossibly costly for most remote rural families.

Two more comments about finance and the credit society. First, it has long been argued that getting a degree enhances job prospects and earning potential. The Graduate Careers Council of Australia (GCCA) vigorously demonstrates that even with 'universal' participation (strictly speaking an APR of around 50 per cent) graduates continue to enjoy material benefit which makes debt for a degree a sound investment. Second, it tends to escape general notice that education has joined white goods, cars, houses and other purchases in a now normal pattern of deferred payment, another manifestation of the debt society. The larger implications of deferring the cost of paying for today's education as well as other consumables have not been openly considered.

From mass higher to universal tertiary – the new diversification

In examining changes in higher education our gaze tends to flicker between the system as a whole and different individual institutions. Here we consider briefly whole system features and emergent trends, before turning yet more briefly to relevant significant tendencies at institutional level.

The OECD seminar referred to earlier in this chapter heard Minister Kemp speak of universal participation in higher education. He was using Trow's meaning accurately (40 per cent threshold) but he could with more accuracy have claimed universality for the tertiary sector or system, since with the inclusion of TAFE the level was more like 90 per cent. In the 1970s and 1980s Australia did indeed think in tertiary system terms. Its Commonwealth Tertiary Education Commission, CTEC, had three Councils, one each for universities, the colleges of advanced education, and TAFE. With the abolition of the binary divide and also of CTEC, the term tertiary fell somewhat out of use. More importantly, attention focused for a while on the HE sector mergers. Only a little later, as now in England, did attention turn to the HE–TAFE dichotomy which some called the new binary divide.[14]

Comprehensive discussion of the politics and language of access must, however, take in the whole of tertiary or post-secondary provision. It can then examine not only APR and older participation rates, special access courses and routes, and so forth, but the articulation, pathways and credit accumulation and transfer that prevails, or is absent, across the whole larger sector. The contrast with New Zealand, which inaugurated its new Tertiary Education Commission (TEC) in 2003 after a lengthy period of consultation and public policy paper, is sharp. TEC draws the whole of post-school education including adult and community learning, polytechnics which are analogous to TAFE and to UK further education, and the universities together under one planning and funding body. In the UK the term tertiary may slowly be gaining purchase as the importance of FE as a vehicle for higher education, including Foundation degrees, is more fully appreciated and valued. But administrative and funding separation (in England between the Higher Education Funding Council HEFCE and the Learning and Skills Council LSC) makes integrative planning, and integrated planning to widen participation, well nigh impossible.[15]

Australia was half way to integrated planning funding across the old tripartite tertiary structure but that became a victim of the Dawkins reforms. The more comprehensive approach would not only address the nightmarish complexities caused by different funding systems for further (TAFE) and higher education and the resulting barriers to smooth progression and credit transfer, but it would also make it easier to tackle more fundamental questions about who has access to which parts of the total tertiary system, how, at what time and with what results – and even if there is the will to do so, to act on the results. Australia appears less lucid than the UK in debate about widening participation. The UK debate has moved beyond mere admission into HE. First, it has moved on to retention, performance, outcomes and the longer-term employment and other benefits, which different kinds of HE offer. Second, it is asking about the longer-term social and educational effects of different curricula and learning opportunities in different kinds of colleges and universities. It is hard to say with confidence in a dispersed country with diverse local discourses just how far these issues are being addressed. It does seem, however, that clear thinking as well as sensible planning is likely to prove easier in New Zealand's new context of 'universal tertiary for lifelong learning'. Instead Australia, like Britain, has what now seems to be unfortunately named 'universal higher' planning separated from other planning and funding, data-getting and evaluation, in the larger and increasingly interacting and interdependent sector.

One way of widening access in Britain at present is to provide more higher education within further education, which is now running at 11 per cent in England but far higher in Scotland. The use of FE as an alternative delivery vehicle for managing growth also protects HE institutions from the need to expand too rapidly. Although the arrangements between TAFE and HE vary between states, there is not the opaqueness and particular difficulty that accompany indirect funding of English colleges through their university franchise partners. Another comparison will present itself as the new associate degree in Australia is taken up, a little later in time than the yet to be proven Foundation degree in Britain. A third kind will be invited by the review of the 14–19 curriculum taking place in the UK under Mike Tomlinson. There is no such contemporaneous inquiry in Australia, where work-based learning and school work experience have gone further already, but arrangements for school years 14–19 and TAFE vary between states, with differential impact on school–university and TAFE–university connections. What seems clear, glancing across this bunch of issues, is that the political economy of mass higher education and wider participation in Australia and the UK at large really will have to move in the New Zealand (or Scottish) direction.

Impacts of mass higher education on the university and the system

Of course 'massification' has meant huge changes to all institutions, even the most historic and prestigious, across many dimensions of their structure, management, internal life and behaviour. Here we take brief note of three only.

First, as alluded to earlier and well illustrated by a content analysis of the Australian (and in a small way New Zealand) equivalent of *The Times Higher Education Supplement* over the past three years, is what we might call the rediscovery of teaching. Teaching has probably always been taken more seriously, maybe enjoyed more, in the Australian HE environment, and on both sides of the pre-1989 binary divide, than in the UK where the status and career importance of research tends to overshadow it more.

Shroud-waving about 'teaching only' universities and the recreation of the colleges (of advanced education) notwithstanding, *Campus Review* records much professional interest and engaged deliberation about how to teach, and about related issues such as staff development. There is certainly cynicism and weariness about government pressure and untrusted purpose,[16] and about students' apparently ever narrower interest only in what will be on the examination paper and what will be useful in job-getting.

Despite these familiar but louder themes, and a well documented general fall in morale as resources keep contracting, and teachers are blamed for failure from examination performance to graduate under-employment, interest in and passion about teaching and students seems to hold up. There are many local and national awards for teaching excellence. All in all, the society and its academic community appear to have responded to massive expansion and the reality that so large a cadre of university academics cannot all be (and are not all needed as) great researchers by recognising and (re)valuing teaching and learning support at the heart of the professional role. This is not to say that the subject of role segregation is not divisive and a source of concern to the professional associations (Coaldrake and Stedman, 1998). Nonetheless, one consequence of moving from elite to universal is the (re)instatement of teaching at the heart of the professional role.

A second main impact concerns the student as learner and prospective graduate. It is increasingly normal, if still widely offensive to both students and staff, to refer to the former as clients or customers, and to talk up their exercise of consumer choice through their purchasing power in this role. Despite Australia's rapid slide towards litigiousness, especially but not only in the health sector where a litigation crisis has caused practising obstetricians to disappear, there are few cases where students have taken action as aggrieved student clients, fewer *pro rata* probably than in the UK.

On the other hand the commonest attitude of students to their studies is, as anecdotally but widely reported, highly utilitarian. They are there to acquire a bundle of marketable skills and a ticket to employment rather than for a rewarding and intellectually challenging higher education.[17] The fact that so many people go to university, and that for so many people it is simply a part-time aspect of their normal life, possibly for many years, also makes it, not always in a bad sense, normal. Being a student is much more a part of daily life for people at work, in the club and on the street than it yet feels to have become in England, more like 'college' perhaps in the United States. Australia has entered the time of the unspecial student, the time when the 'academic community' is inseparably entangled with and in this sense lost within the normal wider world; conversely, the ordinary workaday world has irreversibly penetrated and permeated the university, demolishing the cultural walls of the smaller system.

Third, the change also alluded to earlier concerns the quite sudden and widespread adoption of *engagement*. As part of the identity and work of the university this is seen as a viable means to survive and adapt as the proportion of public 'core' funding falls, possibly down to a third or less. The concept as developed especially through the Association of Commonwealth Universities applies to all universities in the era of the knowledge society. In Australia it was eagerly taken up by the 'modern' or new and regional universities as possibly giving them a distinct identity and mission which might partly offset disadvantage in terms of wealth and reputation. The interest, however, runs wider. Engagement, including what at the Royal Melbourne Institute of Technology (RMIT) was termed 'the scholarship of engagement' as a distinct form of practice alongside Boyer's now established 'four scholarships', features in many conferences and was embraced in 2003 by, among others, BHERT.

At one level engagement appears a different focus of policy and discourse from access and wider participation, and so it is in one important sense. Its subject of focus is community, place, the local economy, social and economic development. It is more 'organic' and 'systemic' in intellectual framing and the implications for organisational behaviour than most essentially individual focused access discourse. It also connects naturally with the slightly earlier notion and language of Mode Two Knowledge Production (Gibbons *et al.*, 1994) with which it shares some common lineage. That way of looking at knowledge makes the university a partner, co-producer and joint user of new knowledge with others in its natural region.

Although the origins and fields of discourse are separate, regional engagement almost inevitably involves examining participation rates, social capital, skill formation and the exclusion of different classes and groups from higher education and the knowledge society. The more *engagement* gains purchase in national and institutional policy-making, the more it is likely to strengthen the agenda for widening participation from a different direction. For the federal government this is likely to be a strictly economic calculation, but for others at more local levels of administration and for many in academe the agenda is larger, and more generous in intent. If it continues to gain support and energy it may even over time move the Australian system closer to that of New Zealand. Here the civic and social role and responsibilities of the university are enshrined in legislation. It may be no coincidence that New Zealand shows itself more committed both formally and in institutional behaviour to the equitable inclusion of – in their case Maori and Pasifika – under-represented peoples among its student numbers as well as in its national cultural mix.

One could conclude ruefully with *the university in ruins* (Readings, 1996). Or one could speculate, as many do today, that as virtuals, corporates, reclassified Australian TAFEs, British colleges and Kiwi polytechnics, 'universities' of this and for that, all crowd the stage and debase the currency, the term university will soon be drained of all meaning.

Alternatively one could celebrate the extension of higher education towards truly universal accessibility as it takes more diverse forms to reach ever more parts of a society in need of lifelong learning.

Let me end instead with a cautionary anecdote. Not long ago I was puzzled to find in the small land of New Zealand what seemed to be two essentially identical national clubs or networks to do with access. They had much the same name and functions. Neither seemed aware of the existence of the other. When the penny dropped it became obvious that one was chalk, the other cheese. One was about getting older, poor, educationally excluded second chance adults from different homeland communities, working class and rural, Pasifika and Maori, into university through piecemeal part-time study. The other was to provide very expensive residential full-time pre-university education for full-fee international students who would then become an income stream for the parent universities of which they were wholly owned subsidiaries – prep schools for the rich. What's in a name?

Notes

1 For an excellent and challenging consideration of the corruption of public language and its invasion of private space read Don Watson's *Death Sentence. The Decay of Public Language* (2003).

2 Martin Trow's elite–mass–higher characterisation postulated an age participation rate (APR) about 15 per cent as crossing the elite to mass threshold, while above 40 per cent moved into universal. As Watson (2004) points out, this is doubly obsolete. Many systems have jumped from elite to universal with barely a pause, and it omits the participation of those beyond the immediate post-school cohort. APR and total system size are central to issues of access, and as this chapter argues we need now to be thinking of more literally universal (say 90 per cent) participation in *tertiary* education, side-stepping for separate consideration just what constitutes 'higher'.

3 The lead headline in the *Sydney Morning Herald*, 2 January 2001, reporting on Australia's centenary federation celebrations.

4 Contrast New Zealand's major participatory nationally telecast consultation in 2001, *Catching the Knowledge Wave* with the Australian Bicentennial in 1988. The original Australian theme was *Living Together* (shades of Aborigines and immigrants), which was arbitrarily dismissed by the Prime Minister in a Christmas Day broadcast, in favour of *The Australian Achievement*.

5 As a further twist on the other hand, if they improved the SSR they were vulnerable for having reduced their efficiency.

6 In the 1970s mention of university mission in Australia still invited ribald humour about missionary position.

7 OECD's 2003 *Education at a glance* indicators show Australia at the head of the field in tertiary graduation as a proportion of population, led possibly only by the United States.

8 New or post-1989 universities from the former college of advanced education sector, known first as *regional*, now call themselves *modern* universities. This term was used in England by the former polytechnics but the Coalition of Modern Universities (CMU) is becoming a Campaign for Mainstream Universities, (post-)modernising the image while protecting the acronym.

9 The Round Table vision for higher education in 1998 was subtitled 'the global imperative'. Starting with internationally competitive graduates, it moved through Lifelong Education, Research and research training, Internationalisation, Interaction, Access, Diversity, to unspecified Community services and partnership.

10 The Royal Melbourne Institute of Technology (RMIT) University is unfashionable in its mission to 'make a difference' and to inspire its students to do likewise. It places value on social and environmental (ecological or sustainability) measures and good governance as well as on the financial.

11 At the same time government has tried to break up national pattern bargaining between universities and unions, driving each institution to make its own 'enterprise agreement', and pushing beyond this for workplace agreements between employers and individual members of staff.

12 Undergraduate fees can be paid up-front for a significant discount, allowing more wealthy families to buy their children's higher education more inexpensively and not to enter working life with a debt.

13 At least 25 per cent among the institutions that lead on this indicator.

14 The use of language is as always instructive. Binary carries emotional energy from the days when CAEs resented the market disadvantage that went with not being called universities. TAFE partisans in turn energised their case by borrowing the same term to stress inequities of per capita funding and treatment compared with the enlarged HE sector. In another twist, however, it is held old-fashioned to talk about TAFE. In its stress upon the vocational and its desire to draw in and support the private sector in competition with the public, the government prefers to use VET – vocational education and training. Since HE is also overwhelmingly vocational this is a triumph of politics over clarity and good sense.

15 In both Scotland and Wales the two funding councils are moving at different rates towards integration but there appears to be little prospect for this in England.

16 Mutual distrust between university staff and federal government is high, although institutional heads working through the AVCC have managed a more effective *modus vivendi* with Minister Nelson than with his two predecessors. The suggestion that more has meant worse is, however, muted on both sides, with only the occasional maverick academic breaking ranks, usually in spectacular fashion. Governments wish to assert that their policies – and economies – have not lowered standards. Universities and staff are reluctant to allow that standards have fallen and quality has suffered, since this is bad for business. The two parties thus close ranks especially against media assaults on supposedly falling standards that break out periodically, particularly in the annual recruitment and admissions round when University Admission Index cut-off scores are tracked with ghoulish interest.

17 As in Britain, many lecturers tend to appreciate older 'non-traditional access' students who often show more intellectual curiosity, so changing the culture of seminars to everyone's benefit.

References

Australian Vice-Chancellors' Committee (AVCC), *1999: University Facts* (Canberra: AVCC, 1999).

Australian Vice-Chancellors' Committee (AVCC), *Our Universities, Our Future: An AVCC Discussion Paper* (Canberra: AVCC, 2000).

Barnett, R., *Realizing the University in an Age of Supercomplexity* (Milton Keynes: Open University Press, 2000).

Boshier, R., 'How the "free market" destroys a good idea: the rise and fall of life-long learning in New Zealand' (University of British Columbia, Vancouver: paper presented at the UCLA Conference, 2000).

Brown, R., 'Diversity in higher education: has it been and gone?' (Goldsmith's College, London: professorial lecture, 1999).

Charlesworth, M., 'The university: death or transfiguration?' (unpublished conference paper, 1998).

Clark, B., *Creating Entrepreneurial Universities. Organizational Pathways of Transformation* (Oxford: Pergamon, 1998).

Coady, T. (ed.), *Why Universities Matter* (Sydney: Allen and Unwin, 2000).

Coady, T., 'Universities must be vigilant to corporate funding', *Sydney Morning Herald* (18 December 2000a).

Coaldrake, P., 'Reflections on the repositioning of the government's approach to higher education, or I'm dreaming of a White Paper', *Journal of Higher Education Policy and Management* 22, 1 (2000), pp. 9–21.

Coaldrake, P. and L. Stedman, *On the Brink: Australia's Universities Confronting Their Future* (Brisbane: Queensland University Press, 1998).

Council on Higher Education: Size and Shape of Higher Education Task Team, *Towards a New Higher Education Landscape* (Pretoria: Council on Higher Education, 2000).

Dawkins, J., *Higher Education: A Policy Statement* (Canberra: AGPS, 1988).

Department for Education and Skills, *The Future of Higher Education* (London: DfES, 2003).

Department of Employment, Education and Training (DEET), *Diversity and Performance of Australian Universities* (Report No. 22) (Canberra: DEET, 1994).

Department of Employment, Education and Training (DEET), *Diversity in Australian Higher Education Institutions* (Report No. 26) (Canberra: DEET, 1996).

Department of Industry, Science and Resources (DISR), Industrial Innovation Working Group of the Learned Group for the National Innovation Summit, *The Innovation Scenarios* (Canberra: DISR, 1999).

Fraser, M., 'Don't publish and be damned', *The Australian* (23 February 2000).

Gallagher, M., 'The emergence of entrepreneurial public universities in Australia', paper presented to the IMHE General Conference (Canberra: DEETYA, 2000).

Gibbons, M., C. Limoges, H. Nowotny, S. Schwartzman, P. Scott and M. Trow, *The New Production of Knowledge* (London: Sage, 1994).

Group of Eight, *Imperatives and Principles for Policy Reform in Australian Higher Education* (Canberra: Group of Eight, 2000).

Hoare, D. (chair), *Higher Education Management Review* (Canberra: AGPS, 1995).

Kemmis, S., S. Marginson, P. Porter and F. Rizvi, *Enhancing Diversity in Australian Higher Education* (Perth: University of Western Australia Press, 1999).

Kemp. D., *Knowledge and Innovation: A Policy Statement on Research and Research Training* (Canberra: DEETYA, 1999).

Marginson, S., 'Diversity and convergence in Australian higher education', *Australian Universities Review*, 1 (1999).

Marginson, S. and M. Considine, *The Enterprise University* (Cambridge: Cambridge University Press, 2000).

OECD, *Thematic Review of the First Years of Tertiary Education: Australia* (Paris: OECD, 1997).

Partridge, P., 'Tertiary Education – Society and the Future', in J. Wilkes (ed.) *Tertiary Education in Australia* (Sydney: Angus and Robertson, 1965).

Readings, B., *The University in Ruins* (Cambridge, MA: Harvard University Press, 1996).

Stevenson, S., C. Evans, M. Maclachlan, T. Karmel and R. Blakers, *Access. Effect of Campus Proximity and Socio-economic Status on University Participation Rates in Regions* (Canberra: Department of Employment, Education, Training and Youth Affairs, 2000).

Stevenson, S., M. Maclachlan, and T. Karmel, *Regional Participation in Higher Education and the Distribution of Higher Education Resources Across Regions* (Canberra: Department of Education, Training and Youth Affairs, 1999).

Tertiary Education Advisory Commission (TEAC), *Shaping a Shared Vision*, Initial Report of the Tertiary Education Advisory Commission (Wellington: TEAC, 2000).

Vanstone, A., *The Australian Research Council and the Higher Education Council*, discussion paper (Canberra: DEETYA, 1996).

Vanstone, A. *Higher Education Budget Statement* (Canberra: DEETYA, 9 August 1996a).

Watson, D., *Death Sentence: The Decay of Public Language* (Canberra: Knopf, 2003).

Watson, D., 'A new university world? National and international perspectives on changes in higher education' (Green College, Oxford: lecture series, 2004).

West, R., *Learning for Life: Review of Higher Education Financing and Policy* (Canberra: DEETYA, 1998).

3 The politics of access to higher education in France

Cécile Deer

Introduction

An important aspect of higher education in France and elsewhere lies in the fact that it does not form part of compulsory education. This explains why access to higher education, more than any other educational level, has often been the subject of heated social debates, political antagonism and economic concern. In western industrialised countries, four main factors have an influence on access to higher education: the political environment, the dominant beliefs concerning the social distribution of opportunity, the economy and the structure of the educational system (Halsey, 1991). The situation in France may be seen as that of a wealthy economy set in a liberal and pluralistic political environment, where there has been a dominant belief in the importance of education. This last aspect is exemplified by the universal nature of primary and secondary education provision and the gradual rise of the legal school leaving-age to sixteen (in 1959).

Over the last twenty years, higher education in France, as in most Western European countries, has expanded rapidly. A glance at longitudinal national statistical records illustrates this evolution (see Table 3.1). Growth at tertiary level has been directly related to an increase in the

Table 3.1 Evolution of the number of registered students in France since 1960

Year	Total number of registered students
1960–61	309,000
1970–71	850,000
1980–81	1,181,100
1990–91	1,717,100
2000–01	2,161,100
2002–03	2,209,100

Source: Ministère de l'Education Nationale, de la Recherche et de la Technologie, *Repères Références Statistiques sur les Enseignements, la Formation et la Recherche* (MEN Direction de la Prospective, Paris, 2003).

participation rate at upper secondary school level (i.e. in the *lycées*). In particular, there has been a significant increase in the participation rate among girls at all levels, although as in most European countries this has not been distributed evenly across all subject areas (Baudelot and Establet, 1992). To determine the key influences behind the rapid expansion of the higher education sector is, however, not an easy matter and several combining causes may be identified to explain this evolution. In the 1960s there was certainly a growing demand from society for more open access to higher education. This was driven by the discourse that a higher education was a socially divisive luxury commodity that entrenched social inequalities through an accumulation of social and cultural capital in the hands of the dominant elite (Bourdieu, 1970). It could therefore only be right to make it available to all those who could participate intellectually. Greater opportunities for the lower social classes at tertiary level were equated with their right to benefit from a higher education, often understood as the pinnacle of the intellectual experience. The endorsement of these values at central political level meant that expansion could take place and, since the mid-1970s, the legitimisation of the policy of expansion has also been the result of proactive government initiatives. Participation in higher education has been allowed to grow on the grounds that it was beneficial both to society and to the economy and this form of political reasoning combined with the social demand.

Since the education reforms and legislation of 1968, which imposed on French universities the principle of non-selectivity at entrance, access to higher education has increased as a direct function of expansion at secondary school level. More particularly, this has been the case at upper secondary level, where steering expansion has been initiated essentially by political decisions. As a result, the universities have had little influence on the quantitative and qualitative aspects of their student recruitment. Access to *baccalauréat* level increased from 34 per cent in 1980 to 68.5 per cent in 1995 and reached close to 70 per cent in 2002.[1] From the second half of the 1980s, participation in higher education grew rapidly and today France has reached a stage of mass higher education with between 35 per cent and 40 per cent entry rate to type-A tertiary education and 21 per cent entry rate to type-B tertiary education in 1999.[2]

Increased access rates to higher education have been debated around the notions of 'selection' and 'elitism'. The corresponding social question has evolved around the ideas of *equality* and *equity*, two contested concepts which have been defined in various ways. Regarding higher education, supporters of equality have been content with opening access as widely as possible in order to make up for the differences in the socioeconomic origins of students. In France, this approach is related to an aspect of the post-war Republican ideal embedded in the 1946 Preamble of the current Constitution:

> The Nation guarantees equal access to instruction, vocational training and culture for children and adults alike. The organisation of free and secular public education at all levels is a duty of the State.[3]
>
> (Preamble to the 1946 Constitution and reaffirmed in the 1958 Constitution)

Free access to public sector higher education may therefore be regarded as a constitutional right for any *baccalauréat* holder. However, the *laissez-faire* meritocratic approach which has long been equated with this notion of equality has been increasingly questioned and there have been growing calls for greater equity, that is to say greater chance of equality of outcome throughout the educational system, rather than just equality of access. This approach first concerned the upper secondary school sector but inevitably affected the higher education sector too. With increasing success rates at upper secondary school level, the real value of the 'gold standard' that the *baccalauréat* represents in France has been repeatedly questioned. We will not enter this debate here; suffice it to say that the gradual build-up of pressure for access to tertiary education for all parts of society has decisively influenced the way that the structure of French higher education has developed and this is where any discussion of access must begin.

The qualitative and quantitative aspects of expansion at upper secondary school level and their impact on access to higher education

In recent decades, it would be fair to say that undergraduate studies in France have gradually become – *de facto* if not *de jure* – the final stage of the official, organised state system of national education. Quantitative changes in recruitment have been accompanied by qualitative changes of two sorts: those of a social nature, as people with more varied social backgrounds have gained access to upper secondary education and those of an educational nature, as this expansion has been achieved through modifications in the schools' programmes and curricula.

Conditions of access to higher education in France today are largely a legacy of the events that took place in 1968. A few weeks before the outburst of student violence that would shake much of France's traditional social and political boundaries and would prove particularly disruptive for those in the faculties, President de Gaulle and his government had come to the conclusion that entrance to university should become more selective (Prost, 1992a). In the aftermath of the riots, the parliamentary majority was no longer in a position to implement such a reform and, since then, the *baccalauréat* has remained a qualification that has legally entitled its holders to enter the first year of a university course.

The pull factor which has driven the increase in participation rates at upper secondary school level in France during the 1980s and the 1990s has been the result of policies devised at central government level to increase qualification rates for future generations. All major political parties have implicitly adhered to this policy. At the same time, parents who themselves benefited from higher education in terms of social mobility have been eager to see their children move further up the social ladder through higher education. This growing expectation on the part of an educated population has had an impact on the increasing demand for tertiary education throughout the 1980s and especially the 1990s.

At the beginning of the 1980s, government experts forecast a significant fall in the demand for secondary schooling (Commission du Bilan, 1981: 179). They were partly right for, between 1980/81 and 1984/85, the number of students in the *lycées* increased by only 5 per cent. In this context, the signing of the European Act in 1985 had the effect of a political wake-up call. France's still rather sheltered national economy would soon have to face compulsory price deregulations as well as European and international competition. Restrictive economic and financial policies, such as the control of the financial market introduced by the Socialist government after its election in 1981, would no longer be a feasible option. A majority of unskilled jobs in traditional industries such as shipbuilding, car manufacturing or mining were already fast disappearing and it was expected that this trend would accelerate as new sectors of activities replaced traditional ones. The understanding was that the European Act heralded a new competitive environment in which the quality of the workforce, and therefore its overall level of education, would become a key factor in a country's international competitiveness. If the French Republic was to produce the kind of manpower a 'post-industrial' economy required, education – including higher education – would have to be a national priority. 'Education, education, education' could have been the motto of the Fabius government (1984–86). For a government which had more or less avowedly decided to put an end to its Keynesian experiment, this understanding presented other more immediate advantages since the unemployment rate, which the new government had pledged to curb, was still very high, especially among young people (Mission Education-Entreprises, 1985). As more economic liberal measures were out of the question, the emphasis on education was an important source of political legitimacy for the left-wing coalition in power, all the more as it pleased their traditional core voters, many of whom were teachers.

In 1985, the Secretary of State for National Education, Jean-Pierre Chevènement, set two targets for the French national education system: first, every school-leaver would be provided with recognised professional qualifications by the year 2000 and, second, 80 per cent of an age cohort would reach *baccalauréat* level. In spite of predictable accusations that this policy of expansion was at best badly devised, at worst demagogical, these objectives have been endorsed by Chevènement's successors, regardless of their political affiliation. In 1989, with Lionel Jospin as Education Minister, they became legal national requirements (Journal Officiel, 1989).

However, the general understanding at central political level was that any increase in numbers that occurred within the existing framework of the general and technical *baccalauréats* would be of little value since these diplomas were not designed to prepare students for direct employment. Central to government's vision, in a classical top-down approach, was the creation of new types of *baccalauréat* which would be vocationally-oriented and which would lead directly to the job market. The introduction of vocational options in 1965 had already led to a sharp increase in access to the *baccalauréat* by making it possible for holders of vocational certificates to continue their studies up to this level. The government's plan was that the new types of vocational *baccalauréat* would be the main vehicle through which government participation targets at upper secondary school level would be met and that these qualifications would be prepared in the vocational *lycées*.

The vocational *baccalauréats* were officially created in December 1985 and it was anticipated that most of the growth in the participation rate encouraged at upper secondary school level would take place in this new sector. This forecast turned out to be optimistic. In particular, it did not take into account the kind of social phenomenon which, for the sake of expediency, is commonly referred to as 'academic drift'. The newly created vocational *baccalauréats* did not at first encounter the expected success, partly because the students and their parents interpreted the situation differently: encouragement from the government for an increased percentage of an age cohort to reach *baccalauréat* level meant greater access to the more highly prized *baccalauréats* of an academic type, which were more widely recognised as the qualification that led to higher education. The *Instituts Universitaires de Technologie* (IUT) were even threatened with financial penalties by one education minister if they continued to recruit general *baccalauréat* holders rather than the technological *baccalauréat* holders for which these higher education institutions were originally planned. Today the normal path to long-term higher education remains the general *baccalauréats* with 66 per cent of those with these qualifications going to university, 10 per cent to the *Classes Préparatoires aux Grandes Ecoles* (*CPGE*) and the remaining 24 per cent choosing to go on to short-term forms of higher education (*IUTs, Sections de Techniciens Supérieurs*, paramedical studies).

At the beginning of the 1980s, roughly one-third of secondary school pupils attended a *lycée*. Ten years later, more than half did so, a clear progression towards the 80 per cent participation rate targeted by Jean-Pierre Chevènement. However, the quantitative forecast was more accurate than the qualitative one, for the social engineering devised at the top by government for the general population did not match the type of social progression sought by parents for their children. Between 1985 and 1990, the student population in the traditional *lycées* increased by 32 per cent.

This steep rise had not been foreseen, let alone planned for, and was in essence the result of the socio-economic environment. For Antoine Prost, observer and historian of the French system of education, this was a case of direct impetus given at government level to vocational secondary education reinforcing the demand for general and technical secondary education (Prost, 1992). (see Table 3.2)

The creation of vocational *baccalauréats*, however, accentuated the trend towards higher qualifications and redefined the place of vocational education within the national system of education. The *Brevet d'Enseignement Professionnel* (BEP) became as much a stepping-stone to studies at *baccalauréat* level and beyond as a final diploma preparing for entrance into the job market. The evolution in the vocational *lycées* has increased this tendency. Since the level of funding was rarely on a par with the extra funding needed for genuine vocational forms of education, financial choices had to be made in terms of courses they offered. Courses leading to the highest diploma, namely the *baccalauréats*, were given priority, as this was a way both to satisfy public demand and to enhance the status of the establishments and their staff. By 1990, the official targets set in 1985 had been surpassed. The next stage was a move in the curricula towards a more general content in comparison to their original vocational character in order to equip the many students who wanted to pursue their studies with an appropriate kind of knowledge.

Developments at upper secondary school level have seen central government plans being diverted by the converging interests of pupils and their parents and the regional authorities (which were given responsibility for the *lycées* following the decentralisation laws at the beginning of the 1980s). This development has had a direct quantitative and qualitative impact on the development of a higher education sector where universities are not officially allowed to be selective. This also explains why the expansion of higher education was late in penetrating the political agenda and why, until recently, it had not been a topic for sustained national debate in France. In a way, expansion at tertiary level 'happened', with those who have tried to steer actively the form of this expansion, such as Alain Devaquet, Claude Allègre or Jacques Attali, encountering strong opposition from the student population.

Table 3.2 Percentage of students studying at *baccalauréat* level

	1980–81	1990–91	1995–96	2002–03
General *baccalauréats*	22.1	33.4	36.5	33.9
Technological *baccalauréats*	11.9	17.6	20.9	21.1
Vocational *baccalauréats*	0.0	5.0	11.1	14.0
Total	34.0	56.0	68.5	69.1

Source: Ministère de la Jeunesse, de l'Éducation et de la Recherche, *L'état de l'école* (MEN Direction de la Prospective, Paris, 2003).

Alongside this 'proactive' picture explaining the rise in access to and participation in French tertiary education in recent decades, there is a more 'negative' factor to be taken into account in the form of persistently high rates of unemployment. This has been particularly true among young people, who have had to remain longer in education both by default and in order to secure greater opportunities to find a job. High youth unemployment in France may be explained by various factors concerned with demographic trends and forms of job market protection and regulation (OECD, 1998: 249).

In governmental spheres, whatever the relative importance of the different causes of expansion at upper secondary school level, growth was intended to occur through new qualifications, which were vocationally oriented. However, what has been modified in the process is the definition and status of upper secondary school qualifications and this has had a knock-on effect upon the next educational stage that is higher education. The central government's target was missed because of a demand which it was not in a position to control. Control would therefore have to take place further up the educational ladder in terms of access and selection.

The politics of access to higher education in France: legitimising access and expansion, protecting selection

It is well known that those from poorer social backgrounds remain relatively excluded from higher education expansion. However, the political debate in France has not focused particularly on this issue as the main parties have been reluctant to face its consequences from within their own sets of ideologies. The themes that have been used to justify expansion have varied over time. In a first stage, the discourse was driven by a notion of social equality, before becoming more a question of national economic performance and wealth creation. This was accompanied by a shift from the notion of equality to those of equity and diversity. At this later stage, the discourses on expansion have diverged more than ever before, cutting across political parties and professional/social allegiance.

In France, increased access to higher education has generated scepticism, not so much along the lines of 'more means worse' but of 'how expansion could be better than it is'. The economics of educational expansion have rarely been discussed openly in terms of private and social rates of return but are increasingly debated in terms of fitness for purpose in relation to graduate employability and opportunities. Proponents of the 'more means worse' argument have had to employ it in a subtle, covert manner or face accusations of being retrograde, elitist anti-republicans and it is more common to find the issue being debated along the lines of 'why more access means less equality/equity'. Prominent sociologists, historians and educationalists (Pierre Bourdieu, Raymond Boudon, Pierre Merle, Roger Establet, Christian Baudelot and Philippe Merrieu amongst others) have investigated the field and provided influential interpretations and criticisms which have fed the debate both in France and internationally.

Expansion in secondary education has made the questions of access and selection in higher education politically sensitive. Underpinned by rhetoric and *profession de foi*, the stances adopted in relation to the question have been informed by differing types of normative ideals concerning how higher education should contribute to the shaping of society. For some, an ideal social organisation is an ordered one consisting of a clear hierarchy of individuals. This favours selection by merit, particularly at the level of higher education, regardless of initial conditions. In France, the ultra-Republicans on the right or on the left would adopt such a stance. Another way to conceptualise the problem has been to see society as emerging from class struggle. Although it is contentious today, this stance was particularly influential in educational matters before the 1980s with strong state organisation being particularly approved of by teachers who sought to reconcile a Marxist discourse with the Republican ideal.

In 1968, French students protested against selection at the point of entry to university on the grounds that it was a principle which bent to capitalist criteria. Consequently, the government had to yield to public demand and the *Loi Faure*, which reorganised the university sector after May 1968, had to reject the notion of selection at entrance to the university. At that time, the prevailing idea at government level was that there would never be enough students and that, if there ought to be selection, it may as well take place within the universities rather than outside. There was already a sense that non-selection was regarded as a custom, almost as a right that could not be taken away. The idea that universities might even be opened up to able people without a *baccalauréat* led to the Vincennes University experiment, where non-traditional students were admitted and a pedagogically innovative form of higher education was developed by such renowned figures as Michel Foucault. Since then, however, the notion of selection has been a major bone of contention between the different protagonists in the French higher education debate.

Those who regard the university as being intrinsically non-selective, mainly the students, their parents and a proportion of the teachers, see it essentially as a public service to which access should be open and free to anybody with the relevant qualifications. For them, the Republican ethos means that the state has the duty to plan and provide enough university places for all those who wish to participate, regardless of the place and studies chosen. Following this logic, and the law that goes with it, it has been possible for the universities to be condemned for setting physical aptitude tests to select candidates at entry to training for physical education teachers (STAPS). In this context, the increasingly vexed question of who pays for expansion and how the costs should be met provides an interesting constitutional debate in that, according to France's written constitution, education is said to be 'free' at the point of delivery. However, does this concern only compulsory education or all state-provided education? At present, higher education is mainly paid for by taxpayers' money and the university fees for mainstream undergraduate and most postgraduate programmes remain nominal (around £100 per year), although students have to pay for social security. Maintenance grants may come in various, sometimes undiscriminating, guises such as accommodation grants (*Aide au Logement*) but direct bursaries are few and hardly generous. Meanwhile, the debate continues between the government and the student union representatives about conferring a special social status on students that would allow them to claim certain benefits and be more independent from family support. To summarise the situation, we may quote an *Inspecteur Général de l'Administration de l'Education Nationale* reflecting upon the current situation of higher education in France, especially after its latest expansion in the form of local university centres or branch campuses:

> [We should now ask ourselves] what the limit of compulsory education is. *De facto* it goes as far as undergraduate level.
>
> (Simon, 1996: 511)

Those who openly advocate stricter selection, and these are mainly academics often in a position of power, express the fear that a university education will merely become an extended form of secondary education. For them, in order to preserve the specific nature of a university education, the *baccalauréat* should not be considered to be an automatic passport to higher education (Schwartz, 1987). Many more, especially among politicians, refuse to consider the unpopular option of selection at entrance and prefer to concentrate their attention on the orientation and channelling of pupils at secondary level, on the regionalisation of short-cycle programmes (Fauroux, 1996; Laurent, 1995) or on the popular notion of lifelong learning. But those who advocate these solutions also add that major changes need to occur in order to make these ideas work: the variety of courses on offer needs to expand significantly to cater for the variety of needs expressed, links between courses have to be officially established and traineeships and hands-on experience should be more systematically organised. At the centre of most of these proposals lies the idea of locally based, non-selective tertiary education institutions, detached from the broader university system and mainly staffed by qualified secondary school teachers (*agrégés*). Needless to say, student unions are radically opposed to this vision. They have already warned the ministry that they would oppose the reorganisation of the second cycles in the university.[4] This proposal is also denounced by those who oppose it as a form of *secondarisatision* of higher education (Couteyron, 1996–97: 63–5).

From reading the parliamentary debates and official reports, the notion of tighter selection at entrance to the university may be regarded as virtually taboo in political debates in France. The reason for this is not only to be found in the events that took place in 1968 but also, closer to today, in the 1986 rioting against the Devaquet Bill. However, it may be argued that the debate surrounding selection is a purely conceptual one, not to say a red herring. In reality, selection is not only present but is fierce and has been the backbone of the organisation of the French higher education system, not to say its *raison d'être* according to the 'screening' interpretation of the role of higher education.

First and foremost, there are the public and private *grandes écoles*, which are greatly diverse in status and which are, in some cases, the remit of ministries other than the Ministry for National Education. In comparison to the universities, little detailed information and empirical evidence is available for the *grandes écoles*. Some facts, however, speak for themselves. In 1980, the *classes préparatoires* and the *grandes écoles* together made up about 5.5 per cent of the recruitment in higher education. In 1997/98 this percentage still represented only 6.6 per cent of the total (Ministère de l'Education Nationale, de la Recherche et de la Technologie, 1998: 153). Entry to most *grandes écoles* requires two years spent in the *classes préparatoires* of the *lycées* or, exceptionally, in the *école* itself. The *baccalauréat* is necessary but not sufficient to be admitted to a *classe préparatoire*. A file containing copies of reports from *baccalauréat* classes and teachers' assessments must be submitted. In this way, school pupils are already pre-selected for entry for the *classes préparatoires* where, for two to three years, they prepare for the stiff competitive examinations for entrance to the *grandes écoles*. In some of these, for example *l'Ecole Normale d'Administration* (ENA) or *Polytechnique*, there is a further selection process, as ranking at the end of the period of study also determines career opportunities. Successful candidates are not always able to choose which of the *grandes écoles* they join, or even their area of specialisation, given that places are allocated according to academic performance in examinations and that there is a clear hierarchy of institutions. The original purpose of the *grandes écoles* system was to serve the interests and needs of the state machinery through the rational selection and vocational training of its administrative, political, technical, academic and, ultimately, social elite and this remains largely the case today. There is no need to dwell on this for it has been consistently shown and often denounced by numerous French and foreign observers (Bourdieu, 1989; Crozier and Tilliette, 1995; Suleiman, 1978; Shinn, 1980). On average more than twice as much public money is spent per student in the government maintained *grandes écoles* (circa £8,000) than per university student (circa £4,000).

What is interesting is the type of pressure this elite sector has had to face in France, where 'blind' written competitive examinations followed by an oral examination have traditionally been presented as the fairest possible meritocratic selection process (Serres, 1999: 7). With unified expansion at upper secondary school level and a persistent lack of diversity in the social recruitment of the *grandes écoles*, the claim that this type of selection process promotes fair access to the *élite* has been an increasingly difficult stance to maintain. In 2004, the decision by the *Institut d'Etudes Politiques* in Paris to establish special links with some *lycées* in the Parisian suburbs is a good example of this unease. However, at national level, any meaningful pressure on the social and academic Malthusian logic of the French elites at tertiary level has come from external – and largely uncontrollable – forces in the form of persistently poor economic performance, European integration and globalisation. These have increasingly exposed the drawbacks of 'academic selection for academic selection's sake' and of certain aspects of the *grandes écoles* system. The main criticisms levelled are that the *grandes écoles* are too small and too conservative in their recruitment practice, too much closed in on themselves, promoting 'old boy networks', and over-specialised in their training often at the expense of good research.

Socialist governments have not been unaware of such criticisms. In the 110 propositions of his election manifesto before the 1981 elections, François Mitterrand had pledged to create a 'great, unified, secular public service of education'. This was vague enough to give some hope to those who opposed the duality of higher education in France and a short-lived attempt was made in 1984 to unify the system. However, it was to prove a statement essentially directed at the private school sector (where over-direct government action was later to result in failure). The Left was thus clinging to one of its traditional political mantras whilst successive Socialist Cabinets continued to recruit graduates from the *grandes écoles* as leaders in the state-owned industries, as political advisers and in various other positions in the power structure of the French state, including public television and privatised companies (Chagnollaud, 1991).

While the *Loi Savary* in 1984 reiterated the right of the *grandes écoles* to be selective, some attempts were made at democratising recruitment in top public institutions. A different type of competitive entrance examination for *l'ENA* was designed to allow second-grade civil servants and certain elected representatives to be admitted to the ENA according to their service record. However, this triggered accusations that such a form of recruitment would lower standards, with some going as far as denouncing it as a breach of the sixth article of the *Déclaration des Droits de l'Homme et du Citoyen*, according to which the civil service should be open to all according to talent. Moreover, those recruited through this new form of admission procedure have officially complained that they have not been treated on equal terms with their younger colleagues. This has meant a poor final ranking and limited career opportunities in the highest spheres of the civil service. In 1995, the reform initiated by Claude Allègre in the curriculum and syllabus of the *classes préparatoires* was introduced. These prepared access to the engineering *grandes écoles* so that 'doing' could be judged more on a par with 'thinking'. However, the *grandes écoles* were able to fend off the ministerial move and continue to give priority, through the way they set their examination papers, to recruiting 'theoretical' rather than 'pragmatic' minds. In practice, pupils with a general scientific *baccalauréat* rather than a technical one continued to be favoured.

The structural impact of the *grandes écoles* has become clear whenever the political centre has deemed it necessary to reinforce the position of the universities within the higher educational spectrum and so boost their credentials in an increasingly depressed job market for young people. Significantly, the decisions to create selective diplomas and programmes within the universities have been taken at central level and have been the result of successive ministerial decisions. The message that has been sent by governments is that selection is the answer to the difficulties faced by the universities. This had already been the case with the creation of the University Institutes of Technology (IUT) in 1966. This was also the case with the *magistères* created by Jean-Pierre Chevènement in the mid-1980s, with the development of the *Nouvelles Formations d'Ingénieurs* or with the *Instituts Universitaires Professionalisés* (IUP) created by Claude Allègre, the idea of which was to allow the universities to compete directly with the *grandes écoles*. The *magistères* in particular were planned as selective degrees *within* the universities, admissions procedures being based on previous achievements. Designed as an indivisible block of three years after two years of university studies, they were intended to combine the acquisition of basic knowledge, an introduction to research and its practical application within a professional framework. However, most *magistères* are now proposed by the *Ecoles Normales Supérieures*, which form part of the *grandes écoles* system, while the *magistères* proposed within the mainstream universities find it hard to establish a reputation, in particular because of the ambiguity of their status, which lies between a university diploma and a national one (Comité National d'Evaluation, 1995: 64–70).

A similar phenomenon may be identified in research activities. Although the *grandes écoles* have not traditionally been geared towards research, a significant evolution of the last few years is that they have increasingly integrated this aspect of higher education into their programmes. This development, encouraged by the central government, has been necessary to maintain their status, not least in relation to their positioning on an ever-competitive international stage. In this way, the traditional selective dualism of the French higher education system has remained.

Further occurrences of selection in French higher education may be noted. Since 1970, there has been a highly competitive examination with a *numerus clausus* at the end of the first year in medicine and pharmacology. Some universities, like *Paris Dauphine,* an experimental university set up after 1968, or certain university programmes do not even try to hide the fact that they apply forms of selection for their recruitment. Finally, in other subjects studied at university such as sciences, the liberal arts or the humanities for which access is automatic, drop-out rates have run high (around 50 per cent at the end of the first cycle of studies in some subjects). Drop-out rates are well-known to be higher in free open-access systems like the French one (OECD, 1997), although, in the case of France, the figures need to be reduced by the number of students who register at university as a safety net against failure in the *classes préparatoires* or as a 'waiting room' before taking other competitive examinations for public services (nurses, midwives, etc.) that are usually taken at *baccalauréat* level. Although elevated drop-out rates in non-selective university programmes may be regarded as a direct result of the existence of parallel selective routes, the rates remain nonetheless high in France and as A.H. Halsey puts it: 'dropping out is socially selective though with decreasing severity' (1993: 138). Central government and the academic profession were able to ride on this 'decreasing severity' until the mid-1990s when the expansionist trend exposed its financial and human costs. This is when the discourse of orientation started to be heard more distinctly.

As a result, the message sent by governments has been twofold. While it gave indications that selection was good practice by allowing the setting up of various selective programmes, it also tried to deliver another message, namely that selection was wasteful. At first, this discourse had the advantage of satisfying student unions but, as expansion gathered speed, it also became a genuine preoccupation for central governments as the bulk of students not carrying on to the next stage of their studies were weighing the system down with considerable financial consequences. This has been partly due to the freedom that *baccalauréat* holders have to register in any higher education programme on offer at their local university regardless of their previous qualifications. Students can be of highly varied strengths in any given subject, which explains why the first year at university has gradually become an orientation year. Thus the reform of the first cycle initiated by Alain Savary at the beginning of the 1980s, while creating the two-year DEUST (*Diplôme d'Etudes Universitaires Scientifiques et Techniques*), was also designed to facilitate the progression of students during their first two years at university. The universities were asked to abandon a disciplinary-based rigid credit accumulation system and to reorganise their activities so as to facilitate the adaptation of students, their reorientation and their acquisition of a number of basic skills. Since then, this type of policy has been endorsed by Savary's successors and it has justified the reorganisation of the first academic year into two semesters. However, the universities have been able to resist the change by paying lip service to a reform that transgresses traditional disciplinary and departmental divides and increases administrative loads (Kergomard, 1995: 126).

The quality of a university undergraduate programme in France has for a long time been measured by its rate of failure (Allègre, 1993: 21). Beyond the continuation of traditional structures, the existence of the much admired, strictly selective *grandes écoles* system, which has been generally supported by parents, students, politicians and academics alike, is not foreign to this. Moreover, in an open university system, it is easier to suspect high success rates of being a 'dumbing down' of degrees, which would result in an undermining of the social position of university teachers, than to consider it a sign of good pedagogical practices and of adaptation to the needs of students. Moreover, if the latter explanation were true, it would represent another threat for academia in the form of a radical overhaul of the student–teacher relationship. More than one hundred years ago, Matthew Arnold praised the poor level of pastoral care provided by teachers in the French *lycées* as a guarantee of their self-cultivation (Arnold, 1892: 288). Today, the situation, both in the universities and in the *classes préparatoires* is not very different and this is an important source of power in the hands of the academic profession. As Claude Allègre, a former Education Minister and an academic himself, states:

> From the beginning, the French university has been built and organised by and for the teachers. In the traditional conception, the professor is at the heart, at the centre of the institution. He owns the knowledge and hands it down ... to those who are capable of receiving it! In such a conception, students are not pupils, they are disciples, privileged people allowed to benefit from the teaching of the master. Through it they are themselves distinguished. Among the disciples the master chooses those few that he judges capable of becoming in turn the future masters.
>
> (Allègre, 1993: 12)

Of course, a former minister may be suspected of promoting a particular agenda with such a statement but personal accounts and empirical evidence support this particular analysis. The relationship is epitomised in the persistence of the age-old lecture-hall format still used for the delivery of most courses at undergraduate level, which has been criticised in a pamphlet written by a group of leading academics (ARESER, 1997: 73). Of course, it may be said, leaving aside methods only recently made possible by information technology, that this has been practically the only way to teach large numbers of students with the number of staff available. Nevertheless, it must be noted that this formal barrier erected between the teachers and the students has helped to shelter university teachers from the impact of rising undergraduate numbers.

It is only since the recognition of the overall human and financial wastage caused by high drop-out and failure rates (especially at undergraduate level) that performance-based approaches have been considered as a possible way of measuring the value of higher education. At the beginning of its activities in 1985, the *Comité National d'Evaluation* was anxious to stress that its task was not to evaluate individual or even departmental performances but that whole institutions were their sole units of inspection. In July 1989, the central authority officially stated that 'the public service of education is designed and organised around the pupils and the students' (Journal Officiel, 1989a). This was intended to represent a major shift in the way education was to be legally envisaged in France. Five years later, with Lionel Jospin as Education Minister, drop-out and failure rates in the first-years of over-crowded universities were emerging as one of the major issues French universities had to face. Claude Allègre, then special adviser to Lionel Jospin, denounced them as a major source of financial wastage and, in 1997, the *Direction de l'Evaluation et de la Prospective de l'Education Nationale* (DEP) published for the first time university league tables based on rates of access to the *licence* (L'Edudiant, 1998) an almost Copernican revolution in French academia.

Equality of access versus equality of outcome

Since education in France is at all levels a public service by constitutional right, the traditional Republican discourse has focused on the notion of equality, that is to say the equal availability of goods and people within the system (Walford, 1994: 13). This principle is also to be found in the equal public subsidies for food, accommodation and various student activities. All students benefit from indirect subsidies through tax allowances for their parents, low prices for food through the *Restaurants Universitaires*, cheap leisure and reduced-price accommodation through non-means-tested accommodation grants. A number of ministers are concerned in the areas of housing, taxes, family policy, transportation and health. Each year, students studying towards national degrees have to pay registration fees, the amount of which is fixed annually by ministerial decree. With such an approach, monitoring the access of specific parts of the population on the basis of ethnic origins or religious affiliation is not only considered as irrelevant but also as philosophically and politically unwelcome. Pushing the argument to its limits, it is recalled that the last time France had any form of social monitoring based on ethnic or religious origins was under the Vichy régime. The whole system has developed 'naturally' – others would say blindly – without any special attention to the various cat-egories of the population gaining access to it and, especially, without any official attempt at developing affirmative action to try to redress social imbalances in access. The monitoring of ethnic minorities, genders or social classes are specific cases in point. In France, it is the egalitarian approach which has been favoured by the government, students and higher education institutions alike. This public discourse on minorities, genders and classes is striking but too pervasive to be linked to particular sets of interest within the higher education system itself without falling into an unjustified form of conspiracy theory. Education systems are embedded in a broader ideological context which they themselves partly produce (Archer, 1996).

In France, expansion has revealed the persistent and, at times, growing inequalities in selection and access at tertiary level. Central government has been slow to realise the threat such a situation poses to their legitimacy as a 'natural' organiser and decision-maker in higher education. In particular, the *grandes écoles* in France were allowed to select whom they wanted the way they wanted whilst expansion was taking place in less-well funded institutions. Then, towards the end of the 1980s, central government took a closer look at the political liabilities that failure to curb certain inequalities might represent and tried to take action. This meant that it intervened directly by creating selective programmes within the universities that would allow a minority of their students to compete with the products of the *grandes écoles* on the job market. In this sense, selection within the universities was chosen as a way to equity. The government encouraged the reorganisation of the programmes so that students could be given a greater chance to complete their degree in three years, thus seeking to minimise the cost of academic selection. At the same time, it did not impose major changes on the *grandes écoles* system itself. In particular, the radical move to generalise preparation for the *grandes écoles* within the universities was not initiated. Abolishing the competitive examinations themselves seems entirely out of the question for the moment as they are constitutive of the French state as it currently operates.

Increased access rates and their impact on the student population as a social group

As may be expected, the widening of access to higher education to this degree could not take place without modifying social interactions. In 1967 there were some 580,000 students in post-secondary education in France, with 500,000 in the public universities alone. The majority of these were in Paris. This was the time when Pierre Bourdieu and Jean-Claude Passeron, in a seminal study on the sociology of French higher education, described the student population as an 'anomy', a group of resentful individuals with nothing in common but their shared middle-class origins and unfulfilled expectations (Bourdieu and Passeron, 1964). By 1981, however, more than one million people were studying at tertiary level. More than a quarter of eighteen to twenty-two-year-olds continued to tertiary education, which meant that a fifth of this class age attended a university. This was mass higher education in the making. The student status had become a privilege *per se*, sufficient to establish a clear distinction from the rest of young people. Students had become a specific social group with its own particular agenda (Baudelot *et al.*, 1981). Today, the situation is again different. With over two million students, representing more than a 50 per cent participation rate among the eighteen- to twenty-two-year-olds (more than 35 per cent in public universities alone), French higher education has become a fully fledged mass system (Trow, 1972: 63) with social categories which were not previously concerned with higher education now seeing their off-spring gain access (see Table 3.3). But expansion has also taken place at the expense of unit costs, in particular in university programmes which are non-selective at entrance. In some instances, students have to arrive well in advance for their lectures in order to secure a seat in overcrowded

Table 3.3 Higher education: rates of access

	Rates of immediate access to various HE programmes after the baccalauréat *(2002)*	Rates of access to the first year of university BA degree programmes[b]
General baccalauréats[a]		
University (without IUT)	63.5	66.3
Instituts Universitaires de Technology (IUT)	11.7	
Classes Préparatoires aux Grandes Écoles	13.8	
Sections de Techniciens Supérieur	8.7	
Others	8.9	
Technological baccalauréats		
University (without IUT)	17.7	23.4
IUT	9.8	
CPGE	1.1	
STS	46.4	
Others	3.5	
Vocational baccalauréats		
University (without IUT)	5.8	8.4
IUT	0.6	
CPGE	0.0	
STS	12.9	
Others	0.5	
Total		
University (without IUT)	39.4	56.8
IUT	9.0	
CPGE	7.5	
STS	20.3	
Others	5.8	

Source: Ministère de la Jeunesse, de l'Éducation et de la Recherche, *L'état de l'école* (MEN Direction de la Prospective, Paris, 2003).

Notes
a Students can be registered for more than one higher education programme so the total numbers/percentages may be higher than those for the individual programmes combined.
b At least two years of study in higher education is required before proceeding to the first year of the BA programme but up to five years is permitted for those who fail examinations or do not complete courses.

lecture halls. By the beginning of the 1990s, French universities could be depicted as being increasingly chaotic and anonymous organisations where students either sank or swam (Lapeyronnie and Marie, 1992). Today it seems that the experiences and attitudes of students vary greatly according to their place of study, the kind of studies they undertake and the type of establishment they attend (Galland *et al.*, 1995) which illustrates the kinds of diversification the French higher education system has undergone as access rates have increased.

A striking feature of the French higher education landscape is the wealth of data that has been made available on the student population as a social category, dealing with their experience of the system, their way of life or hardship. From ethno-methodological studies to surveys carried out on a national basis through the refinement of the statistical tools of the *Direction de l'Evaluation et de la Prospective*, the student population has been a major focus of attention. This is not unconnected to the repeated outbursts of student anger in 1986, 1993 and 1995 and needs to be opposed to the dearth of information concerning the academic profession and its evolving situation in the face of such changes. Apart from the handful of books that have been written by French academics over the last twenty years and which are essentially based on personal experiences, it is very difficult to know what French academics make of the changes that have affected their profession, given the silence which is maintained on the subject as noted in the mid-1990s when François Bayrou organised his *états généraux* of the university (Union Federale Universitaire, 18 June 1996).

A major change has been the gradual de-politicisation of student unions and the repositioning of their action and activities. In spite of declining union affiliation, French students have repeatedly demonstrated their considerable capacity for taking an active part in the social debate. However, a discourse that revolved around general moral and political concepts in the 1960s has gradually been replaced by a wish to secure and foster students' particular interests. Students have become a social category, whose demands have little to do with the broader aspects of political life but whose form of action still takes place mainly at a national political level. In this sense, those who hastily compared the 1986 demonstrations to the 1968 riots were largely mistaken, for the 1986 demonstrations and the ensuing ones were not an attempt to overthrow the existing system but were signs that the growing student population wanted to experience similar conditions to those enjoyed by previous generations. For example, one of the central aims of the French student unions is for the different kinds of public aid that students currently receive through various channels to be reorganised into means-tested lump sums paid directly to them. The idea behind this is the recognition that young people should not be forced to be financially dependent on their parents to be able to study in satisfactory conditions at the higher level. The unions' central demand is that students be officially granted a special social status. Not surprisingly, this demand has met with a lukewarm response on the part of successive governments as it has been calculated that this would cost over nine billion euros. Moreover, parental associations are also against it, as families are entitled to allowances until their 'child' is twenty-two. Others who oppose the project fear that it would contribute to the creation of a privileged caste of young people. This worry is reinforced by surveys such as the one carried out by the UNEF-ID – the main student union close to the Socialist party – at the end of the 1990s which showed that, while 85 per cent of students agree with the idea of means-tested mandatory grants for students, only 67 per cent of them agree with the idea that such financial help should be granted to young job-seekers (Delberghe, 21 January 1998).

One notable feature of student actions has been the extent to which the traditional student unions have become less representative of the student body and have been at times superseded by apparently spontaneous uprisings of student groups which reject any explicit political allegiance. This shift has been part of a broader trend within French society, an evolution which has seen established unions being overtaken by coordinated movements formed around professional categories and without any declared political affiliation and, more recently, by new unions. In the case of the student population, besides the fact that this trend reflects the general evolution in terms of the demands of categories, it has not changed the political essence of their actions or the centralised focus of those actions. It is always the political centre which is called to account and which has to answer their demands. In this sense, one can meaningfully speak of student power, a fact which is illustrated by the wealth of attention this category of the population has received from the media, sociologists and successive governments in the wake of students' public actions and demonstrations. However, if students remain politically influential in extra-curricular matters, they have little say in the day-to-day running of courses and programmes. Alain Devaquet, as a former higher education minister addressing teaching colleagues who were contemplating the American model with envy, asked whether they were also prepared to accept being regularly assessed and ranked by their audience as their American colleagues were (Devaquet, 1987). Two of his successors, François Bayrou and Claude Allègre, took up this idea by mentioning the possibility of establishing course feedback procedures, cautiously adding that these should operate purely on the level of information. In short, we may say that, in a context of increased access and *in relation to students*, French academics are still largely free to decide upon the content and form of the knowledge they wish to transfer. This situation also needs to be related to the fact that the student population is relatively homogeneous in terms of age profile, the needs of mature students being essentially catered for on the fringe in specific vocational university

programmes or outside the higher education sector in continuing education institutions (e.g. *Groupements d'Etablissements pour la Formation
Continue* – GRETA).

Conclusions

The pressure that growth in access has exerted on the original fabric of
higher education has meant that the different stakeholders have vied
to ensure that their interests are taken into account while the central
authorities have made sure that their own interests have been advanced.
The various groups have subscribed to certain values designed to justify
their demands. As numbers have grown, the student population has
seen its stake in the system increase but their reinforced influence
has been channelled through existing structures. So far, it has mostly
been the student population which has had to yield as the academic profession has maintained its core practices with the implicit assent of the
political authorities. This explains why students have fallen back on an
attitude of categorical defence punctuated by sporadic expressions of
anger.

In France, widening access has not turned elitism and canonical academic excellence into suspicious terms, nor have the assumptions on which
these ideas are based been questioned. This explains why access combined
with 'blind' selective academic criteria have remained a way to objectify
obvious types of social selection and reproduction through education. The
situation has spurred recent localised attempts at introducing some sort of
'social positive discrimination', for example at the *Institut d'Etudes Politiques* in Paris. As in Britain, although for different reasons, the question
of how to resolve mass and elite systems of higher education remains
problematic.

Mass higher education has certainly changed the purpose of the French
universities, taking them beyond their traditional roles of the transmission
of knowledge (teaching) and the expansion of knowledge (research)
because it has partly changed the reproductive tendency of the higher education sector. However, while certain actors within the expanded HE
sector have developed outside traditional beliefs and expectations, others
have continued to fight to preserve them. The latter group has not been
put under any great pressure by what has happened to the former and
both have coexisted with the active collaboration of the central public
authorities.

Notes

1 In 2002, the pass rate was 78.8 per cent, (i.e. 61.2 per cent of the age cohort) with
   78.6 per cent of those successful going on to higher education; Ministère de la
   Jeunesse, de l'Éducation et de la Recherche, *L'état de l'école* (MEN Direction
   de la Prospective, Paris, 2003), pp. 52–3.

2 Ministère de la Jeunesse, de l'Éducation et de la Recherche, *L'état de l'école* (MEN Direction de la Prospective, Paris, 2003), pp. 58–9; OECD, *Education at a Glance: OECD Indicators* (Paris: OECD, 2001), p. 155.

Type-A refers to theory-based HE programmes preparing advanced research degrees. In France, this means mainstream university programmes. Type B refers to technical and/or vocational shorter HE programmes. In France, this includes the University Institutes of Technlogy (IUT), the two to three years of preparation for the competitive entrance examinations for the *grandes écoles* and miscellaneous types of selective vocational higher education.

The 21 per cent in Type-B higher education quoted in the OECD document does not take into account the 20 per cent of *baccalauréat* holders who go on to a *Section de Techniciens Supérieurs*.

3 All extracted quotes are translations by the author.

4 French universities are organised in three successive cycles. The first cycle represents the first two years and leads to the DEUG. The second cycle includes the third year (*licence*) and the fourth one (*maitrise*). The third cycle leads to the doctorate after a year of training in research methodology (DEA). This means that the whole system is organised around *baccalauréat* +2 and +4. Student union representatives oppose a *baccalauréat* +3 and +5 reorganisation that would effectively bring the French system closer in line with foreign ones on the grounds that it would devalue previous qualifications.

References

Allègre, C., *L'âge des savoirs: pour une renaissance de l'Université* (Paris: Gallimard, 1993).

Archer, M.S., *Culture and Agency: The Place of Culture in Social Theory* (Cambridge: Cambridge University Press, 1996).

ARESER, *Quelques diagnostics et remèdes pour une université en péril* (Paris: Liber-Raison d'agir, 1997).

Arnold, M., *A French Eton: Or Middle-Class Education and the State: To which is Added Schools and Universities in France* (London: Macmillan, 1892).

Baudelot, C. and R. Establet, *Allez les filles!* (Paris: Seuil, 1992).

Baudelot, C., R. Benoliel, H. Cukrowicz and R. Establet, *Les Etudiants L'Emploi, la Crise* (Paris: Maspero, 1981).

Bourdieu, P., *La reproduction: elements pour une theorie du systeme d'enseignement* (Paris: Editions de Minuit, 1970).

Bourdieu, P., *La noblesse d'Etat: grandes écoles et esprit de corps* (Paris: Editions de Minuit, 1989).

Bourdieu, P. and J.-C. Passeron, *Les Héritiers: les étudiants et la culture* (Paris: Editions de Minuit, 1964).

Chagnollaud, D., *Le premier des ordres. Les hauts fonctionnaires XVII–XX siècle* (Paris: Fayard, 1991).

Comité National d'Evaluation, *Evolution des universités, dynamique de l'évaluation. Rapport au président de la République, 1985–1995* (Paris: La Documentation Française, 1995).

Commission du Bilan, *La France en mai 1981* (Paris: La Documentation Française, 1981).

Couteyron, A., *S'orienter pour mieux réussir* (Paris: Les rapports du Sénat 1996–1997, n. 81, pp. 63–5).

Crozier, M. and B. Tilliette, *La crise de l'intelligence: essai sur l'impuissance des élites à se réformer* (Paris: InterEditions, 1995).

Devaquet, A., *L'amibe et l'étudiant: université et recherche: état d'urgence.* (Paris: Odile Jacob, 1987).

Delberghe, M., 'L'UNEF-ID sonde les attentes dans les faculté', *Le Monde* (21 January 1998).

L'Etudiant, *Le palmarès des premiers cycles.* 195 (April 1998), pp. 42–53.

Fauroux, R., *Pour l'école*, Rapport de la Commission présidée par, (Paris: Calman-Lévy/La Documentation Française, 1996).

Galland, O., M. Clémençon, P. Le Gallès and M. Oberti, *Le monde des étudiants* (Paris: Presses Universitaires de France, 1995).

Halsey, A.H., 'An international comparison of access to higher education', *Oxford Studies in Comparative Education*, 1, (1991), pp. 11–36.

Halsey, A.H., 'Trends in access and equity in higher education: Britain in international perspective', *Oxford Review of Education*, 19, 2 (1993), pp. 11–36.

Journal Officiel, *Loi n.89-486 du 10 juillet 1989 d'Orientation de l'Education*, art. 1, 1989.

Journal Officiel, *Loi n.89-486 du 10 juillet 1989 d'Orientation de l'Education*, art. 20, 1989a.

Kergomard, A., *La mutation universitaire: Clermont 1948-1993* (Paris: L'Harmattan, 1995).

Lapeyronnie, D. and J.-L. Marie, *Campus blues. Les étudiants face à leurs études* (Paris: Le Seuil, 1992).

Laurent, D., *Universités: Relever les défis du nombre* (Rapport remis à Mr le Ministre de l'Enseignement supérieur et de la Recherche) Groupe de réflexion sur l'avenir de l'enseignement supérieur, 1995.

Ministère de la Jeunesse, de l'Éducation et de la Recherche, *L'état de l'école* (Paris: MEN Direction de la Prospective, 2003).

Ministère de l'Éducation Nationale, de la Recherche et de la Technologie, *Repères et Références Statistiques sur les Enseignements et la Formation* (Paris: MEN, 1998).

Ministère de l'Éducation Nationale, de la Recherche et de la Technologie, *Repères Réferences Statistiques sur les Enseignements, la Formation et la Recherche* (Paris: MEN Direction de la Prospective, 2003).

Mission Education-Entreprises (Bureau d'Informations et de Previsions Economiques), *Quels hommes and quelles femmes pour former l'entreprise de demain? Prevision Des qualifications a l'an 2000* (Paris: BIPE, 1985).

Organisation for Economic Co-operation and Development. *Education at a Glance* (Paris: OECD, 1997).

Organisation for Economic Co-operation and Development, *Education at a Glance: Indicators 1998.* (Paris: Centre for Educational Research and Innovation, OECD, 1998).

Preamble to the 1946 Constitution. (Reaffirmed in the 1958 Constitution).

Prost, A., *Education, société et politiques: une histoire de l'enseignement en France de 1945 à nos jours* (Paris: Seuil, 1992).

Prost, A., *Lecture historique et lecture sociologique – Éducation, société et politiques: une histoire de l'enseignement en France de 1945 à nos jours* (Paris: Seuil, 1992a).

Schwartz, L., *Où va l'université?* (Paris: Gallimard, 1987).

Serres, M., 'Choix', *Le Monde de L'Education*, 269, (April 1999), p. 7.

Shinn, T., *L'École polytechnique: 1794-1914* (Paris: Presses de la Fondation Nationale des Sciences Politiques, 1980).

Simon, J., 'La décentralisation du système éducatif', *Revue Française d'Administration* Publique, 79 (1996).

Suleiman, E., *Les élites en France. Grands corps et grandes écoles* (Paris: Seuil, 1978).

Trow, M., 'The expansion and transformation of higher education', *International Review of Education,* 18, 1 (1972).

Union Federale Universitaire, *Synthese de l'intervention de Francois Bayrou, Ministere de L'Education Nationale et de l'Enseignement Superieur et de la Recherche: Les Etats Generaux de l'Universite* (Paris, Sorbonne: 18 June 1996).

Walford, G., *Choice and Equity in Education* (London: Cassell, 1994).

4 *Bildung* or *Ausbildung*?[1]
Reorienting German higher education

Hanna Ostermann

Introduction

Rarely did the publication of an OECD report have such an impact in Germany as the PISA study (Programme for International Student Assessment in secondary education) in 2001. This study placed Germany in its educational achievements in basic skills such as reading competence or mathematics of 14- and 15-year-olds only among the low twenties of the thirty-two participating countries. Not only did this survey show up deficiencies in academic achievements, but it also highlighted greater inequality between different socio-economic and ethnic groups in terms of educational opportunities and achievements than in other countries. This study had the jolting effect, the 'Sputnikschock', which former Federal President Roman Herzog in his speech at the Berlin Forum for Education in November 1997 had found sadly missing in regard to the diminishing reputation of German higher education abroad. Due to the PISA study the early 2000s may well have become another key stage in educational policy-making in Germany, comparable possibly in its impact with the reform period of the 1960s and 1970s which changed the landscape of secondary and higher education.

Over the years federal and state governments of all political persuasions have stressed the importance of education. The current federal government was no exception when it assigned a key role to education and research in its aims to keep Germany's position as a leading nation in an increasingly global economy, to reduce unemployment and to retain a generally high standard of living. Because of the poor results of the PISA study, political and media attention currently focus on pre-school, primary and secondary education. Whereas discussion about the aims and objectives of higher education have been conducted for many years now, this has largely taken place away from the public eye. Only in the late 1990s, and to a lesser extent in 2003, a series of student strikes attracted much media coverage and sparked off a relatively short-lived public debate about higher education. Overcrowding (in the winter semester 2001/02, approximately 1.8 million students were sharing roughly 1 million places (Decker and Beck, 2001: 23)), funding and quality issues are the major areas of concern and have led some critics of the system to portray higher education as a mass system distinguished by quantity rather than quality. At the same time, doubt is expressed more frequently about Germany's ability to produce sufficient numbers of graduates to safeguard the country's survival as a leading economic power, in spite of all its mass universities.

This chapter will briefly sketch the development from an elite to a mass education system, then look at the federal context and current government policies for reforming higher education. The current reform debate is driven by the aim to increase access and to widen participation while at the same time improving the quality of higher education. Of special interest within this reform agenda is the move away from the Humboldtian tradition of the pursuit of scholarship, which has informed the German university system since the nineteenth century, to a more regulated stratified model of undergraduate and postgraduate tuition along the lines of the Anglo-American system. These changes involve not only course organisation but also encourage a stronger vocational orientation in the university sector. Furthermore they broaden access requirements for higher education together with more control for the institutions in the selection of their students. Apart from examining the above changes, this chapter will look at the debate to what extent students should contribute to funding their education.

The historical context

With steady economic recovery after the destruction of the Second World War, student numbers in Germany[2] rose quickly, from 110,000 in 1950 (FRG without Saarland and Berlin) to over 200,000 (FRG including Berlin) in 1959. In relation to the size of the population that meant three times as many students as in 1933 (Ellwein, 1997: 244). The political foundations for the transition from an elite to a mass system, however, were laid later, in the 1960s and 1970s when the evolving interest in higher education was reinforced by a general debate about the nature and aims of education in Germany. Key terms such as Georg Picht's 'Deutsche Bildungskatastrophe' (crisis in German education) (1964) and Ralf Dahrendorf's education as 'Bürgerrecht' (a civil or constitutional right) (1965) characterised the differing points of view in this very public discussion, a discussion that is echoed in many ways by the present debate.

On the one hand the debate was driven by economic considerations focusing on the country's need for a highly qualified workforce in order to compete in an increasingly technological age, a need which the education system at the time was unlikely to satisfy. On the other hand the arguments centred on equal opportunities and the wider participation in the educational process of women and of socially disadvantaged groups. The latter arguments stressed the right of individuals to develop their academic potential to the full without consideration for the demands of the labour market. Whereas motives and arguments for reforming the educational system may have differed, the changes demanded looked very similar. They included increasing the number of young people taking higher qualifications as well as increasing the openness of the system in order to accommodate late developers and to provide opportunities for individuals to 'upgrade' their educational aims and achievements at any stage in their educational or professional careers – demands which are repeated in today's suggestions for reform.

Between 1965 and 1975 the state responded to concerns about the potential lack of highly qualified employees and the demand for greater social inclusion with a massive expansion in the school and the higher education systems. As a result, the number of students taking the *Abitur* (A-levels), the standard entry requirement for higher education, increased dramatically as did the number of A-level students entering higher education. From 8 per cent of the relevant year group entering higher education in 1960, this figure had risen to roughly 25 per cent in 1990 (Peisert and Framheim, 1990: 6). The rise in absolute student figures was even higher than the percentages suggest. It coincided with demographic changes – the year groups with particularly high birth rates had begun to reach university age – and with changes in studying patterns, which meant students were beginning to take longer to graduate.

The general trend among A-level students in choosing a university education continued to be upward, even though demand for university places fluctuated because of the country's changing economic situation and employment prospects for new graduates. These fluctuations, but particularly the fact that the birth rate was declining, again led to a slow down in university expansion. Relying on the assumption that from the 1990s onwards student numbers would drop again, the *Länder* passed the so-called *Öffnungsbeschluss* in 1977, the decision to keep university access open to anyone with the relevant qualifications, in fact a constitutional entitlement, but without equivalent funding for the institutions. Accepting that demand for university places would continue to rise for a number of years to come, it was decided that rather than providing more places, the expected demographic student 'bulge' should be 'tunnelled' (*Untertunnelung*). In effect this meant that for roughly a decade universities were expected to operate above capacity, as further expansion was not considered viable in view of long-term demographic developments (see Arbeitsgruppe Bildungsbericht, 1994: 671). As is known only too well today, this assumption has proven to be a miscalculation.

With increasing general affluence the interest in university education has remained at a higher level than predicted, even though there have been fluctuations in response to the situation on the labour market. Unemployment rates and income among graduates still compare very favourably with those of lesser-qualified people. In addition, the rising number of well-qualified people has gone hand in hand with a change in the type of work in many sectors and with it the expectations of employers (Arbeitsgruppe Bildungsbericht, 1994: 668), which in turn has encouraged more young people to opt for a degree. Another contributing factor has been the rising number of graduates among parents which has affected the choice of their children's career paths. Besides, the social status of a graduate is still higher than that of a non-graduate. This means that the *Öffnungsbeschluss*, which had been conceived as a temporary strategy, by now has resulted in permanent overcrowding and underfunding of German universities, although not all universities and all subjects are similarly affected. Ironically, the *Öffnungsbeschluss* partly resulted in its direct opposite, the *numerus clausus*. Particularly popular subjects and institutions were forced to limit student numbers and introduced restricted or delayed access, that is, a selection process based on a points system which includes A-level results and waiting time and, for male students, national service. This *numerus clausus* may be determined locally by the higher education institution itself for all the courses where demand exceeds the institution's capacities. For the subject areas with a shortage of places nationwide, such as medicine or pharmacy, both the required A-level marks and the allocation of places are set and managed through a central organisation for the whole of Germany. While everybody who has the necessary entry requirements is entitled to a university place, the introduction of the *numerus clausus* means that this place is not guaranteed either for the subject, the institution or the time of the applicant's first choice.

The federal context

In the document *Bildung, Forschung, Innovation – der Zukunft Gestalt geben (Education, Research, Innovation – Shaping the Future)* the Federal Ministry for Education and Research states the government's central aim as: the best education, vocational training and opportunities for lifelong learning for every individual irrespective of postcode or income (see Bundesministerium für Bildung und Forschung, 2002: 2). In order to implement reforms and to achieve its aims in higher education, the government has offered the federal states a *Pakt für die Hochschulen* (Pact for Higher Education). Because of the specific political nature of the Federal Republic, the federal government is not able to decide or dictate educational policies but depends on the cooperation of the federal states, the *Länder*. Article 30 of the Basic Law guarantees the individual states sovereignty in matters cultural and educational (*Kulturhoheit*) which include the organisation of schools and of the higher education sector. Educational policies in each federal state are informed by a general framework based on the ongoing process of negotiation and agreement through the *Kultusministerkonferenz (KMK)*, the Standing Conference of the Ministers for Education and Culture. The education system is now a largely unified system but there are local variations which in the primary and secondary sector can be substantial. For higher education the sovereignty of the federal states has been diminished much more over the years, while the federal government has increased its influence, in particular through the introduction in 1976 of the Framework Act for Higher Education (*Hochschulrahmengesetz*), which has since undergone several amendments, increasing federal responsibility, for example, for both the grant system and the university building programme.

An example of the increasingly close cooperation between the federal government and the *Länder* for all levels of education is the creation in 1999 of the *Forum Bildung* (Forum Education) consisting of the federal minister and the *Länder* ministers for education as well as representatives of employers, trade unions, churches, lecturers, students and trainees and apprentices. The cooperative nature of this body is probably highlighted best by the joint chairmanship of Edelgard Bulmahn, the Federal Minister for Education and Research (SPD), and Hans Zehetmair, the Bavarian Minister for Science, Research and the Arts (CSU), each representing a different end of the political spectrum, and is summed up in the preamble of the *Forum's* 2001 recommendations: 'The diversity offered by German federalism has a stimulating effect on educational reform. However, it is important to make sure that, on an international level, the German education system is perceived as a whole' (Forum Bildung Working Party, 2001: 4). Attributing a 'stimulating effect' to federalism may well be understood as a polite euphemism here. More often it is probably seen as, for example, a 'föderales Gerangel', a federal scramble (Poschardt, 20 June 2003), a term that focuses more on the never-ending discussions on the distribution of responsibilities and on the vested interests of the different political parties, both of which can ultimately have a paralysing effect when it comes to changes to the system. Decisions by the *KMK* have to be unanimous and tend to settle on the lowest common denominator in the *Länders'* search for a consensus (von Hammerstein *et al.*, 2002). Minister Bulmahn herself is much more direct in her press statement of the 25 June 2002 (see Bundesministerium für Bildung und Forschung, 25 June 2002) in which she introduces her five-point action plan in response to the PISA study. Here she describes education as a 'national task' which should and will be the responsibility of the Federation. According to her, decades of 'Kirchturmpolitik' (parochial policies), quarrelling about competencies, and party politics have done little, apart from – by implication – leading to Germany's poor showing in international league tables. However, as will be shown later in the context of funding, curtailing the cultural sovereignty of the *Länder* may be rather easier in theory than in practice. Nevertheless, the government's signing up to the Bologna Agreement means that certainly in higher education the states have to present a largely unified front, even if differing political aims and objectives of the 16 *Länder* governments may well continue to affect the detail and speed of the implementation of changes. How successful initiatives such as the *Forum Bildung* and the *Pakt für Hochschulen* are going to be remains to be seen.

In its 2001 recommendations the *Forum Bildung* concentrates on five major areas for improving education in Germany. These recommendations, which already inform government policy, are access to education in general, the acquisition of skills relevant in a knowledge society, lifelong learning, constant improvement of the quality of education programmes, and the motivation and ability to learn independently. As far as financing the system is concerned a combination of 'public funding and funding based on collective agreements with financial input from the individual concerned' (Forum Bildung Working Party, 2001: 5) is seen as the way forward. What changes are envisaged or already being implemented for higher education and how these may impact on access will now be examined in more detail.

Increasing access to higher education

The percentage of entrants into higher education among the relevant year group in Germany rose from 27.7 per cent in 1998 to 35.6 per cent in 2002, which in spite of its rising tendency is well below the OECD average of 44 per cent.[3] Discussions about increasing access and widening participation are largely driven by the needs of the labour market. The interdependence between economic growth and a high level of education is stressed again and again. According to Minister Bulmahn, Germany needs more qualified people and therefore a higher percentage of A-level students and graduates (see Bundesministerium für Bildung und Forschung, 25 June 2002). It is estimated that the demand for highly qualified employees in Germany will increase by 2.4 million by the year 2015, of which nearly one million would have to be graduates, a need which cannot be fulfilled with current graduate numbers. The government therefore aims at reaching a figure of at least 40 per cent of each year group embarking on a higher education degree within the next few years (Bundesministerium für Bildung und Forschung, *Bildung, Forschung*, 2002: 5).

However, in 2001, the *Kultusministerkonferenz* predicted a rather different trend. While according to their estimates the number of young people achieving the *Abitur* would increase further until 2008, the percentage of A-level students who would actually enter university would not keep pace. The increase in new entrants to higher education since 1992/93 has occurred largely in the eastern states, after substantial changes had been made to the former GDR institutions of higher education (55.8 per cent in Sachsen-Anhalt or even 157.3 per cent in Brandenburg). This masked the only moderate increase (9.8 per cent in Lower Saxony, 8.1 per cent in Baden Württemberg) or even decline (−13.9 per cent in Saarland, −10.4 per cent in Schleswig-Holstein) in the western states. The *KMK* therefore expects that the number of first-year students is likely to have peaked and may even drop by 2015 (Decker and Beck, 2001: 8).

In order to reverse this negative trend in university entry figures, a variety of marketing initiatives have been launched addressing very specific groups of potential students. For example, in sciences and engineering where a major demand for qualified graduates is anticipated, the as yet largely untapped potential of women is targeted. Equality of the sexes here, though welcome, is not the objective itself. Another target group is that of foreign students in an attempt to promote Germany as a destination for international students.

The government's dilemma is obvious. On the one hand universities are already suffering overcrowding and underfunding, the interest in entering higher education among A-level students is predicted to be reaching a plateau, and yet more graduates are needed to safeguard Germany's economic future. What is intended therefore is not a new broad expansion programme as happened in the 1960s and 1970s, but rather a reform of existing structures: through substantial changes to the organisation of degree programmes, better tutorial guidance for students to cut the high drop-out rate (27 per cent according to the 2002 *HIS*-study (Heublein, *et al.*, 2002: 5)) and a reduction in the time it takes to graduate (currently up to 14.1 semesters – in 2000 the average age of graduates was 29 years but with substantial variations between subjects (see Decker and Beck, 2001: 25–6)). This would allow a faster throughput of students within existing facilities. In addition to structural changes, the government is also looking at curricular reforms and at changing entry requirements by introducing mechanisms which allow professional or vocational qualifications to be considered for entry into higher education or to be accredited towards a final degree.

The cost factor

Tuition fees for higher education in Germany were abolished in the 1970s, perceived as socially unjust. All that students have to pay each semester is a small registration fee which covers administrative costs and may include the cost of a subsidised pass for public transport. With increasing student numbers and continuous serious underfunding, however, ministers for education have started to look at other sources of income, and at one in particular: the debate about the reintroduction of student fees began in the late 1990s and was one reason for the wave of student protests in 1997.

The current federal government is strongly opposed to charging students for their education and managed to rule out tuition fees for a first degree in an amendment to the Framework Act for Higher Education in 2002. Minister Bulmahn stressed that equal opportunities in education – irrespective of parental income – had to be paramount again and rejected the idea that her point of view simply echoed an ideological credo from the 1970s (Bulmahn, 19 July 2001). She stated that in view of the growing demand for highly qualified employees in Germany neglecting the poorer social groups would not only be socially unfair but above all economically absurd. Her ruling out fees for a first degree, however, is not as absolute as it may appear at first glance. On average students in Germany now take up to seven years to graduate, due partly to overcrowding and partly to a change in studying behaviour. Unlike the strictly regulated Anglo-American systems of higher education, the German system allows students much more freedom in the organisation of their degree programme including the decision of when to register for final examinations. Legislation, on the other hand, is based on the *Regelstudienzeit*, the length of time it can be reasonably expected for students to complete their degree, normally eight to nine semesters in the arts and humanities, for example. It is this discrepancy between the ideal and the actual length of degree courses which allows a certain flexibility in the interpretation of the entitlement to free higher education.

The difference in opinion on tuition fees is between the Federation and the *Länder* rather than between government and opposition, and at *Länder*-level goes across party lines. The federal states, not the Federation, are responsible for financing higher education in their region and it is in the area of finance where the regional differences in Germany's higher education system are most obvious. Some federal states do not charge any fees at all, in Bavaria students only have to pay for a second degree, Baden Württemberg introduced a fee of just over €500 per semester from the fourteenth semester onwards, other federal states followed suit in 2003 or planned for 2004 the implementation of a charge for students who take too long to graduate. The amount to be paid in all these schemes is around €500 per semester. Yet another initiative is that of *Studienkonten,* learning or learning time accounts. These basically work in two ways. On initial enrolment students are either given vouchers for seminars and lectures which can be redeemed over fourteen semesters (e.g. in Hesse). If students need more vouchers, then they will have to purchase them. Or students are given a time account, in Rhineland Palatinate, for example, of eighteen semesters. Once this credit has been used up every session has to be bought for approximately €25 per double session (see Ringling, 2003: 36).

All these initiatives have one major aim apart from bringing in additional funding. They are intended to reduce the long study periods in Germany thus relieving the overcrowding at universities. However, for many federal states these fees for overlong study periods do not go far enough to alleviate their financial problems. They argued that the general ruling out of tuition fees for a first degree infringes their constitutionally guaranteed cultural sovereignty and took the government to the Federal Constitutional Court. (The verdict is expected in 2004.) This could mean the end of free degrees in the near future but not necessarily in the form of payment upfront. The Hamburg Senator for Science, Jörg Dräger, for example, presented a model of delayed payment along the lines of the Australian way of 'learn now, pay later' of approximately €2,500 a year (Koch, 2003: 76–8). The money would have to be paid back in instalments once graduates have found employment where they earn above a certain threshold.

An argument in favour of tuition fees is the belief that they would stimulate competition among universities thus increasing the overall quality of higher education courses. The government, too, wants to see more competition among and within higher education institutions, however, not through fees but through more financial and organisational autonomy for institutions. The danger that competition and fees might lead to a two-tier system of increasingly elitist institutions on the one hand and those for the less well-off and/or less able students on the other – an 'educational Darwinism' (Lange, 1997: 10) – rather than a general improvement of quality is seldom mentioned. The Federal Minister for Education, Edelgard Bulmahn, has yet another suspicion. She fears that income from fees would not necessarily be invested in higher education but would simply disappear into the general budgets of the impoverished *Länder* (Koch, 2003: 77).

Proponents of tuition fees, among them not only desperate finance ministers but also employers, for example, justify them as a personal investment in the student's future, as job prospects with a degree are generally still better than without. The government sees this very argument as a vindication of its opposition to fees, as graduates are likely to be higher earners in future and would repay their debt to society through higher taxes (ZDFheute, 29 October 2002). The income of German graduates four years after graduation is on average 25 per cent higher than that of non-graduates. With the exception of graduates in social sciences or the humanities, they are generally also far less at risk of becoming unemployed (Schmidt-Klingenberg, 2002: 155) or staying unemployed for long, even though a degree does not offer the same protection against unemployment as it used to.

In contrast to the government's position, proponents see a system in which everyone has to contribute to their higher education as fairer than a system financed through taxation. Their assessment is that the current system disadvantages low-income groups whose children are less likely to benefit from higher education but that their taxes contribute to financing the degrees of the already better off, a position that is supported also by the influential *Sachverständigenrat,* The German Council of Economic Experts, an independent advisory body. The *Deutsches Studentenwerk*, the national umbrella group of the individual students' associations or student services, on the other hand believes that students contribute enough to their higher education as it is, as parents and students together already pay for nearly 80 per cent of students' expenses during their degree programmes (Deutsches Studentenwerk, 16 May 2003). The *Studentenwerk* also fears that tuition fees might deter potential students from low-income and less-educated groups, which confirms the federal government's concern that fees would be counterproductive in terms of increasing student numbers. The government and the *Studentenwerk* both believe that this increase can only be achieved through unlocking the potential in low-income and less-educated groups.

The percentage of students from a working-class background in higher education compared with their representation in the total population is already unfavourable. In 2000, there was 40 per cent of the total population classified as working class but only 12 per cent of all students came from that background, whereas 47 per cent of all students were from families of civil servants and self-employed professionals who only represented 21 per cent of the total population (Decker and Beck, 2001: 21). The *Deutsches Studentenwerk* distinguishes between four socio-economic categories: 'high', 'upper middle', 'middle' and 'low'. According to the *Studentenwerk*'s latest survey, the *16th Sozialerhebung* from 2001, a regular survey of the social background and living conditions of students, 33 per cent of students in 2000 were from the 'high' category, an increase of 2 per cent since 1997; for the other groups the trend was slightly downwards – from 27 to 26 per cent for the 'upper middle' group, 29 to 28 per cent for 'middle' and 14 to 13 per cent for 'low' income groups (Deutsches Studentenwerk, 19 July 2001: 9). Children from lower-income families in percentage terms are therefore very much under-represented in higher education. The fact that the proportion of students from the high-income group has nearly doubled since 1982 whereas that from the 'low' income group has decreased by 10 per cent since then seems to indicate that the education system in Germany is not as open as had always been believed and that socio-economic background can be a determining factor in shaping an educational career.

The financial situation of the family is not all-important but has a profound effect on career choice and studying behaviour. The *16th Sozialerhebung* found that 86 per cent of all students receive financial support from their parents. The more affluent the parents the higher the parental contributions in terms of the overall percentage of the students' income and in the actual sums paid. Nearly two-thirds of students contribute to their own upkeep through, for example, part-time jobs; 24 per cent receive state support. In her press statement of 19 July 2001 accompanying the publication of the *Sozialerhebung*, Minister Bulmahn added that 15 per cent of students interrupted their studies in 2000, of whom 27 per cent quoted taking up full-time employment and 28 per cent financial problems as the reasons for their decision, which can be interpreted as further justification of the Minister's opposition to tuition fees.

In addition to ruling out tuition fees for first degrees, the federal government actively tried to encourage greater participation in higher education. The 2001 reform of the *Bafög* grant system and the simultaneous introduction of *Bildungskredite* (student loans) were supposed to provide a financial incentive. *Bafög* is the combination of a grant and a loan system. Depending on parental and personal income, students can currently receive a monthly maximum sum of €585 for the duration of the *Regelstudienzeit*. Of that sum they have to pay back 50 per cent after graduation up to a maximum of €10,000. Apart from a slight increase in the monthly allowances, in the 2001 reform the payment of child benefit was also disregarded in the means testing for *Bafög* eligibility and the thresholds for parental income have been raised. Students who qualify for *Bafög* will now also receive it wherever they study in the EU. *Bildungskredite* are similar to the UK student loan system. Students can apply for a loan at favourable interest rates for particular situations, for example work placement abroad or the purchasing of expensive course books. This loan of €300 a month for a maximum period of twenty-four months is granted independent of student or parental income and has to be paid back in instalments starting four years after the first payment. The idea is to reduce the number of students having to take on part-time work thus allowing for a speedier progression towards graduation (Bulmahn, 19 July 2001). In its aim to encourage more young people to enter and to complete a degree programme the government sees the *Bafög* reform and the *Bildungskredite* as two major initiatives complementing structural and curricular reforms of higher education.

Increasing access and widening participation through diversity

Higher education institutions

In the winter semester 2002/03 Germany had 359 higher education institutions of which 172 were universities or academically equivalent institutions and 187 *Fachhochschulen* including twenty-nine specialised *Verwaltungsfachhochschulen* (universities of administrative sciences). *Fachhochschulen* are comparable to the new universities in Great Britain. Of particular relevance in terms of access to higher education are the mainstream state universities in particular and *Fachhochschulen*, which together are the destinations for the large majority of A-level students in Germany.

The discussion on reforms in higher education centres largely on the universities whose portrayal in the media has become increasingly negative. They are characterised as 'ineffective' and 'resistant to reform' (Hielscher *et al.*, 2002: 56), or as 'mediocre', leading to the demise of excellence, and anti-elitist (Bölsche, 2002: 122–3). These may be quotes from just one publication but they reflect the general coverage in the media fairly well. Concern about the state of university education, however, is not confined to the media. The problems of overcrowding and underfunding are undisputed and generally believed to be at the source of many of the difficulties German universities are facing, not just in terms of student numbers but also of quality. The relative ease of access to higher education through the constitutional entitlement to a university place has encouraged large numbers of A-level students to opt for a degree, including those who may not necessarily be intellectually able enough or those who are still uncertain as to what career path to take. As a result the drop-out rate is high, on average 27 per cent (Heublein *et al.*, 2002: 5). This average hides substantial differences between genders and between subjects and also the reasons for dropping out. In modern languages and literary studies, favoured more by women than men, at universities the drop-out rate was 41 per cent. Uncertain job prospects and poor learning conditions at universities, such as lack of structure in degree courses and insufficient tutorial guidance, are seen as the key reasons (Heublein *et al.*, 2002: 27). The high drop-out rate in information technology, on the other hand, is largely due to the growing demand for IT specialists on the labour market which encourages students to take up employment before completing their degree (Heublein *et al.*, 2002: 29).

Other criticism focuses on the content of many degree courses. Employers, in particular, but students too, keep complaining that university graduates receive a very theoretical academic education and are poorly prepared for the world of work. This was one reason why in the 1970s the federal and the *Länder* governments initiated a major building programme of *Fachhochschulen* which were founded as an alternative to universities with 'their educational goals and profiles ... adapted especially to the needs and requirements of professional life' (Federal Ministry of Education, 1996: 3). Often regarded by traditional universities as inferior institutions academically, *Fachhochschulen* nevertheless have become an attractive alternative for students. Unlike universities they concentrate on a limited number of subjects, above all business studies, engineering and social sciences, and are much smaller in size. Their course programmes are more prescriptive thus allowing – or forcing – students to graduate faster, they are increasingly internationally oriented, offering exchanges or dual qualifications with institutions abroad, and often have good contacts with industry and commerce.

While the academic and social prestige of *Fachhochschulen* is still lower than that of a university – for example, a *Fachhochschule* is not allowed to award PhDs and only a university degree is accepted as the entry qualification for the higher civil service – they are nevertheless popular with students because they promise good job prospects in industry and commerce. The average drop-out rate in these institutions, with 22 per cent in 1999, is lower than in universities (30 per cent) (Heublein *et al.*, 2002: 5). In addition to the different structure and orientation of *Fachhochschule* courses, a contributing factor may also be that they attract a higher percentage of applicants who already have work experience and start with clearer ideas of their career path (Heublein *et al.*, 2002: 26). Employers, too, value the practical approach in *Fachhochschulen* and would not only like to see their numbers extended but also the range of subjects taught at each institution expanded (Landesvereinigung der Arbeitgeberverbände Nordrhein-Westfalen, 11 March 2002).

If the *Fachhochschule* sector is extended with more weight on a practical focus, this may well result in a reorganisation of higher education with a clear distinction between academically orientated institutions and applied or labour-market-orientated ones. Chancellor Schröder's policy statement in his inaugural speech in the German parliament (10 November 1998) indicates this direction. His government was to 'encourage application-oriented research' asking higher education to serve the needs of the labour market more. As he makes no special mention of *Fachhochschulen* this points towards an overall change in orientation, especially for universities. *Fachhochschulen,* on the other hand, seem to want to go in the opposite direction by becoming more like universities. The fact that on the international stage they now call themselves 'Universities of Applied Sciences' highlights their intention to make the difference between university and *Fachhochschule* less distinct. The high demand for *Fachhochschule* places, in fact, is already a good indicator of their rising status. In the winter semester 2002/03 approximately 523,000 of the nearly 1.95 million students in Germany were enrolled at *Fachhochschulen* (Statistisches Bundesamt, 27 November 2002). Ironically, *Fachhochschulen* often ask for better A-level results for their *numerus clausus* subjects than universities do with the result that students who initially opted for a *Fachhochschule* degree course in the end settle for a university course because they were not good enough for the *Fachhochschule* of their choice.

Private education, in the school as well as in the higher education sector, has always played a minor role in Germany. The number of private universities may have increased dramatically from nineteen in the winter semester 1992/93 to forty-four in 2001/02 but the number of students enrolled is very small with 24,600 or just 1.4 per cent of all students in Germany (Decker and Beck, 2001: 23). Like *Fachhochschulen,* private institutions concentrate on very few subjects, often their degree programmes are centred around just one subject area – business studies or subjects with a business orientation being among the most prominent. Their degrees are very rigorously structured taking three to four years until graduation, include industrial placements and academic or work placements abroad, are often taught in English and French as well as German, and are very much performance-orientated. All this is supported by a very favourable staff–student ratio of one to eight at private universities, compared to one to twenty-six or more in the public sector. The drop-out rate is only one tenth of that in public universities (Stegelmann, 2002a) and job prospects for graduates are excellent. However, as private institutions only cater for students in their hundreds rather than thousands, their success rate simply cannot be compared with that of the large state universities with up to 60,000 students or more.

Apart from size, there are two other major differences between the state sector and private institutions. Private universities charge hefty fees and, unlike the public sector universities, they can also choose their own students. Many private universities therefore have acquired the status of elite institutions, partly because of their size and their selectivity, partly because their aim is to 'produce' recruits for top-level management positions. In spite of their high fees, they claim to be socially inclusive with various mechanisms in place to allow access for intellectually deserving candidates from less affluent backgrounds. Even though the differences between state and private institutions are obvious, the academic success of private universities means they are often cited as examples of good practice to be borne in mind when considering changes in state higher education. Two important characteristics of private universities, the rigorous degree programme structures and their close application to the labour market, are being taken up in all suggestions for reform in the public sector.

While the federal government rejects all moves towards (social) elitism, nevertheless it is now trying to create centres of excellence in the state sector which are to be comparable to institutions like Oxford or Harvard. In January 2004 it launched a competition which invited higher education institutions to bid for money in order to encourage institutions to become more competitive internationally. In an initial round any university or *Fachhochschule* can make a bid for money from federal funds. Out of a shortlist of ten institutions a jury consisting of national and international experts will eventually choose those institutions which are deemed worth supporting. The federal government is making available up to €50 million over five years for the winning institutions. In order to arrive at and to sustain a high level of quality in research and teaching generally the competition is to be repeated in a few years' time in order to keep the pressure on the winning institutions and to offer others a further chance to move into the top league (see Bundesministerium für Bildung, 25 August 2004.

Structural and curricular changes

The 1998 amendment to the Framework Act for Higher Education paved the way for the introduction of Bachelor and Masters degrees in the German higher education system. This new degree structure – either three years for the Bachelor degree plus two years for the Masters degree or four plus one – with a clear focus on core rather than broad content of the subject together with key or transferable skills for the Bachelor degree and specialisation and research for the Masters – is a major part of the reform process and is heralding a considerable change especially for the universities. Until 1998 the vertical structure of undergraduate and post-graduate programmes – with the exception of doctorates – was not part of the German system which is very much orientated towards a first degree. German university education is based on the Humboldtian tradition which has been the guiding principle since the nineteenth century. It stresses the ideal of scholarship, the pursuit of knowledge (as a means of developing the individual's character) and intellectual abilities. This involves the unity of research and teaching and the principles of *Lehrfreiheit* (academic freedom for lecturers in what they research and teach) and *Lernfreiheit* (allowing students a considerable amount of flexibility in what areas they want to focus on within a degree programme and in the length of time they want to take until sitting final examinations). An important aspect in the light of today's reform debate is the extent to which the Humboldtian tradition of scholarship and its independence of any vocational or societal needs with the state enabling this pursuit of knowledge through financial support for the universities should or can still apply.

As the focus in university tuition has always been on scholarship – leading to the academic *Diplom* qualification – rather than vocational or professional training, the state has taken responsibility for the examination process for those subjects which generally provide graduates for the civil service (including teaching) or for those professions which are regulated by the state such as medicine or pharmacy (Peisert and Framheim, 1990: 82). This examination, the *Staatsexamen*, is not a professional qualification as such, rather the entry qualification for a transitional phase outside the university in which the graduate is prepared for the requirements of the chosen profession (Ellwein, 1997: 247). A graduate with *Staatsexamen* intending to become a teacher, for example, would progress to a teacher training course, run by the education authority and after eighteen months or two years, depending on the federal state, would sit the second *Staatsexamen*, the professional qualification for the teaching profession. With increasing student numbers this process has become more and more prolonged. Students take longer to graduate and often immediate progression to teacher training cannot be guaranteed because of insufficient numbers of training places. This division between theoretical and practical instruction has led to considerably longer periods of education and training than in other countries, and does not even guarantee employment at the end of the training process.

The introduction of Bachelor and Masters degrees with their time-limiting structure and above all the Bachelor degree's stated nature as a professional qualification has been widely welcomed, especially outside academia. It is seen as a major step on the way to adapting higher education with its nineteenth-century tradition, originally aimed at a small elite, to the requirements of today's mass system. Proponents see a number of immediate benefits. The introduction of a two-phase degree structure complies with the Bologna Agreement of creating a uniform higher education sector in Europe, which also means that Bachelor and Masters degrees promote a stronger international orientation of the German system. On the one hand the German *Diplom* qualification or the *Staatsexamen* are little known or understood abroad, on the other hand the lack of a vertical system of undergraduate and postgraduate tuition has made it unattractive for foreign graduates to continue their education in Germany. They are often slotted into *Diplom* programmes, which means that achieving a Masters equivalent in Germany can take several years, rather longer than in the Anglo-American system. Bachelor and Masters degrees also improve study opportunities as well as job opportunities for German students abroad.

Another benefit that is expected is that the time limit of three or four years for the Bachelor degree will reduce the length of time until graduation for first degrees, thus releasing graduates onto the job market much more quickly. Masters degrees on the other hand, it is intended, will offer a better opportunity for lifelong learning and for upgrading qualifications after a period of professional activity in line with the changing demands of the labour market. Guido Westerwelle, leader of the FDP, the German Liberal Party, in addition, sees the economic long-term benefit of reducing education and training times should it lead to a cut in national insurance contributions, thus reducing labour costs in Germany (Poschardt, 20 June 2003).

For the federal and state ministers of education the new degree structure offers the possibility of increasing graduate numbers in Germany without increasing the number of higher education places. They expect that the Bachelor programmes especially will help to reduce the high drop-out rate among German students. The 2002 *HIS-Abbruchstudie*, a government-commissioned study on the scale and reasons for changing courses or dropping out of higher education, seems to confirm the ministers in their belief. Students on a first-degree programme who had left higher education without a qualification – 24 per cent from universities and 20 per cent from *Fachhochschulen* (excluding foreign students) (Heublein *et al.*, 2002: 5) – cited as the main reasons for their decision the lack of structure in their chosen courses, the lack of practical application and the length of time needed until graduation. Eighteen per cent of university drop-outs stated lack of motivation because of disappointment with the course in comparison with 11 per cent of *Fachhochschule* drop-outs (Ederleh, 2003: 10). As *Fachhochschule* courses are generally shorter and more vocational in orientation this may well strengthen the argument for Bachelor degrees. On the other hand the lower drop-out rate may arise from the fact that the percentage of mature students or students who already have a vocational qualification and practical experience is higher at *Fachhochschulen* (Heublein *et al.*, 2002: 26). With a faster graduation rate those university places which up to now have been occupied by long-term students will become available sooner. Ministers also hope that the shorter time-scale and the more professional orientation of Bachelor programmes will be more attractive to potential students from lower socio-

economic and less-educated backgrounds thus making the aim of a participation rate of 40 per cent more realistic.

However, the introduction of Bachelor and Masters degrees in
Germany is not without its critics, more so among academics and students
than among politicians and employers. The clear break with the Humboldtian tradition is seen as a violation of academic freedom and the time-
limit and the stronger focus on skills rather than scholarship has led to
derisory remarks, such as calling the Bachelor degree a 'Discount-
Examen', an exam on the cheap, or the degree course a 'Schmal-
spurstudium', a slimmed-down version of lesser value or just another
expression for dumbing down, as quoted in a web-based information pool
for present and future students (Campus, Bachelor und Master,
www.nebenjob.de/campus). When in 1997, students protested against the
stricter enforcement of the *Regelstudienzeit,* they argued that that meant
the 'Verschulung' of higher education, that is the 'demotion' to school-like
tuition, which expresses similar fears to the negative comments above. The
German Academic Exchange Service, therefore, stresses the importance
of curricular reform alongside structural changes. Bachelor degrees are
not a 'Studium light' (*DAAD Magazin*, 1999). No one would argue against
the focus on transferable skills but the extent to which the needs of the
economy or a very utilitarian approach should shape the curriculum of
higher degree courses is controversial. Chancellor Schröder's call for
'bringing education more in line with the labour market' is supported by
the *BDA's* (*Bundesvereinigung der Deutschen Arbeitgeberverbände* – Con-
federation of German Employers' Associations) proposal to establish
mechanisms for a dialogue between employers and higher education institutions in order to define, and redefine, what content and skills are needed
for various degree programmes (BDA, 16 September 2003). Some academics, on the other hand, argue that it is exactly the experience of scholarly
activity which provides the skills needed and that concentrating on 'future
professions' rather than 'future activities' would be less desirable or even
counter-productive (Daxner, 1996: 94, 96).

The introduction of the new vertical course structure causes concern
also in other respects. Exemption from tuition fees currently applies only
to first degrees. Having to pay for an MA may eventually open the door to
fees for all degree programmes and deter graduates and practitioners from
returning to higher education for postgraduate study. There are also fears
that higher education may become impoverished if – as seems the case –
the Bachelor degree is aimed at the majority of students, whereas the
Masters programmes are intended for a minority. The *BDA* fully supports
the new structure but argues against a politically determined quota for the
transition from Bachelor to Masters degrees (BDA, 16 September 2003).
Instead they stress the need for academic lifelong learning and have
developed together with the *HRK* (*Hochschulrektorenkonferenz* – the
Conference of German Vice-Chancellors) and the *DIHK* (*Deutscher*

Industrie und Handelskammertag, the Association of German Chambers
of Industry and Commerce) a ten-point programme for enabling lifelong
learning at higher education institutions in line with market needs.

To date there are already over 1,500 Bachelor and Masters degree
courses on offer in Germany, the percentage of students enrolled on them,
however, is small, only 3 per cent in the winter semester 2002/3, among
new entrants the figure was 6 per cent. To foreign students these degrees
seem particularly attractive. Ten per cent of new entrants into higher education from the immigrant population in Germany opted for Bachelor and
Masters degrees. These figures seem to encourage the view that the new
degree structure is attractive to population groups for whom higher education is not an obvious choice. The same goes for foreign students coming
to Germany to study. Of these students 17 per cent enrolled on a Bachelor
or Masters degree (Statistisches Bundesamt, 17 October 2003). Awareness
of this alternative to the traditional degrees is only just beginning to rise
among A-level students. It is also too early at this stage to judge their
acceptance by employers. While their associations are in favour, individual
employers may still rely on the qualifications they know. The parallel
existence of new and traditional degree structures and as yet unknown
benefits in the labour market may well encourage new entrants into higher
education to opt for familiar degree programmes. In fact, in *UniWelt*, a
special Hamburg higher education supplement of the daily *Die Welt*, students were advised that the traditional option may still be the safer bet
(*UniWelt*, 13/15 April 2003: 5). Rather than reforming the system this parallel structure may actually be a hindrance to reforms leaving the decision
to students and at the same time burdening the higher education institutions which opt for keeping both routes with the need to administer two
systems (Witte *et al.*, 2003: 3).

Yet another complication in the practical conversion of the degree
structure is the fact that among the new degrees currently offered by universities and *Fachhochschulen* only a minority are accredited (*Stern
Spezial*, 2003: 61). In 1998 the *KMK* established the *länderübergreifende
Akkreditierungsrat*, a single validation panel for all Bachelors and Masters
degrees which provides a nationwide mechanism for quality assurance. A
non-accredited degree is likely to be worth less than a traditional *Diplom*
and would not encourage many students to take up this new offer. In view
of the above, it is unlikely that structural reform will contribute substantially in the next few years to realising the government's aim of increasing
and widening participation in higher education.

Changes in entry requirements for higher education

Germany's relatively poor showing in graduation rates among the OECD
countries (19 per cent of the age cohort compared to the average 26 per
cent) is better than it looks at first glance. It is partly explained by the dif-

ferent organisation of the education and vocational training systems in Germany where many advanced professional and vocational qualifications are obtained in the *duale System* rather than in higher education as in many other OECD countries. This dual system combines practical training on the job with theoretical instruction in vocational schools or colleges, takes generally three years and has strictly regulated examination procedures. A successfully completed apprenticeship with added years of work experience also provides the basis for achieving higher vocational or professional qualifications, again under the umbrella of the *duale System*. All these qualifications are counted in the upper secondary graduation rate and in this Germany actually performs above the OECD average of 64 per cent with 83 per cent of twenty-five- to sixty-four-year-olds having at least one upper secondary qualification (Bundesministerium für Bildung, 16 September 2003: 3). Employers see the *duale System* as a major positive factor for the German economy, in its importance for them even above higher education (Institut der deutschen Wirtschaft Köln, 2002: 7). Originally intended for school-leavers with qualifications below A-levels, apprenticeships or traineeships have now become increasingly popular destinations for A-level students, too. In 1999, six months after leaving school, 26 per cent of A-level students decided not to go to university at all, and six per cent wanted to complete an apprenticeship or traineeship first before entering higher education (Stegelmann, 2002: 68). Reasons were, for example, fewer good job prospects for young graduates and the attraction of earning money immediately. Those students who wanted to go to university after their apprenticeship believed that practical experience together with a degree would enhance their job prospects.

While the *duale System* enjoys a high reputation in Germany and abroad, it is believed that it alone will not safeguard Germany's survival as a leading economy. The high percentage of upper secondary graduation is seen as an indicator of a more traditional industrial or manufacturing society whereas a modern service and knowledge society can only be developed and sustained by a larger number of higher education graduates (Institut der deutschen Wirtschaft Köln, 11 April 2002). In its attempt to increase access to higher education, the federal government announced its intention to broaden access requirements, a step which has found general approval. This was, for example, one of the recommendations of the *Forum Bildung* which suggested easier transfer from the dual system to higher education by acknowledging prior learning in the vocational system.

However, it is not only the opportunities for lateral transfer that are under discussion but also the value of the *Abitur,* the standard entry qualification for higher education. Neither universities nor students feel that achieving this qualification is adequate preparation for a degree course (Schmidt-Klingenberg, 2002a: 81–2). Not only that but because of the federal structure of the school system there is a lack of comparability and transparency in the acquisition of the *Abitur*. In most federal states it takes nine years of secondary school for the *Abitur,* in some it is eight. There is also a discrepancy in the way the testing is carried out. Some federal states have devolved the process down to school level, in others it is centrally administered for all schools in their region. According to an IW-survey 80 per cent of professors would be in favour of selecting their students themselves rather than just accepting the *Abitur* as an entry qualification (Bölsche, 2002: 123). Nevertheless, this happens only in a few institutions. This is partly because of the additional workload involved, partly because higher education institutions are limited in the criteria they can apply. While universities and *Fachhochschulen* are allowed to introduce a locally determined *numerus clausus* for all subjects in which demand exceeds supply in their institution, A-level results have to count for 51 per cent in their decision of whom to accept. In the most popular subjects – medicine, pharmacy, dentistry, business studies, veterinary medicine, psychology and biology – applications for a university place are considered on a nation-wide basis, students are allocated to places by a central organisation, the *Zentralstelle für die Vergabe von Studienplätzen*. The extent to which higher education institutions are to be involved in this central selection process is under discussion again. Currently they can decide on 24 per cent of places. The *HRK* would like to see 100 per cent involvement for the institutions, the *Länder* suggested a compromise of 50 per cent, while the government has postponed the decision until 2004. Applicants who fail to meet the criteria are entered in the *Losverfahren,* a lottery system which reallocates places which were not taken up. This is widely seen by academics as lowering standards and negating their participation in any selection process. In fact, there is general consensus among academics and politicians alike that a university-based selection process would increase the quality and the efficiency of higher education. The former chair of the *KMK*, Dagmar Schipanski (CDU), finds it unacceptable that universities should have to take A-level students who only just passed their exam (Schmidt-Klingenberg, 2002a: 85). Hans Joachim Meyer (CDU), Minister for Education in Saxony, is even tempted to abolish the automatic entitlement to a university place, which the *Abitur* confers, as he fears it will eventually ruin higher education. Thomas Oppermann (SPD), Minister for Education in Lower Saxony, believes that by allowing universities to select their students the competition between students for university places would increase, as would the competition among universities for students, thus improving quality (Bölsche, 2002: 123).

While a stronger selection process is likely to contribute to reducing the high drop-out rate by weeding out unsuitable candidates from the beginning, it is unlikely to contribute to the government's aim of increasing the participation rate in higher education and highlights the importance of making entry requirements more flexible.

Conclusion

Lateral transfer from vocational training to higher education together with the introduction of Bachelor and Masters degrees probably constitute the most radical break with tradition and may well be comparable in their wide-ranging effects to the expansion programme of the 1960s and 1970s. Experience in the secondary school system would suggest, however, that especially the broadening of entry requirements could take some time to be accepted. The secondary school system in Germany is still charac-terised by a fairly rigid tripartite division into *Hauptschule, Realschule* and *Gymnasium,* with the highest social prestige attributed to the *Gymnasium* and its academic orientation. Whatever type of school children attend largely maps their professional career. The lateral movement from one type of school to another exists in theory but in practice the direction is more often 'downwards' rather than 'upwards'. The idea of comprehensive education has not been widely accepted in Germany, where comprehen-sive schools exist but are not the norm. The fact that an increasing number of A-level students now consider taking the vocational route and the success of the *Fachhochschulen,* on the other hand, could be taken as encouraging indicators that attitudes are changing.

Reshaping the character of higher education and the debate about access has to be seen against the background of a globalised economy, high unemployment and slow economic growth in Germany. One major focus of the debate in 1960s and 1970s was on equal opportunities and social justice. With rising economic problems, however, there seems to be a shift from seeing access to higher education as a civil right to seeing it as an economic necessity. Mature manufacturing industries are evolving quickly into service and knowledge-based organisations, a process which started in Germany rather later than in other developed nations. Increas-ing access to higher education, widening participation and promoting life-long academic learning will need to ensure that the higher education system provides highly qualified employees in sufficient numbers to guar-antee Germany's survival as a leading economic power.

Recent enrolment figures are encouraging. Numbers of first-year stu-dents have started to grow again, rising steadily since 1998, in absolute and in percentage figures. In the winter semester 2002/3, 37.5 per cent of the relevant year group entered higher education, only two years previ-ously the figure stood at 33.5 per cent (Statistisches Bundesamt, 27 November 2002). In the winter semester 2003/4, the total number of stu-dents enrolled reached the two million mark for the first time. The reasons for this increase are speculative. The Bafög reform of 2001 may have encouraged more A-level students to opt for higher education again, as the government claims, or prospective students may be assuming that career prospects in times of high unemployment will be better for graduates. Alternatively, insufficient numbers of traineeships and apprenticeships may have limited their choice and therefore made a degree course more attractive or even the only alternative. In Northrhine Westphalia increased student numbers are attributed to the introduction of Bachelor degree programmes (Gillmann, 21/22 November 2003). Yet another, rather more negative reason, might be rising unemployment in Germany. Rather than being without a job, A-level students may prefer to spend their time at university instead of at the job centre (von Randow, 4 December 2003).

While Minister Bulmahn expressed her delight at the increase in student numbers, public protests and demonstrations by students and academics, for example in November and December 2003 in Berlin, indicate that this satisfaction may be somewhat one-sided. Student numbers may be rising but some state governments, which have to bear the costs for this increase in numbers, have already seen themselves forced to reduce funding for higher education in their attempts to balance their budgets. Other states are contemplating a similar solution. Higher education institutions are faced with cuts in funding between 2 per cent as in Lower Saxony or even 7 per cent as in Berlin. This happens at a time when the staff (professor)-student-ratio has already risen from one to 49.3 in 1995 to 51.2 in 2002. As a result the number of *numerus clausus* subjects across the range of higher education institutions has increased substantially, creating another obstacle for the government in its aim to achieve a participation rate of 40 per cent. Detlef Müller-Böling, Director of the *CHE* (Centre for Development in Higher Education) sees a contradiction in government policy which cannot easily be solved, if at all: on the one hand the government set the target of increasing student numbers, at the same time it ruled out tuition fees without providing alternative sources for the appropriate funding of universities and *Fachhochschulen* (Wiarda, 4 December 2003).

In spite of an increase in educational funding of 25 per cent since 1998, according to the government's own figures, the financial situation of higher education institutions has improved little. Neither does it look likely that this situation will change quickly. In response to the poor results for Germany in the PISA study, the expansion of all-day schools has been given immediate priority, including the availability of necessary funds, whereas for higher education the government hopes to achieve improvements largely through efficiency gains rather than expansion. This prospect of continuing underfunding of higher education has led *HRK* President, Peter Gaethgens, to express the warning that while the German higher education system needs to become truly a mass education system, it is by no means ready yet for this challenge (Gillmann, 21/22 December 2003).

After many years of reform debates, German higher education now seems to have reached a crossroads. It is generally accepted that changes to the system have to be made. The nineteenth-century Humboldtian tradition originally intended for a small elite, cannot apply unchanged to a system which is aiming at a participation rate of around 40 per cent. Traditional degree structures are still being offered in parallel to the new Bachelor and Masters degrees. At the same time there are attempts to create internationally competitive top institutions; this seems to indicate that, while the reorienting of German higher education has begun, the discussion about the extent of *Bildung* versus *Ausbildung* and the related questions of access are not yet over.

Notes

1 Although translated into English as 'education', the German term 'Bildung' has another implication. It implies the development of the character and intellect of an individual through scholarship, in contrast to 'Ausbildung' which means 'training' with a particular vocational destination in mind.
2 All developments before 1990 outlined in this chapter relate to West Germany. The situation and the developments in the GDR are largely neglected here because, with unification, the structures of the former East German higher education system were replaced by the West German ones and have had little impact on the current debate.
3 OECD figures as quoted in *Bildung, Forschung, Innovation*, p. 5. According to figures published by the Federal Statistical Office Germany (press statement of 29 November 2002) the percentage of entrants into higher education was 29.2 per cent in 1998 and 37.5 per cent in 2002.

References

Arbeitsgruppe Bildungsbericht am Max-Planck-Institut für Bildungsforschung, *Das Bildungswesen in der Bundesrepublik Deutschland: Strukturen und Entwicklungen im Überblick* (Reinbek: Rowohlt Taschenbuch Verlag GmbH, 1994).

BDA, 'Bologna-Prozess mit Nachdruck vorantreiben – Memorandum zu den Abschlüssen Bachelor und Master vorgestellt', *Presseinformation* 16 September 2003 – PI 55/03, www.bda-online.de [11 March 2003].

Bölsche, J., 'Pfusch am Kind', *Der Spiegel*, 20 (2002).

Bulmahn, E., Statement anlässlich der Pressekonferenz 'Die wirtschaftliche Lage der Studierenden in der Bundesrepublik Deutschland 2000' (Berlin, 19 July 2001).

Bundesministerium für Bildung und Forschung, '5-Punkte-Program "Zukunft Bildung" als nationale Antwort auf PISA' *Pressemitteilung 129/02* (25 June 2002).

Bundesministerium für Bildung und Forschung *Bildung, Forschung, Innovation – der Zukunft Gestalt geben: Bildungs- und forschungspolitische Schwerpunkte des Bundesministeriums für Bildung und Forschung in der 15. Legislaturperiode* (2002)

Bundesministerium für Bildung und Forschung und Kultusministerkonferenz, *OECD-Veröffentlichung "Bildung auf einen Blick": Wesentliche Aussagen der OECD zur Ausgabe 2003* (16 September 2003).

Bundesministerium für Bildung und Forschung, *Brain Up!* Deutschland Sucht seine Spitzenuniversitäten, http://www.bmbf.de/de/2129.php [25 August 2004].

Campus, Bachelor und Master, www.nebenjob.de/campus [9 August 2003].

DAAD Magazin, 'Bachelor und Master – was ist das eigentlich?' (Thema des Monats März 1999).

Daxner, M., 'Towards mass higher education', in S. Muller (ed.) *Universities in the Twenty-First Century* (Providence, Oxford: Berghahn Books, 1996).

Decker, J. and M. Beck, *Hochschulstandort Deutschland 2001* (Wiesbaden: Statistisches Bundesamt, 2001).

Deutsches Studentenwerk warnt vor Einführung von Studiengebühren' *Nachricht* 16 May 2003 www.campus-germany.de/german [9 September 2003].

Deutsches Studentenwerk, *Zusammenfassung der 16. Sozialerhebung* (19 July 2001).

Ederleh, J., *Studienerfolg an Fachhochschulen: Sonderauswertung aus der HIS-Studienabbruchstudie* 2002 (zusammengestellt zur 33. Jahrestagung des Bad Wiesseer Kreises, 29 May/1 June 2003).

Ellwein, T., *Die deutsche Universität: Vom Mittelalter bis zur Gegenwart* (Wiesbaden: Fourier Verlag, 1997).

Federal Ministry of Education, Science, Research and Technology, *The Fachhochschulen in Germany* (Bonn: 1996).

Forum Bildung Working Party at the Office of the Bund and Länder Commission for Educational Planning and Research Promotion, *Recommendations of the Forum Bildung* (10 November 2001).

Gillmann, B., 'Hochschulen melden Rekordzugänge', *Handelsblatt,* 225 (21/22 November 2003).

Heublein, U., R. Schmelzer, D. Sommer and H. Spangenberg, *Studienabbruchstudie 2002: die Studienabbrecherquoten in den Fächergruppen und Studienbereichen der Universitäten und Fachhochschulen* (Hannover: Hochschul-Informations-System, HIS Kurzinformation A 5/2002).

Hielscher, A., J. Koch and C. Schmidt, 'Uni zum Wohlfühlen' *Der Spiegel,* 30 (2002).

Institut der deutschen Wirtschaft Köln, *Informationsdienst* no. 14, 4 April 2002, www.iwkoeln.de [26 March 2004].

Institut der deutschen Wirtschaft Köln: Werner, D. *Arbeitsmarkt und Bildung am Standort Deutschland: Bewertung und Reformbedarf im Spiegel einer Unternehmensbefragung* (Köln: Dokumentation 3/2002).

Koch, J., 'Studium auf Pump', *Der Spiegel,* 17 (2003).

Landesvereinigung der Arbeitgeberverbände Nordrhein-Westfalen, 'Fachhochschulen stärken – Kapazitäten ausbauen' *Meldung* vom 11 March 2002, www.arbeitgebernrw.de-aktuelles-Bildung [8 September 2003].

Lange, J., 'Transparenz und Effizienz – veränderte Rahmenbedingungen für die Hochschulen', in J. Hollerith (ed.) *Leistungsfähige Hochschulen – aber wie? Beiträge zur Hochschulreform* (Neuwied, Kriftel, Berlin: Luchterhand, 1997).

OECD, Education at a glance – OECD Indicators 2003 (Paris: OECD, 2003).

Peisert, H. and G. Framheim, *Higher Education in Germany* (Bonn: Federal Ministry of Education, Science, Research and Technology, 1990).

Poschardt, U. 'Universitäten auf der schiefen Bahn', *Welt am Sonntag,* 29 (20 June 2003).

Ringling, A. 'Im Westen wird bummeln teuer', *Stern Spezial,* 1 (2003).

Schmidt-Klingenberg, M. 'Billige Bildung', *Spiegel Special,* 3 (2002).

Schmidt-Klingenberg, M. 'Zeugnis ohne Wert', *Der Spiegel,* 3 (2002a).

Statistisches Bundesamt 'Studienanfängerquote im Studienjahr 2002 jetzt bei

37.5%', *Pressemitteilung*, 29 December 2002, www.destatis.de/presse/deutsch [25 March 2003].

Statistisches Bundesamt – Hochschulstatistik, Wiesbaden, 27 November 2002.

Statistisches Bundesamt '6% Studienanfänger in Bachelor- und Masterstudiengängen 2002' *Pressemitteilung*, 17 October 2003, www.destatis.de/presse/deutsch [2 December 2003].

Stegelmann, K. 'Ein echter Vorteil', *Spiegel Special*, 3 (2002a).

Stegelmann, K. 'Entscheidung ohne Reue', *Der Spiegel*, 28 (2002).

Stern Spezial, 'Überall anerkannt', *Stern Spezial*, 1 (2003).

UniWelt, 'Das sollten Studenten schon jetzt beachten', *Das Hochschul-Special der Welt und* Welt am Sonntag (Hamburg, 13/15 April 2003).

von Hammerstein, K., J. Koch, A. Neubacher, N. Pötzl, U. Schäfer and G. Steingart, 'Die blockierte Republik', *Der Spiegel*, 39 (2002).

von Randow, G., 'Freiheit für die Unis!', *Die Zeit*, 50 (4 December 2003).

Wiarda, J.-M. 'In zehn Jahren Dritte Welt', *Die Zeit*, 50 (4 December 2003).

Witte, J., U. Schreiterer, L. Hüning, E. Otto and D. Müller-Böling, 'Argumente für eine rasche und konsequente Umsetzung auf Bachelor- und Masterstudiengänge an deutschen Hochschulen', *Positionspapier I zu Bachelor- und Masterstudiengängen* (Gütersloh: Centrum für Hochschulentwicklung, April 2003).

ZDFheute 'OECD: Zu wenig Akademiker in Deutschland', 29 October 2002, www.heute.t-online.de/ZDFheute [29 September 2003].

5 The value of higher education in a mass system

The Italian debate

Simonetta Michelotti

Introduction

In November 2001 the Italian university system entered a new phase. The reorganisation of the courses of study offered nationwide is the final phase in the reform of university self-government and regulation which began in 1989. The intention has been to remedy some of the dysfunctions, which were the consequence of the liberalisation of access to higher education that began in 1969. In particular, the aim has been to introduce corrective measures to:

1 Lower the high number of dropouts.
2 Lower the average age of graduation.
3 Increase the number of graduates.
4 Provide graduates with more vocational qualifications.

The 'new university' intends to bridge the gap between the social and cultural demand for wider access to higher education in Italy and the low number of students who actually graduate.

The debate concerning the right to free access to the Italian university has persisted in spite of the demand for radical change. In fact, free access to university is considered to be a basic individual right in Italy. However, even if the principle is widely shared, the actual infrastructure of Italian universities cannot cope with the current challenge of nearly 1,700,000 student enrolments (Comitato Nazionale per la Valutazione del Sistema Universitario). Moreover, expectations of solving the crisis of higher education in Italy, in terms of both controlling its growth and improving its quality, remain low. However, at this point in time to abandon the task is difficult, or as Guido Martinotti has put it 'that which must be done is impossible to do, but at the same time it seems impossible to do otherwise' (2002: 11).

Central to the new phase in Italian higher education is the principle of university self-government as set out in Article 33 of the Italian Constitution, ratified in 1948 but never really put into effect. Not surprisingly, the reform of university governance is part of a much larger move towards the decentralisation of the entire system of public administration, which began in Italy with the so-called 'Bassanini Law' of 15 May 1997 (*Gazzetta Ufficiale*, no. 113, 17 May 1997). But the move towards a self-governing university system potentially clashes with the policy of free access to university education, which had begun over thirty years earlier. At that time the middle classes, whose economic opportunities had increased because of the expansion in the so-called 'Golden Age' of the 1950s and 1960s, started to demand free access to higher education. And it is certainly no coincidence that this demand overlapped with the events of 1968: the combination of international political conflict and local social unrest, endogenous and exogenous events, created a potent cocktail that has had a profound impact upon the subsequent development of Italian higher education (Marsiglia, 1993: 141).

The rise and impact of mass higher education

The decision to liberalise access to higher education in Italy was, therefore, induced by the spirit of the times: it was felt that educational opportunities had to be expanded to reinforce the positive trends in Italian society established in the years of post-war reconstruction and reinforced by 'the Golden Age'. There were also important political implications: in the twenty years following the fall of the fascist regime and the beginning of the new democratic Republic, Italians had developed strong opposition to any social policy that had restricted access to its benefits. This was also true for higher education, and from the beginning of the 1960s the application of selective admissions criteria was considered politically incorrect (Zecchino, 4 November 2001).

The obstacles to mass access to university education were in theory mainly cultural since formally the only selective criteria that were applied concerned the type of secondary school diploma a student had obtained. In practice, however, the means of selection was also socially biased because the lyceum diploma, which allowed access to all university degree courses, was generally obtained by the offspring of the upper and middle classes, while the lower class tended to enrol their children in vocational schools, where they could learn a trade (Marsiglia, 1993: 130). However, the selective criteria for university education were not severe and students with vocational high school diplomas could enrol for a university degree, although their choice of courses was restricted.

The general socio-cultural barrier to access has been reinforced by both self-imposed and formally agreed restrictions. Vocational courses have never attracted a large number of students (Guerzoni, 18–19 June, 1999) possibly because they have been considered inferior programmes or possibly because the entrance examination they impose discourages students. Of the mainstream degree programmes only medicine, veterinary sciences, dentistry (since 1980), communication sciences and architecture (since

1992) have entrance examinations. The reason being that the number of students seeking enrolment to these courses has been so high as to risk bringing teaching to a standstill. Alternatively, in some cases the European Union had issued precise regulations that limit admission to some courses (Directive 89/48, CEE, 21 December 1988).

There is a history of *numerous clausus* and limited enrolments in the Italian higher education system and the distinction between them is important. *Numerous clausus* is determined by national or regional planning decisions based on economic and social factors that affect the whole country, such as the supply of staff, the quality of facilities and the availability of equipment in the universities. Limited enrolments, on the other hand, are decided by each university and they may vary on a yearly basis. In fact they are one of the manifestations of university self-government (Vinigiani and Santoro, 2002: 1055).

However, regulations limiting access to university pale into insignificance compared with the general liberalisation of access. For example, Law No. 910 – 'Urgent Measures for University Reform' – was enacted in December 1969 and essentially guaranteed enrolment to university for all students with the five-year secondary school diplomas (*maturità*). And since the 1960s the Italian higher education system has expanded rapidly in quantitative terms (Marsiglia, 1993: 135): the number of institutions has risen from twenty-seven to seventy-seven, the number of students enrolled expanded from 270,000 in 1960/61 to 1,700,000 in 2001/02, and the academic staff has grown from a few thousand (about 4,000) in the 1960s to currently about 50,000 (Comitato Nazionale per la Valutazione del Sistema Universitario). This growth was symptomatic of the country's increased well-being as reflected in the declining role of agriculture in the national economy, the rise in the importance of the industrial and service sectors and, above all, in the increase of per capita income, which permitted the population the 'luxury' of dedicating more time to education (Crainz, 1996). This same growth, however, highlighted several problems, synthesised in the report introducing the new university legislation of 1999 (Ministero dell'Università e della Ricerca Scientificia e Technologica, 1999):

1   The higher education system in Italy was represented mainly by the universities.
2   The system was excessively rigid and offered mainly four-year degree courses whose contents were regulated by national rules.
3   The difference between the legal course length and the longer periods of time generally required to graduate was caused by the lack of planning in the organisation of the degree programmes and students' excessive workloads.
4   The excessive length of degree courses and the lack of intermediate diplomas were the main causes of the high number of student dropouts.

5   The lack of correlation between higher education and the employment market created an excessive number of jobless graduates.

The problems with Italian higher education had become very evident towards the end of the 1980s, when new external elements, such as the spread of Information and Communication Technology (ICT) and the process of cooperation and harmonisation among European systems of higher education, led to an inevitable comparison between the Italian and the international situation. Moreover, the question of whether Article 33 of the Italian Constitution had in reality ever been applied was inevitably raised. It was clear that Italian higher education had grown remarkably but within an obsolete straitjacket ranging from the legal framework, university structures and organisation to the use of human resources. In particular, it is interesting to note that the efforts to widen university access had failed to increase either the number of graduates (as opposed to the number of students) or their preparation for the world of work.

In other words, quantity did not mean quality or relevance. While Italian graduates could be described as 'scholarly' they lacked the practical experience that would prepare them for the realities of the job market. In some disciplines the number of graduates exceeded the demand for them (for example, in the humanities and medicine), but in others there were large shortfalls (engineering has been the prime example). It became evident that there was a 'funnel effect' in which large numbers entered the higher education system but far fewer graduated by which time they were no longer young adults. Obviously, the system needed changing but the focus was not on those who were excluded from higher education but rather on the quality of its graduates: the knowledge and competences they had acquired in relation to the time it took them to obtain a degree, and whether they could meet the demands of the job market.

Key failures of the mass system

Entrapped in its academic ivory tower, the Italian university offered degree courses which often had irrational workloads and, despite studying full time, students graduated after studying on average seven and half years for a four-year degree course (Guerzoni, 18–19 June 1999). This situation imposed personal costs with important social and economic consequences: delaying entry into the job market, postponing the start of a career as well as marriage and raising a family. In Italy the final school-leaving diploma – *maturità* – is obtained at the age of eighteen and the average period of higher education spans from nineteen to twenty-six. Successful job-hunting generally requires another two years and, thus, for Italian graduates the path from school to university and then into employment is now concluded at the age of twenty-eight. By comparison the average European student obtains the equivalent of the Italian *maturità* at seventeen years of age, a degree at twenty-one, and by the age of twenty-two may already have a job (Universo MURST).

Besides the broader negative social consequences, free access to the old system of university education gave rise to two main problems:

1   For students, because if they selected an inappropriate degree course the Italian university lacked the means of permitting them to transfer to other programmes without losing all of their credits, and lacked procedures to assist students in selecting courses appropriate to their interests and prior qualifications.
2   For institutions, because many universities, with tens of thousands of enrolments, faced impossible situations: teaching came to a virtual standstill (with lectures often attended by hundreds of students) and final examinations that lasted weeks.

Before the current reform of higher education the four-year Italian degree – at least in terms of its length – was about half-way between the three-year first degree programmes of certain European countries and the time it would take to acquire a doctorate. In fact, while the four-year degree course may have been superior to a three-year degree, not only in terms of the number of study years but also its academic quality, it failed almost totally to transmit vocational skills. Consequently this persuaded many students, who had worked laboriously to obtain a degree, not to continue with postgraduate studies (Ministero dell'Istruzione, 2000).

However, there are several reasons behind the high drop-out rate – about 60 per cent of those enrolled, of whom 25 per cent dropped out during the first year of the course (Guerzoni, 18–19 June 1999). First, the course units while sometimes placing excessive workloads on students were often of little relevance to the final aims of the degree programmes. In fact, professors frequently saw their lectures as academic exercises in their own right, imposing large demands on their students but without a clear connection to the aims of the course. Second, evaluation of progress was poor, including weak procedures to support those who had accumulated 'learning debts'. Third, the administrative structures were inefficient and both the physical and the human resources stretched (overcrowded classrooms, libraries and laboratories whose capacity could not meet the demand, especially in the so-called mega-universities, and real problems in creating fruitful professor/student relationships). Fourth, the problems were exacerbated for those 54 per cent of the total student population who worked part-time (Conferenza Permanente dei Rettori delle Università Italiane, 2003), not surprisingly finding it very difficult to keep up with the pace of university studies which even many full-time students found challenging. Fifth, there was a lack of effective control on students' attendance, which, even though it was considered to be vital to the learning process, was almost discouraged so as not to increase the logistical problems. In effect university enrolment provided a 'parking place' or 'social cushion' (Zecchino, 4 November 2001) for those who had yet to decide what to do with their futures.

The reasons for the high number of drop-outs also caused the so-called 'out of course' phenomenon, that is, those students who had failed to complete their degrees in the stipulated time period but were nonetheless still registered as students and continued to pay fees. These students were tolerated by the system because they made a positive contribution to the university balance sheets. In fact, they paid higher fees than regular students, thereby creating a perverse mechanism in which the longer the student was enrolled the more he or she paid.

Even those who laboriously obtained their final degree did so on average three years later than the legal duration of the degree course: this represents 84 per cent of graduates (Trentini, 28 August 2000). What is particularly striking is the impact of mass access upon the numbers actually graduating over the past forty years. In 1960 some 50 per cent of those who were enrolled graduated, in 1980 about 35 per cent finished their studies and an all-time low was recorded in 1985 with only 30 per cent of the total student population of that year graduating. In 2001 the remarkable increase in the numbers graduating (52 per cent) was the result of incorporating graduates in the new three-year university diploma courses that had been introduced in 1990 (Comitato Nazionale per la Valutazione del Sistema Universitario).

Moreover, it is likely that this percentage will increase again as many students who had fallen behind in the old system now have the opportunity to take a few additional course modules in order to graduate with the three-year diploma. This will artificially inflate the number of graduates in Italy, but in some cases there will be a significant gap between the knowledge and skills acquired by those following the new first-level degrees from the start and those who transferred into the new programmes sometimes having completed as much as 90 per cent of their higher education within the old system.

It remains to be seen whether the new system of higher education will more closely match the demands of the job market; whether it will be successful in lowering the number of jobless and underemployed graduates (Guerzoni, 18–19 June, 1999). In fact, only 47 per cent of young Italian graduates find employment in a sector they have studied for, which puts Italy in last place in the European ranking list (*Eurispes-Liberal*, May 2003). Not surprisingly, therefore, Italian graduates are often discontented with their subsequent employment with respect to: salary (49.2 per cent), career opportunities (46.5 per cent), the usefulness of their university studies in the working environment (41.8 per cent), and their job security (37.5 per cent). While such discontent may be put down to the excessive expectations of graduates, nonetheless it is evidence of a significant tension between the experiences of higher education and the realities of work (Trentini, 28 August 2000).

Up to 2001 the regulation of university degree courses laid down a system of degrees and study programmes – there was uniformity throughout the country. The curriculum structure and content of each degree programme was established by national didactic regulations, offering only a narrow margin of choice for both universities and students. This rigidity required long bureaucratic procedures to be followed if the regulations were to be updated, so hindering the efficient introduction of those reforms that would enable the courses to respond to either the evolution of knowledge or the demands of the job market (Guerzoni, 18–19 June 1999). So while the Italian system of higher education was widely appreciated in Europe for the theoretical, historical and methodological knowledge it implanted in its students, it was also recognised that Italian graduates had rarely acquired practical, job-related skills (Schmidt and Michelotti, 2000: 294). And the bureaucratic rigidities in the system made it difficult to change the balance.

The high number of drop-outs, the peculiarity of 'out of course' students, the low number of graduates – especially young graduates – in comparison to other countries, and the low percentage of graduates among employees have all served to diminish, or even cancel out, the allegedly 'democratic' advantages of mass access to higher education (Moratti, 18 July 2001). What meaning does free access have if the number of students acquiring their final degree is so low? And the price for the community is twofold: on one hand it lacks graduates, while on the other hand the state spends considerable sums sustaining inefficient university structures for large numbers of students.

Such a weak system risks marginalising Italy among the developed countries for it is widely accepted that the effectiveness of a nation's higher education system and associated research tradition contribute greatly to its competitiveness (Avveduto *et al.*, May–June 1990). The more people can access education, the better it is for the community, but with the emergence of the 'knowledge society' growth is no longer based on cheap manpower, but on effective teaching and research (Matteucci, March–April 1978), and quality has become the most important issue. The challenge, therefore, for Italy is how to combine quality with its democratic commitment to mass access.

The ongoing reform process

In 1989, in order to overcome the stagnation and inflexibility of Italian higher education, new legislation was passed that granted greater self-governing powers to the universities. Permitting the universities greater autonomy was seen as a key means for renovating the system, in the hope that the quality of university education would be improved by ending the previous centralised management that had caused delays and inefficiency. Moreover, further reforms in 1996 granted Italian universities greater control of the organisation of their degree courses. The universities were granted the right to determine the goals and content of their degree programmes, although still within a national framework set by the ministry. This new system aimed at reducing bureaucracy and enabling prompt responses to the demands for educational change by the local communities in which the universities function. Moreover, to encourage innovation and the modernisation of the higher education system the reforms have aimed to internationalise the content of degree programmes in order to fall in line with the European trends. In fact, a closer look at the basic reform principles would suggest that there has been a drive towards European harmonisation, to follow the principles set out in the Declarations of Sorbonne 1998, Bologna 1999 and Berlin 2003, with the final objective of creating a European system of higher education by 2010 (Ministero dell'Università e della Ricerca Scientifica e Technologica, 16 October 1998).

Thus, since 2001/02 the structure of the Italian university system has been as follows (Ministero dell'Universita e della Ricerca Scientifica e Tecnologica, 1998):

1   Three-year, first-level degree courses, which aim to provide students with a basic command of research methods and general scientific concepts, as well as ensuring that they acquire specific vocational skills.
2   Two-year, second-level specialist degree courses which have the objective of providing the student with the advanced level of education necessary to carry out highly skilled activities in specialised fields.
3   University Masters degrees, which can be acquired in one year by students with either first or second-level degrees.
4   Specialised courses that are organised according to specific European Union regulations (see Directive 82/76/CEE, 26 January 1982), many of which train recruits for the medical professions.
5   Doctoral programmes.

Therefore, the introduction of the three-year degree course has arisen from the twofold demand for harmony with the wider European system of higher education, and the need to aid those who are not interested in undertaking lengthy studies to earn a degree that could turn out to be less than useful. It should be noted that the reforms were intended not only to increase the number of graduates, but also to impart to students more meaningful forms of knowledge and skills. The planning of degree courses around clear educational objectives, and not by merely adding additional courses (a reform as yet only partially implemented) will be fundamental towards achieving this goal. The emphasis will be placed on the quality of the learning process with teaching structured to reflect how educational goals are to be achieved. Furthermore, this must take into consideration a student body that is no longer as homogeneous as it used to be but has different needs that may be satisfied in varying – but equally legitimate –

ways through full- or part-time study in anticipation of lifelong learning (Gruppo di Lavoro Ministeriale, 21 October 1997). It is not by chance that students have been the focal point of the reform (Conferenza Permanente dei Rettori delle Università Italiane, 2003). The most important challenge is to replace the concept of university teaching as the transmission of knowledge as an end in its own right with a system that encourages self-learning and which makes the acquisition of knowledge more accessible by reforming teaching methods (Schmidt and Michelotti, 2000: 296).

By implementing the reforms the new Italian higher education plan (commonly called the '3 + 2' plan to indicate the lengths of the first- and second-level degree programmes) has a double advantage. It awards an academic degree to those who are satisfied with a three-year degree that combines academic and vocational knowledge, while those who intend to continue their studies can use the three-year degree as a springboard for selecting the specialist sector in which they wish to pursue their two further years of studies. This would then put them at the same level as those who, under the previous system, had graduated after a four-year degree programme, but with the additional benefit of having acquired some practical experience along the way.

In theory, every university should be encouraged to improve their teaching methods given the current didactic autonomy of each university. However, there is the danger that the reform of degree programmes could be geared not so much to improving the quality of teaching but rather to attracting more students with the promise of 'effortless success'. The principle income source for the universities remains student fees and given that the Ministry of Education provides funding for teaching on the basis of the number of students enrolled to the number graduating, then the temptation to construct degree programmes that will attract students and teach them in a manner that enhances the prospects of graduation is high. In the context, therefore, of continuing open access to higher education it is difficult to ensure quality control of the new degree programmes even if they are monitored by the National Evaluation System. In effect open access has fundamental economic repercussions that can seriously undermine pedagogical reform.

Mass access and the new system

Times have surely changed when it is no longer politically incorrect for a minister to publicly admit that 'the open doors system has contributed significantly to the problems of the university in the past 30 years' (Zecchino, 4 November 2001). Minister Ortensio Zecchino, who issued the 1999 Act, went on to say with specific reference to Article 6: 'Even though the new system will not close doors to those students who choose university courses that are different from the studies they carried out during their secondary school education, it will surely persuade them to make a more careful and informed choice' (Gobbi, 3 November 1999).

Upon the introduction of the measure, Luciano Modica, President of the Italian Permanent Conference of University Rectors, commented along the same lines: 'This new measure has been welcomed by the academic world since often the greatest difficulties students encounter at the beginning of their university career derive from the complete lack of preparation of those who have chosen courses of study different from their previous academic experience' (Gobbi, 10 September 1999).

However, this measure, as unthreatening as it may seem, created very negative reactions amongst the wider public, who feared that the university was moving towards constructing procedures to limit enrolment. This reaction made it evident that even the simplest of restrictions to free university enrolment in Italy would make the public fear for a right considered untouchable, regardless of its cost, even though key figures in the higher education system itself had long argued that to defend 'the unconditional occupation of academic structures' is not to protect a democratic right since free access had undermined the very fabric of university life (Quagliariello, 1986).

So, although Article 6 of the 1999 Act allows universities to establish entry prerequisites for both first- and second-level degrees (Decree, 3 November, 1999: no. 509), to verify the qualifications that applicants have obtained, and to insist that those students deemed to lack certain necessary qualifications on enrolment should acquire them in their first year of study, it has been for the most part ignored. But what is even more curious is the fact that some interpretations of the legislation deny that the reform has in any way limited access to the university by arguing that to evaluate whether students are prepared for admission to university is not the same as either limiting or managing enrolments (Vinigiani and Santoro, 2002: 1055). It may be concluded that either the declarations made by both the Minister and the President of the Permanent Conference of Italian Rectors went farther than the real intentions of the new regulations, or that their public statements have been misinterpreted.

In fact, up until now Article 6 has been interpreted in the various internal regulations of universities either as an optional measure or it has been applied as a mere bureaucratic ritual (Zecchino, 4 November 2001); that is, the evaluations are carried out but then no practical use is made of the results. Nicola Tranfaglia has written, 'Those who know the Italian University understand that you will not get much out of rules that are not legally binding' (July–August, 1999: 710). It almost seems as if the universities are marking time, fearing that if one university applies evaluative criteria and others do not, it is likely that the 'zealous' university could lose a certain number of potential students who may prefer to enrol where there is no evaluation before admission.

Besides the potential economic difficulties for the universities of imposing Article 6 there is also the genuine fear that changes in the structure of their degrees could mean a decline in academic standards: by luring students back into higher education by apparently 'facilitating' the completion of their degrees; by proposals for obtaining a degree without the heavy workload that was once necessary; and by the continuing need to demonstrate to the Ministry a favourable ratio of students enrolled to those graduating. The danger is that the university could sacrifice quality and move even further away from the goal of providing high-quality recruits for the labour market. Not even the national evaluation process, which is seen as an integral part of the reform strategy (Moratti, 22 July 2003), would necessarily prevent what the enemies of reform call 'the transformation of the universities into glorified secondary schools'. The evaluation procedures are only concerned with the fulfilment of minimum prerequisites, for example, that ministry guidelines for the creation of new courses have been followed, or that the universities have the appropriate number of professors for the planned courses. Neither the means of access nor the course learning structure are part of the evaluative process. Moreover, the universities decide upon their own quality standards to evaluate the course content of their degrees, and it is difficult in present circumstance not to conclude that the key assessment criteria will be the trend of student/customer enrolments in one university as opposed to another.

The new system: a wider evaluation

Within the new system it is now possible to make teaching more efficient because of the changes in the approach to learning; for example, the division of degrees into different stages, and the more flexible use of teaching methods (lectures, laboratory instruction, seminars, exercises, etc.). Moreover, a wider choice of courses – 3,034 compared to 2,443 in the old system (Conferenza Permanente dei Rettori delle Università Italiane, 2003) – offers more flexibility to students, who may be dissatisfied with the study programme they originally chose but can now move more easily from one course to another thanks to the credit-transfer system. New topics of study have been introduced (for example, Informatics and European Studies) and others have been expanded (European languages). Therefore, the basis for the creation of a radically new order exists but what is lacking is the academic world's willingness to respond more positively to the social and economic needs of society. For example, to allow non-academic experts to carry out marginal aspects of the teaching would still be widely looked upon with some disdain, as an unwelcome intrusion into the 'caste system' of the academic world and the 'contamination' of knowledge by those lacking the correct training. This is just one of the problems that have emerged as the system has attempted to reinvigorate the traditional pedagogical model.

Furthermore, universities lack sufficient academic personnel to create a more frequent and efficient follow-up of students by diversifying the traditional teaching modes with other forms of student/teacher contact. In fact, if open access is to be maintained, then students should not be abandoned, as invariably currently occurs, in the initial phases of orientation or whilst trying to pay-off possible learning debts (that is, taking courses that would compensate for shortfalls in their admissions qualifications). Actually, the necessary human resources could come from the increasing number of doctoral students. In fact, in Italy these doctoral students have all the rights of students, and many also have study grants, but they have no obligation to teach or tutor students as occurs in some other European countries. This intellectual workforce, along with research assistants, many of whom are also publicly funded, could be used in supportive teaching activities such as tutoring and student orientation.

The changes aimed at securing a different balance between knowledge and skills should meet the demands of the job market. Hopefully they will bring to an end the suspicion that the graduate *cum laude* faced in the past of being looked upon as someone who was better adapted for conceptual thinking rather than professional work. The methods of evaluation employed in the world of work and the academic world will have converged.

However, the reform process has not been accompanied by either an increase in funding or the construction of new funding mechanisms. In fact in the current regime of university self-government the Ministry makes fewer resources available. Given that, students remain the major source of revenue raises suspicions that reform of the product (the degree programmes) is designed more to please the customer (the potential student) than improve the quality and demands of the learning process provided by the supplier (the university). The reduced workload required to obtain a degree may be considered to be more important than either its quality or cost.

An important obstacle to higher education reform in Italy has been the changeover from a central-left-wing government, that had wanted the reform, to a central-right-wing government, that found itself in the position of implementing the reform process without being fully convinced of its usefulness and, moreover, was sympathetic to idea that universities were in 'cultural decline' (Bertelli, May–June 1999). In fact, the reform itself – and not the failure to implement it effectively – has been considered in certain quarters as a decline in the university's commitment to implanting knowledge in favour of transmitting skills, while at the same time seeking to give academics more privileges.

Letizia Moratti, the new centre-right minister, who took over from Minister Ortensio Zecchino of the centre-left, was one of the first to express her perplexity concerning the philosophy of the reform. At first, Minister Moratti expressed her concerns to the Senate's Committee for Education (Pampaloni, 27 September 2001) about the reform of the faculties of humanities and of law, while in the process voicing some doubts about the future of the entire system. In particular, she questioned whether the three-year course provided sufficient study time to reach degree standard in these fields (De Cesari, 26 September 2001).

Nonetheless, the so-called '3 + 2' system has been substantially confirmed even if some corrective measures have been introduced. For example, after being enrolled in a 'class' of degree courses,[1] the student will follow a common study programme for at least one academic year and will then be assisted by the university to select either a professional learning path (two years of study) or a broader learning path (also two years of study). Minister Letizia Moratti recently appealed for a solution to 'the need for better quality higher education, which at the same time offers more job opportunities' ('Università & Ricerca', 9 May 2003: no. 81–3), but it is not clear at the present time what solution she may propose. Not by simply changing the names of the courses: it is proposed that the second-level degree should be renamed *laurea magistralis*. And certainly not by simply stressing that the universities plan their courses by taking into consideration the needs of the job market thereby enhancing the prospects of pursuing professional careers – which had been strongly recommended as long ago as 1996. But the only sure thing, which has been strongly stressed, is that the present system of open access to higher education will not be changed!

Future prospects

In theory the new system of higher education in Italy is structured to help students to manage their study time more effectively and be prepared for the job market at the age of twenty-two or twenty-three (Universo MURST). However, it is clear that the reform process is far from achieving all the goals that were originally anticipated. While in Italy the higher education system still only coincides with the universities themselves, the emerging parallel system, IFTS (*Istruzione e Formazione Tecnica Superiore* – Education and Higher Technical Training), with courses lasting a maximum of two years and providing a distinctly skills-oriented training for a small number of students, is still in the experimental stage. However, it is a potential threat to the universities especially given their failure to enhance the quality of higher education in the search for ever more students and as they extend the concept of flexibility to its limits in response to student demand which includes the re-enrolment of many students who had apparently dropped-out of higher education several years previously.[2] On a number of points – insistence upon sticking to legal course lengths so enforcing a time limit on the actual duration of studies, drop-out rates, and graduate employability – firm evaluation will not be possible for some time to come. But one thing is certain, the number of graduates will increase in Italy, however, whether their competitiveness on the international job market improves is yet to be seen.

The structure of the new system may resolve some of the problems of higher education in Italy, without touching upon the question of free access. Moreover, if some had felt that all the recent upheaval, as well as potential competition from IFTS programmes, was likely to discourage university enrolment then they have been proven wrong. As of 25 November 2002, there has been an increase over the previous academic year of 4.5 per cent in university enrolments (Università & Ricerca, 28 December, 2002: no. 73–4). Could it be that 'students and their families have renewed their faith in the University system' (Conferenza Permanente dei Rettori delle Università Italiane, 2003) or is it rather that the university is still considered the most desirable 'parking place' or 'social 'cushion' for young Italian adults?

Acknowledgement

The author wishes to thank Drs Salvatrice Massari and Antonio De Luca for assistance in the preparation of this chapter, and Nancy Wittman for help with the translation.

Notes

1 Degree classes are degree programmes which are considered to have similar educational goals.
2 At one time students would lose their academic credit if they had not been assessed for eight consecutive years.

References

Books, journal and newspaper articles

Avveduto, S., M. Rocchi and A. Silvani, 'La formazione nella collaborazione tra Università e imprese', *Il Mulino*, May–June 1990, pp. 455–64.
Bertelli, S., 'Aboliamo l'Università', *Ideazione* (May–June 1999).
Crainz, G., *Storia del miracolo italiano: culture, identità, trasformazioni tra gli anni Cinquanta e Sessanta* (Roma: Donzelli, 1996).
De Cesari, M.C., 'Moratti: per i corsi umanistici va ripensato il modulo 3+2', *Il Sole 24 Ore* (26 September 2001).
Gobbi, B., 'Università avanza la riforma varato il regolamento', *La Repubblica* (10 September 1999).
Gobbi, B., 'Università, si cambia arriva la doppia laurea', *La Repubblica* (3 November 1999).
Marsiglia, G., 'L'Università di massa: espansione, crisi e trasformazione', in S. Soldani and G. Turi (eds) *Fare gli Italiani. Scuola e cultura nell'Italia contemporanea*, vol. 2, *Una società di massa* (Bologna: Il Mulino, 1993), pp. 129–68.
Martinotti, G., 'Il futuro dell'Università italiana', in S. Pontremoli and G. Luzzatto (eds) *Università: la riforma è iniziata* (Milano: La Nuova Italia, 2002), pp. 11–23.
Matteucci, N., 'Università e potere. Le basi culturali per la riforma dell'Università', *Il Mulino*, March–April 1978, pp. 281–97.
Pampaloni, L., 'Le nuove lauree partono', *La Repubblica* (27 September 2001).
Quagliariello, E., 'Il pluralismo universitario nel sistema delle libertà', in E. Quagliariello (ed.) *Questione universitaria tra pubblico e privato* (Manduria: Piero Lacaita Editore, 1986), pp. 11–27.

Schmidt, R. and S. Michelotti, 'Crediti e innovazione didattica', in V. Cerulli Irelli and O. Roselli (eds) *Per una riflessione sulla didattica del diritto* (Milano: Franco Angeli, 2000), pp. 277–310.

Tranfaglia, N., 'Occasioni perdute', *Il Mulino*, July–August 1999, pp. 708–23.

Vinigiani, F.S. and I. Santoro, *L'ordinamento universitario annotato e coordinato*, (Bari: Caccucci Editore, 2002).

Zecchino, O., 'Riforma universitaria, sette note dolenti', *Il Sole 24 Ore* (4 November 2001).

Material available on the Internet

Comitato Nazionale per la Valutazione del Sistema Universitario, 'Rapporti annuali sullo stato delle Università', www.cnvsu.it/indagini/datistat/default.asp.

Conferenza Permanente dei Rettori delle Università Italiane, 'Prima relazione sullo stato delle Università Italiane', (Roma, 25 September 2003), www.crui.it/data/allegati/links/919/1aRelazionepdf.pdf.

De Maio, 'Relazione Commissione De Maio', www.mi.infno.it/rnric/assemblea/DeMaioGiuridico.htm.

Eurispes-Liberal, 'Primo rapporto nazionale sulla scuola' (May 2003), www.eurispes.it/visualizzaRicerche.htm.

Gruppo di Lavoro Ministeriale, 'Autonomia didattica e innovazione dei corsi di studio a livello universitario e post-universitario', (21 October 1997), www.ecno.org/saffi24/docuff/martinot.htm.

Guerzoni, L., 'La riforma dell'istruzione superiore in Italia (1996–1999)', in *The European Space for Higher Education*, (Bologna, 18–19 June 1999), www.murst.it/convegni/bologna99/Guerzoni/Guerzoniit.htm.

Ministero dell'Istruzione, dell'Università e della Ricerca, 'Rilevazione sull'istruzione universitaria 2000', www.miur.it/scripts/IU/etalaudip.htm.

Ministero dell'Università e della Ricerca Scientifica e Tecnologica, 'Nota d'indirizzo' (16 October 1998), www.murst.it/atti/1998/no1016.htm.

Ministero dell'Università e della Ricerca Scientifica e Technologica, 'Relazione alla presentazione del Regolamento in materia di autonomia didattica degli atenei, I perché della riforma', www.murst.it/regolame/1999/adqrel3.htm.

Moratti, L., 'Discorso programmatico del Ministro dell'Istruzione, dell'Università e della Ricerca, Letizia Moratti, alla Camera dei Deputati', (Roma, 18 July 2001), www.istruzione.it/prehome/ministro/programma.shtml.

Moratti, L., 'Intervento del Ministro Letizia Moratti alla conferenza del Comitato Nazionale per la Valutazione del Sistema Universitario' (Roma, 22 July 2003), www.cnvsu.it/indagini/datistat/default.asp.

Trentini, M., 'La riforma del sistema formativo si estende all'università', in *European Industrial Relations Observatory* (28 August 2000), www.eiro.eurofound.ie/2000/08.

'Università & Ricerca', no. 73–4, (Roma, 28 December 2002), www.istruzione.it/prehome/newsletter/newsletter73_74.shtml#ammessi.

'Università & Ricerca', no. 813 (Roma, 9 May 2003), www.istruzione.it/prehome/newsletter/2003/newsletter81_82_83.shtml#universita.

Universo, 'Verso la nuova università', www.universo.murst.it/presentazione/index.html.

Italian laws and European directives

'Bassanini Law' 15 May 1997, no. 127, 'Misure urgenti per lo snellimento dell'attività amministrativa e dei procedimenti di decisione e di controllo', published in *Gazzetta Ufficiale* no. 113 (17 May 1997).

Decree 3 November 1999, no. 509, 'Regolamento recante norme concernenti l'autonomia didattica degli atenei', published in *Gazzetta Ufficiale* no. 2 (4 January 2000).

European Union, *Directive 82/76/CEE* (26 January 1982).

European Union, *Directive 89/48/CEE* (21 December 1988).

6 Access to Dutch higher education

Policies and trends

Frans Kaiser and Hans Vossensteyn

Introduction

This chapter focuses on access to higher education in the Netherlands. Dutch access policies present an interesting case where the government tries to find a proper balance between individual freedom of choice, societal needs and affordability from both a public and individual perspective. Although the Dutch higher education system has in general open access, government deems it necessary to intervene. The main questions we are addressing are why government intervention takes place and what instruments are used.

In the first section, we start our analysis of Dutch access policies by presenting a framework in which the main determinants of access are identified and related to each other. This is followed by our analysis of the reasons why governments intervene to shape access policies and the instruments they employ. This leads on to an overview of the characteristics of the Dutch education system, which precedes a presentation of the key trends in higher education access. In the succeeding sections we discuss some of the ways in which the major instruments of Dutch access policies have been employed: structural reforms to the education system, selection, tuition fees/student assistance, and the use of information. We will conclude with a final reflection on the major access issues in Dutch higher education.

Access to higher education and its determinants

In this section we use 'access' to indicate the number of people who enter higher education. Access policies are the public policies aimed at influencing this number or its composition. To understand the rationale of access policies and to assess its potential leverage, we explore the factors that determine access. Our first hypothesis is that demography is only one factor and that there is an array of other factors that have an impact on the proportion of the population that actually enters higher education. Within that array we distinguish three categories: characteristics of the structure of schooling, individual characteristics and factors related to the (carrying) capacity of the higher education system.

Entrance into higher education requires in most cases a specific type and level of preparatory schooling. National schooling systems may differ in the way schooling is organised and in deciding who meets the entrance requirements for higher education and who does not. For example, secondary education in most countries is divided into a number of tracks, each of which prepares either for the labour market or for specific types of post-secondary education, amongst others higher education. This compartmentalisation in secondary education funnels pupils eligible for higher education.

In addition, not all people who are eligible to enter higher education actually choose or apply to enter. What motivates individuals to enrol is addressed in a wide body of literature, which is dominated by two perspectives. The first is the economic perspective, largely dependent on the human capital theory. In this view individuals will base their choice on an evaluation of the costs and benefits of a higher education degree. The costs include the direct costs of study, such as (tuition) fees and living costs, but also indirect costs like foregone earnings during the period of study. The benefits of a higher education include better employment conditions, such as higher wages (the so-called wage premium of higher educated workers over other employees) and reduced unemployment risks, and some less tangible issues like the consumption benefits of studying, self-development, appreciation of cultural affairs, etc. The original theory was augmented by the introduction of perceived costs and benefits (that may differ from actual costs and benefits) and of the costs of uncertainty (risk). The second perspective in student choice literature is the social/cultural perspective. In this framework, the socio-economic background of people (like gender, ethnicity, parental education, and parental income) has a predominant impact on their educational choices. Authors like Bourdieu (1977) state that such decision-making processes sustain the persistent pattern of social reproduction. The economic and sociological factors have been integrated in the so-called combined models of student choice (Hossler *et al.*, 1999).

Together, demographic, structural and individual characteristics lead to a number of people applying for entrance into higher education. Whether all of them actually can enter higher education depends on the carrying capacity of society. The carrying capacity of a society (a concept borrowed from evolutionary biology) is on the one hand determined by the maximum number of students that society is able – and willing – to accommodate (subsidise) and on the other hand by the maximum number of graduates the labour market is able to absorb. The carrying capacity of a society largely depends on the economic conditions of a country (like economic growth and unemployment rates), the public budget available for higher education, and the labour market demand for highly skilled workers. If the economic situation is bleak and public budgets are under severe pressure, the carrying capacity may deteriorate, which may lead to pressures or policies to limit access to higher education.

The factors influencing access to higher education are tentatively summarised in Figure 6.1.

Access policies: rationales and instruments

Rationales

Why should government intervene in access to higher education? The standard economic answer to this question is to point out that higher education is a merit good, which means that higher education has external effects on society (Barr, 1998). The external effect most often mentioned is the contribution of higher education to economic growth. A higher level of educational attainment in the labour force is assumed to enhance productivity, not only of the higher educated employees but also of those who work with them. Since individuals do not take into account those external effects when deciding to enter higher education, it is argued that government should stimulate access.

Government access policy can have a general character, aiming at the expansion of the entire higher education system, but it can also be

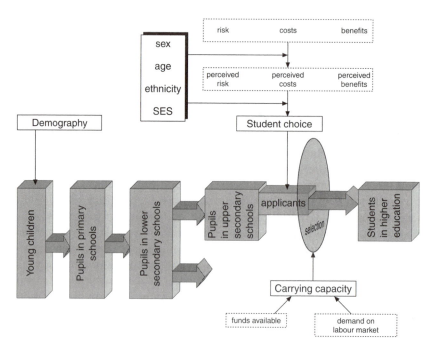

Figure 6.1 Overview of factors influencing access to higher education.

targeted at entrance into specific programmes. For example, the labour market may demand more graduates from specific disciplines like engineering or teacher training than higher education currently delivers. In addition, public intervention may also have a more social character where policies can be targeted at increasing the access of students from specific social groups. Aggregated individual choices may result in inequalities in the student body (regarding gender, ethnicity and socio-economic background) that are socially undesirable. In that case, access policies aim to redress those situations by widening access for under-represented groups.

Instruments

To achieve their goals governments may use a number of instruments. We identify three main types of instruments:

1   Structural reforms, both at the system level and within different education sectors.
2   Restrictive admission policies such as entrance requirements, *numerus fixus* and selection.
3   Non-restrictive measures focusing on the behaviour of students and/or institutions; for example, by offering financial incentives and providing information.

Structural reforms

Structural reforms address changes in the structure of the education system and the organisation and content of programmes, often aiming at removing obstacles to access. In many countries, secondary education is divided into a number of tracks, each of which prepares for the labour market or specific types of post-secondary education. If the boundaries between the tracks are strong, this may lead to a restrictive funnelling of pupils between those who are eligible for higher education and those who are not. The potential negative effects of this compartmentalisation of secondary and higher education on access may be tackled by making these boundaries more flexible. One way would be through the introduction of 'bridging-courses', in which deficiencies preventing access can be repaired. Or by allowing pupils who have fallen out of the higher education funnel to find their way back in again. These suggest possible structural reforms aimed at improving the transition from secondary to higher education.

The major structural reform in the Dutch higher education system has been the construction of processes of differentiation. Differentiation aims at widening the range of choices for students. Many of those processes started in the early 1970s when new types of institutions (non-university) were established to meet the economic demands of society. The creation and expansion of the non-university sector has been very important in the move from elite towards mass higher education. Differentiation has not been limited to institutional differentiation but also comprises differentiation in programmes, subjects or course duration. For example, one of the reasons to differentiate standard course lengths is that courses shorter than the standard degree course can be attractive for students with medium grades. The rigidity of the system may also be tackled by an increase in the flexibility of the organisation of courses. For instance, providing distance education programmes or part-time programmes may create opportunities for more groups of students (adult students, part-time students) to participate. These may also prevent students from getting 'trapped' in a course that turns out to be less relevant from both a personal and a social point of view.

Restrictive admission policies

Restrictive admission policies limit the choices individual applicants have when choosing a higher education programme. These policies may range from general basic entrance requirements to strong selection mechanisms. In most countries a qualifying diploma of secondary education forms the basic requirement for entry to higher education. Without such a qualification entry is possible only in exceptional cases, where 'open access' is permitted. In addition to this baseline requirement, there are two types of restrictive instruments: the *numerus fixus* and selection. The *numerus fixus* is a mechanism that restricts the number of entrants into higher education or into specific studies where the limited capacity of the system does not allow further growth. Such measures are, for example, taken in situations where there has been an excessive supply of graduates onto the labour market – or even to prevent that occurring. A *numerus fixus*, although often determined at the national level, can also be set at the institutional level. Consequently, selection procedures are used to allocate the applicants to the (limited) number of student places available in specific programmes and at specific institutions. Selection can either work as a lottery or with very detailed criteria to define the desired characteristics.

Non-restrictive instruments

Governments may also want to influence (stimulate) students' choices in directions that are desirable from a national perspective. Two types of instruments can be discerned that aim to influence students' preferences for particular courses according to national priorities: the provision of information and guidance, and offering financial incentives.

Information and guidance are used primarily to enhance the transparency of the various course options on the one hand and of the (presumed) labour market demands on the other. Moreover, government may manipulate two types of financial incentives: the direct cost of higher education, that is, tuition fees, and the creation of student support systems. Tuition fees determine what proportion of the teaching costs has to be paid by the students. When a uniform tuition tariff is charged to all students, this price – *ceteris paribus* – will only influence whether students enter higher education or not. But levying differential fees is a way to make particular degree programmes more or less attractive. For example, government can raise fees for those degrees where the enrolment is considered to be too high, whereas fees may be lowered for studies in which shortages are foreseen. Student support systems are usually set up to help students meet the costs of study by removing potential price barriers. Because students from different backgrounds may have different price barriers, student support systems may be set up in such a way that underprivileged groups benefit more from grants and scholarships by the lowering of their direct costs.

Access policies in the Netherlands

With a framework for analysis to hand, we can now turn to the Dutch situation. What is the pattern of access to higher education in the Netherlands and what does Dutch access policy look like? Before addressing these questions we present a brief description of the Dutch education system as visualised in Figure 6.2.

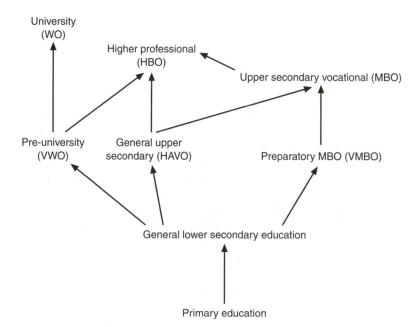

Figure 6.2 The Dutch education system.

The Dutch road(s) to higher education

Education is compulsory up to the age of sixteen. The different types of secondary education have taught the same core curriculum of fifteen subjects in the early years. After the completion of basic secondary education, pupils can follow one of two main pathways: either the VMBO path towards vocational education, or the HAVO/VWO path towards higher education. These routes are the official ways of qualifying for entry into higher education. The five-year HAVO programme gives direct access to the *hogescholen*[1] (HBO). The six-year VWO programme prepares pupils for entry into university education, though VWO-graduates may also enter HBO programmes. Pupils with a HAVO qualification may take a short-cut route into university by successfully completing the first year of a HBO programme and then transferring to a university programme in the same field. A more indirect way into higher education can be taken by pupils in secondary vocational education as those with a MBO-diploma are allowed to enter HBO courses in a similar subject area.

In addition to these possibilities, students can in some cases qualify for higher education without an official pre-entry Dutch qualification. One such major group consists of those with recognised foreign secondary education qualifications, while another opportunity is the so-called *colloquium doctum*, which is an entrance examination for those without an official qualification.

The Dutch higher education system

Public higher education is a binary system and consists of thirteen universities and about fifty *hogescholen* (HBOs). Besides the thirteen traditional research universities, a number of small 'designated institutions' are part of the university sector: a university for business administration, four institutes for theological training, a university for humanistics offering a degree programme in humanistics/humanist studies, as well as several international institutes of education. The latter are formally part of the higher education system, but are usually not included in the educational statistics and they are only marginally influenced by overall higher education policy. In the HBO sector, the number of recognised, but not publicly funded, institutions in addition to the fifty public institutions is considerably larger.

Traditionally, universities have offered either four-year programmes or five-year programmes in science and engineering. Since 2000, new entrants can no longer access these traditional programmes. All new entrants have to enrol in the new three-year Bachelor programmes. In addition to the Bachelor programmes, one- or two-year Masters programmes are offered.[2] The traditional length of the HBO programmes did not change with the introduction of the Bachelor–Master system and the four-year HBO programmes now officially lead to Bachelor degrees.

With regard to access to higher education, we can state that most pro-grammes and institutions in Dutch higher education require only the minimum entrance requirement of holding a qualifying secondary education qualification and so there is open access. However, to enter certain higher education programmes, for example in science and engineering subjects, *hogescholen* and universities often require prospective students to have passed secondary education examinations in particular subjects, like mathe-matics, physics, biology or chemistry. Only in a very limited number of pro-grammes is the number of study places restricted, requiring selection procedures to choose and allocate the applicants. All students in Dutch higher education have to pay tuition fees, which are basically charged at a uniform tariff in the public institutions. Private institutions can set their own tariffs. All full-time students on recognised programmes, both at public and at designated institutions, are eligible for student financial support from the government.

Access trends

In addition to the differences in programmes between the universities and *hogescholen*, there is another marked contrast between the two sectors: the *hogescholen* sector is much larger and has grown much faster. This becomes clear from Figure 6.3. In total, entrance into higher education increased almost sixfold from around 20,000 in the early 1960s to almost 120,000 in 2002. Universities showed a strong growth up till 1970, which

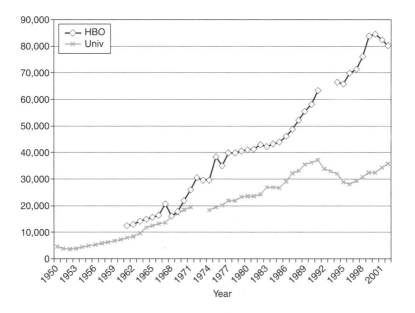

Figure 6.3 New entrants in Dutch higher education, by type of institution (source: CBS Statline, www.cbs.nl).

levelled off during the 1970s and went up again in the 1980s. The 1990s showed a quite remarkable pattern: the number of new entrants decreased during the first half of the decade and then returned to the same starting point. In the *hogescholen* sector there was also a strong growth until the mid-1970s, after which it slackened. In the late 1980s a very strong growth occurred, which has continued into the new millennium, with only a minor setback in the early 1990s. The increase since 2001 is quite remarkable and today the number of new entrants to the *hogescholen* is more than double that of the universities.

A major cause of the rapid growth of higher education arises from the feminisation of higher education in the Netherlands. Figure 6.4 shows that female participation has grown significantly up to the point at which women are no longer under-represented in higher education access.

Next to the feminisation of higher education it is also interesting to see whether different social classes benefited to the same extent from the expansion of higher education. Boosting higher education participation among under-represented groups has never been the real objective of Dutch access policies. This fact is a likely explanation for a lack of structural data on the socio-economic composition of the student body. Only a few *ad hoc* studies provide some historical insights in the backgrounds of students. Since 2000, a new student monitoring system has been set up that provides comparable data and also focuses on the representation of ethnic groups among students. The available data show that access into higher education is skewed to the students whose parents have a higher educa-

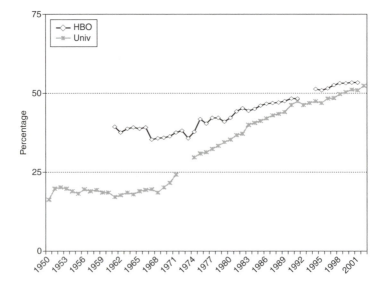

Figure 6.4 Female new entrants as a percentage of total number of new entrants (source: CBS Statline, www.cbs.nl).

tional background (Figure 6.5). This is especially the case for the university programmes (Hofman *et al.*, 2003).

As mentioned above, demography alone can have a substantial impact on access patterns. However, in the Netherlands that is not the case: demographic factors do not account for the typical growth pattern as can be seen in Figure 6.6. If we compare the trend in the number of eighteen-year-olds – which still is the most common age for people to enter higher education – with the trend in new entrants, we can see that the population of eighteen-year-olds has been more or less stable, whereas the number of new entrants has grown almost six times since 1962.

Evidently, there have been major changes both in the capacity of higher education to expand and in students' decisions that have led to this massive expansion. Next to general economic growth and public awareness of the value of a higher education degree, the access policies developed and implemented by the Dutch government may have had a large impact on this massification of higher education. These policies will

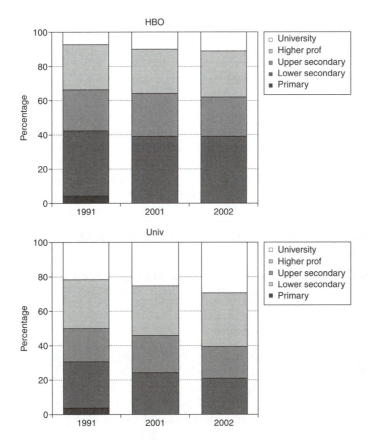

Figure 6.5 Composition of new entrants by educational background of parents.

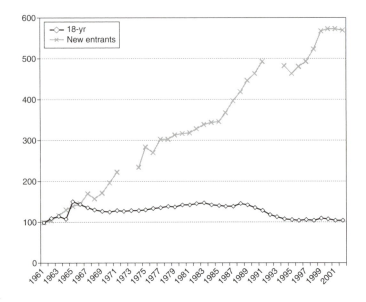

Figure 6.6 Changes in the number of new entrants in higher education and the number of eighteen-year-olds in the population (1962 = 100) (source: CBS Statline, www.cbs.nl).

be discussed below. However, to what extent these policies have had a causal impact on the access trends described above is difficult to determine and is a question the answer to which goes beyond the scope of this chapter. In describing the access policies, we will use the previous divide between structural reforms, restrictive policies and non-restrictive policies.

Structural reforms in Dutch education with respect to access into higher education

A number of reforms in the Dutch education system has been undertaken in order to improve the accessibility of higher education.

Reforms in secondary education

Structural reforms in secondary education have postponed the time at which the decision to select a specific track has to be made and have increased the permeability of the boundaries between tracks.

After the introduction of the Secondary Education Act of 1968, the structure of secondary education remained rather stable until the early 1990s. Then, in 1993/94, a form of basic secondary education (*basisvorming*) was introduced in each of the different types of secondary education.

It more or less means that since then all pupils have been taught the same core curriculum in the early years of secondary education. For each of the fifteen subjects, national core objectives have been formulated. Schools can decide themselves how they intend to reach these objectives. The third year is flexible: either students continue basic education or work towards preparing for the second tier of secondary education (*bovenbouw*). In total, some 80 per cent of the contents of the courses of basic education are determined nationally, the schools themselves – taking into account the needs and wishes of the pupils – can decide upon 20 per cent of the courses. The school advises the pupil and the parents/guardians after two years of basic education what would be the most suitable (upper) secondary education option for the individual pupil.

After the basic secondary education, in principle two paths lie ahead of the pupils. The first being the VMBO route which prepares students for vocational education. In terms of size, about 60 per cent of the pupils choose this vocationally oriented VMBO, route whereas 40 per cent of the pupils opt for the preparatory tracks for higher education, the HAVO/VWO route (CBS, 2002).

The new structure and contents of HAVO and VWO, preparing pupils for higher education, comprised a number of changes in the second tier of secondary education. The first major change meant that the traditional set of six to eight subjects that students could choose for the final examinations was replaced in 1998 by four sets of about fifteen subjects in which pupils have to be examined. These four so-called profiles (*doorstroomprofielen*) prepare each student for a different study programme in higher education. The four profiles are 'culture and society' (preparation for the social sciences, history, languages and culture), 'economy and society' (preparation for economics and social sciences), 'nature and health' (preparation for medical sciences and biology), and 'nature and technology' (preparation for natural sciences and engineering). Each profile includes a compulsory part (50 per cent) meant for general education, a profile part (30 per cent) to prepare for higher education, and a free part (20 per cent) for personal development. The examinations consist of school examinations and national examinations.

A second major change refers to the organisation of the learning process. The traditional organisation of the learning process, which was mainly directed by the teachers, was replaced by a new approach in which pupils learn in a more active and autonomous way, designed to do justice to the differences between pupils. This new approach is termed *studiehuis* (study house) and was introduced in 1998. As a result, pupils are offered different learning routes, dependent on their talents, interests and pace. Furthermore, the teacher should be seen as assisting the whole learning process rather than simply implanting knowledge.

The third change relates to the higher education entrance requirements. Access to particular higher education programmes requires a specific secondary education profile rather than examination success in a few core subjects. For example, the university pharmacy degree programme requires candidates to have completed the 'nature and technology' profile, but, higher education institutions may also admit students from other profiles on the basis of additional qualifications. In the example of pharmacy, pupils with a 'nature and health' profile may be admitted if they have studied chemistry courses in the free part of their profile. A fourth change permits potential deficiencies to be overlooked before one enters a higher education programme, whereas previously a shortfall in qualifications could be made up in the initial months of the higher education programme.

Finally, the content of secondary courses now pays more attention to skills (design, problem solving, communication, cooperation, planning, etc.) rather than factual knowledge. This means that some subject matters disappeared and were replaced by new courses designed to implant, for example, skills in information technology, management and organisation. In addition, all the profiles orientate students towards possible future study plans and professional career choices, so preparing pupils for the decisions to be made after secondary education.

Reforms in higher education

In the 1970s, the government proposed to re-organise university education into two tiers in order to make higher education more accessible to a larger number of students. As a result of this in 1982 a two-tier system was implemented in university education by the so-called Two-phases Structure Act (Tweede Kamer, 1980). The traditional programmes with a regular nominal duration of five years were shortened to four-year undergraduate programmes leading to a 'doctorandus' degree. These formed the first phase in the new university structure. The second phase would have to offer selective postdoctoral programmes with a maximum duration of two years. In practice only a few programmes were established in this second phase. One example was the creation of teacher training programmes in which university graduates could gain a teaching qualification within their field of study by following a one-year programme.

Another important change in the structure of higher education degree programmes was established by the so-called Harmonisation Act. This Act not only equalised the tuition levels of HBO and university students, but it also enabled students who already held a HBO degree to obtain a university degree in the limited period of two years, and vice versa. Before 1988 such students would have been required to complete a full four-year programme (Tweede Kamer, 1987).

In 1995, because the study load in engineering was regarded as relatively heavy and the labour market wanted to have better prepared engineers, technology programmes were required to extend the nominal duration of their degrees from four to five years. In 1997 the same happened for science programmes, such as biology, chemistry, mathematics and physics.

In the wake of the Bologna Agreement, the Dutch government formulated plans to further reform the degree structure. Early in 2002, the Dutch parliament approved a change in the Law on Higher Education and Research (WHW), making it legally possible for Dutch higher education institutions to grant Bachelor and Master degrees from the academic year 2002/03. Under the 'BaMa' system, university students will first follow a Bachelor's programme lasting at least three years and will then be able to enter a specialised Master's programme. The existing regulations on the maximum time students can study will remain in force. The main motive for the Dutch government's implementation of the BaMa structure was that this new system is seen as an essential condition for a modern and internationally oriented higher education system (Ministerie van OCenW, 2000). The BaMa structure is designed to make the Dutch higher education system more flexible and open, so that anticipating new societal developments – for instance internationalisation, globalisation and developments in information and communication technology – is simplified. The system should be flexible enough to meet the needs of students of all ages and open enough to allow Dutch students to study abroad, as well as allowing foreign students to enter the Dutch system.

Open access and selection

Numerus fixus

In general, the Dutch government has a policy of open access to higher education, which actually means that all who meet the basic entrance requirements are admitted to the programme of their choice. However, not all Dutch higher education system has (always) been subject to policies of open access. Because of limitations in the carrying capacity of the system, some programmes have been subject to restrictive entrance policies. These are known as the *numerus fixus* programmes for which student demand exceeds the capacity. For those programmes a *numerus fixus* is applied.[3] There are two types of *numerus fixus*: the institutional fixus and the programme fixus.

In the case of an institutional fixus, a particular higher education institution has a capacity shortage in a particular programme. This unmet demand may be redirected to other institutions that offer the same (type of) programme and that still have some capacity to enrol students. A government agency (the Informatie Beheergroep, IBG) then determines how students will be distributed over the institutions that offer the programme at stake.[4]

The programme fixus (also known as the labour market fixus) is applied when the expected outflow of graduates of a specific programme exceeds the 'expected needs of the labour market'. This particularly goes for programmes like medicine, dentistry, veterinary sciences, physiotherapy, nursing and architecture. Though the 'acceptable' number of new entrants is determined by the government, the professional groups in these branches are often very influential in setting the entrance quota. Consequently, a number of applicants will not be able to take up their preferred course. They have to select a different programme, go abroad, or try again next year.

Over the last few years, the number of institutions and programmes with a fixus has slightly declined and the labour market is absorbing more graduates than ever and the demand for highly skilled labour is expected to increase even further. Apparently, the 'carrying capacity' of the system has substantially increased. A potential explanation is that the previous decades have shown a tremendous growth of the public sector demanding large numbers of highly trained employees, not only in all kinds of government bodies, but also in the health care and education system. In addition the Dutch economy has shown a major transformation from manufacturing industries and agriculture towards a more knowledge-intensive service-economy. Whereas the production industries are moving abroad, the Dutch labour market becomes more and more service oriented. These developments may also partly explain the feminisation of higher education.

Below we elaborate on the mechanisms used to select students.

Selection mechanisms

In 1996–97, there was a heated public debate on the merits and flaws of the lottery system of selection that was used for a long time. The debate was triggered by the rejection in two consecutive years of a student with almost perfect marks (9.9 out of 10) for access to a medical programme. However, other reasons have also persuaded the minister to have the weighted lottery system reviewed. The revised system should enhance the influence applicants have on their chances to be admitted, either by taking into account work experience or by demonstrating high motivation or the input of extra effort. It should reduce the element of chance and thereby the uncertainty for applicants. It was also felt that the then existing system (which was introduced in the 1970s) was no longer in line with the profoundly changed relationship between government and the higher education institutions. Since the late 1980s, higher education institutions have gained much more autonomy than they had in the 1970s. Changes in secondary education, which were to stimulate the development of social and learning competencies, were another drive for the intended change. It was expected that the pool of applicants would become more heterogeneous because of those changes and because of the expansion of higher education.

Weighted lottery

To give everyone an equal chance to enter the *numerus fixus* programmes, a lottery system is used. Those applicants with very good marks on the qualifying secondary education examinations (on a scale of 0 to 10, 8 or higher) have direct access. In 2002, around 9 per cent of the applicants for *numerus fixus* university programmes were admitted on this criterion. The percentage for HBO applicants was around 4 per cent. Other applicants have to participate in a weighted lottery. The weights are determined by the average mark of the qualifying examination. Applicants may participate in a lottery three times. At least half of the applicants accepted have to be allocated by the lottery system. In 2002, 74 per cent of the applicants for *numerus fixus* university programmes were admitted through the lottery system. The percentage for HBO applicants was around 63 per cent.

Decentralised selection

The new 1999 law regulating access introduced decentralised selection. For those places that are not filled by direct (merit based) access or by the central lottery system (see above) higher education institutions may select applicants themselves, using their own criteria. These criteria may (and do) differ by programme. Decentralised selection was to set up to enhance the influence students may have on their chances to be admitted to a programme. Institutions use it to select those applicants with special motivations or specific talents.

In 2002 this experimental regulation was evaluated. The evaluation showed that higher education institutions do not use the decentralised selection to the fullest extent. Only 17 per cent of new university entrants in *numerus fixus* programmes were selected by the institutions themselves. For the HBO programmes, the percentage was twice as high. The number of programmes for which decentralised selection was used was rather limited (twelve in the universities and nine in the *hogescholen*). The time-consuming development of selection criteria and the easing of capacity restrictions were the main reasons for this 'meagre' result.

Apart from (experimental) decentralised selection, higher education institutions may select for a number of specific programmes (twenty-one in 2003). This type of selection has a much longer history. These programmes require specific skills or abilities (for example, art colleges). This type of selection does not necessarily refer to *numerus fixus* programmes.

Non-restrictive policy instruments: tuition, student support and information

Access policies not only concentrate on limiting and selecting the students admitted to higher education, but can also address the conditions of student life and the information about the opportunities in higher education. Research on college choice has taught us that a large number of factors influence the likelihood of attending higher education, such as gender, age, socio-economic background, learning aptitude, student motivation, tuition fees, scholarships and student loans. A number of these factors, such as background characteristics, are difficult to influence by public policies. But, if governments want to have an impact on access to higher education, tuition fees and student support are the major tools, particularly influencing the costs that students will incur. Another tool is the information potential students use in selecting a degree programme. In the following subsections we will address the way in which the Dutch government has used tuition fees and student support to influence the costs of attending college and what information campaigns were set up to focus (potential) students' attention on particular higher education programmes.

Tuition

One of the possibilities for governments to stimulate higher education participation is to reduce the private costs of attendance. Public subsidies to higher education as such can limit the amount of tuition fees students have to pay. The extreme case is that students do not have to pay tuition fees at all, which is the case in several countries, such as in Germany, Denmark, Finland, Sweden, Norway and most Central and Eastern European countries (Vossensteyn, 2003). An argument often heard is that tuition fees may restrict access to higher education, particularly for those from already disadvantaged socio-economic backgrounds. As such, tuition subsidies may be used to widen access for students from such backgrounds.

In the Netherlands tuition fees have been established for some time. Since 1945 students in publicly funded higher education have had to pay a uniform tuition fee, regardless of the costs related to different study programmes. The government annually sets the tuition rate. During the 1980s university students paid slightly higher fees than students in the HBO sector, but in the early 1990s this was equalised again. Students make their tuition payments directly to the higher education institutions, which have full autonomy over this revenue stream. In 2002, tuition fees made up about 17 per cent of institutional revenues in the HBO sector and about 5.5 per cent in the university sector – about 15 per cent of the overall university teaching budget (Tweede Kamer, 2002). This demonstrates that public subsidies to higher education are considerable and private contributions moderate. Figure 6.7 shows the development of the level of tuition fees in the Netherlands since 1945.

The real value of the fees declined in the 1945–71 period. In that period students had to pay NLG 200 (€91) per academic year in nominal terms. After an initial increase to NLG 1,000 (€454) in 1972–73, the level was set at NLG 500 (€227) between 1974 and 1980. Since then, tuition levels have gradually increased up to almost €1,445 in 2003/04. Figure 6.7 shows that particularly in the period since 1986 the increases in the level of fees often exceeded the rate of inflation. As a result, a larger share of the costs of higher education has been gradually shifted to students and their families, which indicates that the Dutch government did not use the instrument of tuition reduction to expand access to higher education. As such, tuition fees have become an issue of continuous discussion. Proponents argue that tuition fees constitute a 'fair' private contribution to the costs of higher education, which brings the individual students considerable future rewards (monetary as well as non-monetary). But the opponents of fees argue that they harm access, particularly for those from lower socio-economic backgrounds. This has led to many heated political debates on where the money has to come from to finance the steadily growing higher education system. As a good Dutch tradition, such debates generally end in compromises that include moderate tuition increases accompanied with full compensation of lower-income students through the system of student financial support. This explains the steady incremental tuition path since the 1980s as shown in Figure 6.7 as well as the development in the system of student support.

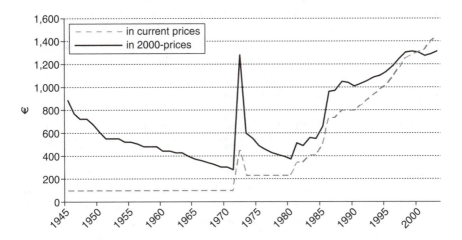

Figure 6.7 Development of tuition fees (€, in current prices and in real 2000-prices) (source: Ministerie van OCenW, time series).

The major discussions on tuition fees in 2002–03 related to the issue of differential tuition fees. The Ministry of Education, Science and Culture took up the discussion for a number of reasons: to allow institutions to charge higher contributions in return for enhanced quality programmes, and to make particular subjects like science, engineering and teacher training more attractive. However, in the first case opponents fear that this would harm access for poor students, and in the second case it is questioned whether abandoning the equity principle, not to mention the public costs involved, can be justified by the expected number of extra students attracted to the desired programmes.

Student support

Besides controlling fee levels, governments have a second financial instrument available to enhance access to higher education: providing financial support to meet the costs of instruction and living. This can be done either with loans or with subsidies (for example, grants, tax benefits or family allowances). Since 1945, successive Dutch governments gradually developed a system of student support, though with a change of focus over the following six decades (de Regt, 1993). In the early days the major drive was to open up opportunities for small numbers of talented low-income students. Between 1956 and 1972, economic growth and the general tendency of democratisation changed the focus to opening opportunities for all. This period laid the ground for the massification of higher education, though student support remained limited to small bursary and loan programmes. Financial support consisted mainly of tax benefits and family allowances for students' parents. Because of the oil crises in the early 1970s, the actual implementation of a far-reaching student support system was postponed. As a result, we can conclude that until 1986 there was the willingness to expand students' opportunities but because of limited government resources, student support was not a very active instrument in encouraging access to higher education. Nevertheless, participation rates considerably increased during this period (Figure 6.3) and the gender imbalance to a large extent disappeared (Figure 6.4).

A new relatively generous system of student aid was implemented by the Student Finance Act (*WSF*) in 1986. This system transformed all indirect support such as tax benefits and family allowances into direct financial support to students themselves. The system established a compromise between students' access and financial independence, transparency and simplicity of the system, and affordability for the government (Hupe and van Solm, 1998). The major characteristics of the system that are still largely in place are reflected in the following basic elements:

- A basic grant (*basisbeurs*) for all full-time students, varying between students who live with their parents and those who do not.

- A means-tested supplementary grant for a limited number (about 30 per cent) of students.
- Loans that can be taken up on a voluntary basis, carrying a below-market interest rate.
- Parental contributions or students' own income. The parental contributions are strongly interrelated with the (parental) means-tested supplementary grants and loans.
- Finally, students can earn up to €9,847 per annum (in 2003) before they start losing any of their grant entitlements.

All components together add up to a given amount that students are expected to need for study and living costs according to annual estimations by the Ministry of Education, Culture and Sciences. From this perspective, no (full-time) students should face any financial barriers for entrance into higher education.

After 1986, on the basis of demographic developments the government expected a decline in the number of students and thus believed that a relatively generous system for students would be feasible from the viewpoint of public finances. But, as shown in Figures 6.3 and 6.6 the opposite happened, and, partly as a result, a large number of additional changes have taken place since then (Vossenteyn, 2002):

- Tuition fees were increased in real terms (see Figure 6.7).
- Basic grants were reduced several times because of growing numbers of students and limited public budgets.
- Supplementary grants were increased to compensate for tuition increases, inflation, and reductions in the basic grants. This is to guarantee access for students from disadvantaged backgrounds (about 30 per cent, based on a means-test).
- The duration of grants was reduced in two successive steps (1991 and 1996) to the nominal duration of courses (four to six years).
- Student loans gained in importance. As with supplementary grants, student loans also covered reductions in the basic grant, increases in tuition fees and inflation. In addition, students have been permitted to replace (assumed) parental contributions with student loans since 1995.
- Performance requirements were imposed. Since 1993 students had to meet performance requirements in order to remain eligible for grants. Under the so-called 'progress-related grant' (*Tempobeurs*) students had to pass 25 per cent of the annual study credits otherwise their grants would be converted into interest-bearing loans (Hupe and van Solm, 1998). In 1996, the progress requirements were intensified through the 'performance-related grant' (*Prestatiebeurs*). Since then, all grants have been awarded initially as loans and only if students pass 50 per cent of the exams in the first year and complete their degree within the nominal duration of the programme plus two years

(six or seven years in total) are their initial loans converted into a grant. In 2000, the time limit to complete a degree was relaxed to ten years for all programmes, particularly to allow students to be involved in extra-curricular activities and part-time work (Ministerie van OCenW, 1999).

- Because of the developments addressed above the emphasis on parental contributions and students' own resources gradually increased. In addition, students' expenditure patterns have gone up, exceeding the standard budget available through student support. Finally, students seem to be debt averse. Consequently there is greater pressure on parents and students who are more likely to have part-time jobs (Vossensteyn, 1997).

Most of the changes implicitly meant budgetary reductions and were aimed at encouraging students to pursue more efficient study patterns. Furthermore, the focus of the support policies have shifted: from opening up opportunities for lower income groups until the mid-1980s, followed by creating a basic income provision for all students in 1986, to the system reverting once again to supporting underprivileged students.

Impact of tuition and support policies on student enrolment behaviour

Until the mid-1980s, student financial support was relatively modest or poor in the Netherlands and thus could not be expected to generate massification in higher education. Nevertheless, rapid expansion of higher education happened during the 1960s and 1970s, also reducing the gender imbalance to a large extent. These developments seem to be the result of general societal tendencies rather than active access policies.

However, the introduction of a relatively generous system of student support in 1986 could be expected to boost access and participation, although its purpose was to guarantee equal access for all students regardless of their backgrounds. There has been a number of studies on student choice behaviour that also looked at the potential relationships between financial support and participation. However, most of these studies indicated no clear relationships between changes in student finance and the composition of the student body (de Jong *et al.*, 1991; de Jonge *et al.*, 1991).

Also the deterioration of student support, particularly during the 1990s, has been studied for its impact on access to higher education (Vossensteyn, 2002). The gradual shift towards cost-sharing in the Netherlands might be expected to have led to changes in student enrolment behaviour; for example in terms of lower participation, the choice of cheaper (shorter) or easier study programmes or higher study progress. However, hardly any such changes in student choice seem to have occurred. Only a few tendencies can be indicated.

First, the introduction of study progress requirements, which meant a serious 'cultural change' had only a temporary effect on participation in higher education. Initially, the number of new entrants to university studies decreased slightly, some (potential) students postponing actual enrolment and some university-qualified candidates entering HBO programmes (de Jong *et al.*, 1996). However, within a few years, the traditional enrolment patterns appeared again.

A second interesting development is that, regardless of the growing emphasis on loans, the number of students actually taking up loans decreased substantially, from 40 per cent in 1991 to about 15 per cent in 1997 (de Vos and Fontein, 1998). One reason is that since 1992 interest has been charged. However, take-up rates have gone up slightly since 2000. Instead of acquiring student loans, students prefer to take part-time jobs which enables them to avoid accumulating debts and even to upgrade their standard of living. Moreover, students are also willing to borrow outside the student loans system, either from family or by having a bank overdraft. Many even take up flexible and temporary loans from private banks to cover extraordinary expenses, such as computer equipment or holidays (Kerstens and de Jonge, 1999).

With respect to the impact of tuition fees, most studies show that the real increases in tuition fees did not seem to impact on access in terms of enrolment patterns. Student choice behaviour in general seems to be price inelastic! Such price-unresponsiveness dates back to the 1980s and continues into the 1990s (Oosterbeek and Webbink, 1995). A simulation model showed that even substantial tuition fee increases will hardly affect enrolment rates, except for students from lower socio-economic families (Sterken, 1995). Furthermore, a recent survey by Felsö *et al.* (2000) indicated that students would not change their preferences in cases where tuition fees were either increased or reduced by €450.

Some simulation studies paid attention to the problem of a declining interest in science and engineering studies. They found that guaranteeing students a job after graduation and increasing engineers' salaries would have a stronger influence in attracting extra students to these studies than increasing scholarships or reducing tuition (de Jong *et al.*, 2001; Felsö *et al.*, 2000). In fact some universities of technology have experimented with giving students additional scholarships but this did not attract extra students.

All in all, various studies, covering different time periods, all come to the conclusion that student choice is not unduly affected by financial incentives, except for students from disadvantaged groups. This more or less confirms the findings of international studies on student choice (Heller, 1997; Hossler *et al.*, 1999).

Information for prospective students

Money is not the only thing that has an impact on the choices students make. Government may also provide (potential) students with detailed and objective information on the basis of which they can make a carefully considered decision on whether to study, what and where. Ideally, the information provision regarding student choice (and access) not only gives insights into what study opportunities there are, but also about the content of programmes, their (relative) quality and what labour market opportunities they open up.

The communication and information strategies of Dutch higher education institutions have developed in three stages (Jansen, 1996). Until the mid-1980s, the information presented to future students was sober, independent, and focused purely on the content of study programmes. In the second stage, from 1985 to 1994, the inflow of new entrants levelled off. Because of governmental cutbacks to the education budget, the higher education sector gradually turned into a market where institutions had to compete for students. A particularly visible manifestation was the appointment of market research personnel and public relations officers as well as the hiring of professional advertising firms. Communication with, and recruitment of, future students became highly professional. Institutions tried to create their own images by conducting large advertising campaigns in newspapers and magazines and by developing information services for secondary school pupils.

In the third stage, since 1994–95, a slight decrease in student numbers, accompanied by a move towards performance-based funding, resulted in institutional policies directed at limiting the actual duration of study and attracting particular groups of students. Under pressure from the increased amount of information available on the quality and performance of institutions, the communication strategies towards potential target groups were focused more on programme content, quality and student performance. The scores in national surveys on student satisfaction, the outcomes of quality assessments, the position of graduates in the labour market, the ICT facilities offered by the institutions, as well as the ranking of cities in terms of attractiveness to students, are all used in promotional campaigns (Jansen, 1996). In the mid-1990s, a number of annual country-wide publications were set up to provide prospective students with objective information and inform them of the outcomes of various studies. *De Keuzegids Hoger Onderwijs*, *De Beste Studies* of the magazine *Elsevier*, and *De Studiekeuze Barometer* convey the outcomes of the quality assurance processes as well as monitoring the labour market position of HBO and university graduates (Ramaekers and Huijgen, 2000; Allen *et al.*, 2000).

Specific information campaigns

Alongside the growth in the general information available for prospective students, particular developments in student choice and in the labour market triggered the government to initiate a number of specific programmes to stimulate the participation of specific social groups and to encourage access into certain degree programmes. The major examples concern the participation of women and enrolments in science, engineering and teacher training.

Female participation

In 1990, the government started a general campaign to make women more aware of their career opportunities within society and to become more independent in both a socio-cultural and a socio-economic sense (van den Broek and Voeten, 2002). The campaign is known as *'een slimme meid is op haar toekomst voorbereid'* (a smart woman is prepared for her future). One of the initiatives was to bring to the attention of women the opportunities that higher education offered.

Science and engineering

Young people show declining interest in science and engineering programmes and enrolments continue to drop. To reverse this trend a number of government campaigns have been started over the past decade and a half. These campaigns have aimed at increasing student participation in technical sciences. The major campaigns were *'Kies exact'* (Choose appropriately, as well as Choose science), which ran from 1987 till 1989; and *'Thea studeert techniek'* (Thea is studying engineering), also running in the late 1980s (van den Broek and Voeten, 2002). The campaign *'Kies exact'*, and as a part of it *'Slaag exact'* (Get an appropriate/science degree), aimed at stimulating secondary education pupils to take final exams in some science and engineering courses in order to prepare for further study in those disciplines. A wide range of channels was used to promote the campaign: brochures, posters, advertisements, billboards and television commercials (van den Broek and Voeten, 2002).

Other campaigns were directed specifically at strengthening interest in engineering, particularly amongst females. In the early 1990s, one such campaign, *'Technika 10 Nederland'*, provided courses for girls in order to interest them in science and engineering. The evaluation of the outcomes of the campaign was ambiguous: in some cases participating girls were more likely to continue their studies, while in other cases they were not.

Between 1995 and 1998 the Ministry of Economic Affairs, the Ministry of Education, Culture and Science, and the Ministry of Social Affairs together set up the *'Actieplan Vrouwen en Techniek'* (Action plan: Women in Engineering) to enlarge the presence of females in engineering and to increase female participation in scientific studies and the professions. Finally, a number of theatre groups promoted engineering by visiting schools, and many professional interest groups have tried to raise the profile of science and engineering.

The effectiveness of the various initiatives to raise the interest and participation in science and engineering programmes is questionable: participation in most traditional science and engineering programmes is collapsing and growing participation in new science and engineering programmes cannot make up for that decline (Kaiser *et al.*, 2003). Yet the campaigns have put science and engineering on the political agenda and awaken the general awareness of the importance of science and engineering for society. Students' choices, however, are still based mainly on personal interest and future employment perspectives. So far, a negative image of science and engineering has made these programmes unattractive to many potential students (van den Broek and Voeten, 2002).

Teacher training

Since 1998/1999 the teacher training sector has received additional attention because of serious shortages of teachers in primary and secondary education. A particular action programme – called *Maatwerk voor morgen* – has been set up in order to attract more people into teacher training education and to improve the attractiveness of the teaching profession. Within this framework, a number of initiatives have been developed.

As such, a few image and recruitment campaigns were started (Lugthart and Vossensteyn, 2001). In 1998, an image campaign was started for primary education (*Goed werk juf, Goed werk meester*) leading to a substantial increase in positive attitudes towards the teaching profession, and also to increased entry into teacher training courses. Subsequently, all those who had left a primary school teaching job were sent a letter asking them to re-enter the teaching profession. This resulted in 3,200 people re-entering the profession and about 1,500 following a 'refresher course'. In 1999/2000 a campaign was started to promote access into secondary education teacher training programmes. Media spots, *Elke dag anders*, emphasised the variety and fun of the teaching profession, trying to reverse the perspective that teaching is a tough and boring job. Furthermore, the opportunity of 'sideways-entry' (*zij-instroom*) commenced in 2000. This meant that people with a higher education qualification working in another sector could enter the teaching profession. Based on an assessment, candidates receive a tailor-made programme including relevant training and teaching practice leading to a formal teaching qualification within a maximum duration of two years. Because the reactions to this initiative have been very promising, a new media campaign has been set up aimed at interesting both younger and mature people in the teaching profession. One of the target groups to be further developed concerns potential students from ethnic backgrounds. A final development has been to reach agreements within both the HBO and university sectors to make teacher training more flexible. This, for example, has resulted in the possibility of following the whole or a part of a teacher-training programme during the Master's degree or after the completion of the Master degree as a tailor-made course.

Reflection

Access to higher education is not an issue that dominates higher education policy in the Netherlands, though it is often referred to in other debates on, for example, funding models, tuition fees and student support policies, and on changes in the programme structures. If we take a closer look at the three rationales for access policy, we can conclude that there is almost no reference to expansion as justifying the need for government intervention. There is some debate on participation rates and the international position of the Netherlands in this respect, but no clear or concrete policy has been formulated to expand the higher education system. It seems plausible that this is because of the traditionally open character of the Dutch higher education system, although it is difficult to corroborate the claim.

The desire to widen access underlies only a small part of Dutch higher education access policies. At the system level, gender imbalances no longer exist. Whether that is because of the campaigns to encourage girls and women to enter higher education is not clear. The major feminisation took place before any active policies were developed in this area. Furthermore, widening access for those from more deprived socio-economic groups is not an ongoing concern. Only when changes are announced in tuition fees and the student support system does the access issue move on to the political agenda. Consequently, changes in fees and student support take into account opportunities for the socio-economically deprived. The under-representation of ethnic minorities is starting to be perceived as a problem. However, official policies focus more on monitoring actual tendencies rather than actively intervening. Recent studies also indicate that the position of ethnic minorities is strongly improving in terms of transition rates between secondary and higher education (Hofman *et al.*, 2003).

Thus the main purpose of access policies has been to steer student choice for economic (macro-efficiency) reasons, and the use of *numerus fixus* is the most invasive instrument for this purpose. Although the labour market fixus is still applied, the scope of this instrument (that is the programmes to which it is applied) has diminished. There have been debates in parliament to abandon the labour market fixus, but to date those debates have had no effect on current policy. Finally, information campaigns have been used to change the image of certain professions and programmes (engineering, teachers) in order to attract more new entrants into those programmes. But again it is difficult to measure their effect with any certainty.

The number of people entering higher education has increased rapidly in the Netherlands. Between 1960 and 2002, the number of new entrants in universities nearly quadrupled and in higher professional education student numbers multiplied by almost eight. Since this development does not originate from changes in demography, the question rises: 'What is the role of government access policies in all this?' If we take a closer look at the three rationales for access policy we arrive at the following conclusions.

Expansion of higher education has not been an issue that has dominated the higher education policy agenda. Though it is often referred to in other debates, for example on funding, tuition, student support and changes in the programme structures, no clear objectives in terms of participation rates or targets for student numbers have been formulated. Within the framework of the EU Lisbon objective, the Netherlands wants to become one of the leading economies within Europe by 2010. High educational attainment levels of the labour force are considered to be crucial in that respect, which can be said to be one of the underlying rationales for the continuing open character of Dutch (higher) education.

All in all, Dutch higher education is shown to be an interesting case where access policies have a rather indirect and often vague character, and where higher education has expanded tremendously over the past decades, partly because of feminisation of participation. The role of access policies in the expansion is hard to pinpoint. There are no large-scale access policies and for those that do exist, there is no clear evidence that links access policies to changes in participation. Students keep coming because higher education institutions have shown themselves to be very flexible in meeting the increasing demand for their services, and because the labour market has shown a seemingly insatiable need for highly educated employees. In view of the fact that some specific sectors – such as teaching, health care, and engineering – still show substantial labour market shortages and that the Dutch economy grows steadily more knowledge intensive, these developments cannot be expected to change in the short run. Open access policy, combined with policies designed purposefully to widen access, will play a role in this, albeit a modest one.

Notes

1 Outside the Netherlands, the *hogescholen* are officially allowed to promote themselves as universities of professional education.
2 This new Bachelor–Master structure does not apply to medical programmes.
3 In 2003, there are thirteen HBO programmes with a *numerus fixus* (5,630 applicants, 3,258 admitted). Most of them are in the health sector. In the university sector, six programmes had an institutional fixus (1,369 applicants, 1,050 places), three had a programme fixus (medicine, veterinary medicine and dentistry) (6,542 applicants, 3,375 admitted). Source: http://www.ib-groep.nl/.
4 The IBG is the government organisation that manages the whole application process for higher education as well the provision of student support.

References

Allen, J.P., G.W.M. Ramaekers and A.E. Verbeek, *WO-Monitor 1999, De arbeidsmarktpositie van afgestudeerden van de Nederlandse Universiteiten*, Researchcentrum voor Onderwijs en Arbeidsmarkt (ROA) (Utrecht: VSNU, 2000).

Barr, N., *The Economics of the Welfare State* (Oxford: Oxford University Press, 1998).

Bourdieu, P., 'Cultural reproduction and social reproduction', in J. Karabel and A. Halsey (eds) *Power and Ideology in Education* (New York: Oxford University Press, 1977), pp. 487–511.

Broek, A. van den and R. Voeten, *Wisselstroom, Een analyse van de bèta-instroom in het wetenschappelijk onderwijs in de periode 1980–2000*, Beleidsgerichte studies Hoger onderwijs en Wetenschappelijk onderzoek, nr. 93, Ministerie van Onderwijs, Cultuur en Wetenschappen (Den Haag: Sdu Grafisch Bedrijf BV., 2002).

CBS, Statline, www.cbs.nl (2002).

Felsö, F., M. van Leeuwen and M. van Zijl, *Verkenning van stimulansen voor het keuzegedrag van leerlingen en studenten* (Stichting voor Economisch Onderzoek der Universiteit van Amsterdam (SEO), Amsterdam: 2000).

Heller, D.E., 'Student price response in higher education, an update to Leslie and Brinkman', *Journal of Higher Education*, 68, 6 (1997), pp. 624–59.

Hofman, A., U. de Jong, M. van Leeuwen, J. de Boom, I. van der Veen, J.A. Korteweg and E. Heyl, *Studentenmonitor 2003, studeren in het hoger onderwijs*, Beleidsgerichte studies Hoger onderwijs en Wetenschappelijk onderzoek 94 (Den Haag: Sdu Grafisch Bedrijf, 2003).

Hossler, D., J. Schmit and N. Vesper, *Going to College: How Social, Economic and Educational Factors Influence the Decisions Students Make* (Baltimore: The Johns Hopkins University Press, 1999).

Hupe, P.L. and A.I.T. van Solm, *Het Zoetermeerse labyrint*, Beleidsgerichte studies Hoger onderwijs en Wetenschappelijk onderzoek 55 (Den Haag: Sdu Grafisch Bedrijf, 1998).

Jansen, C., 'Van onafhankelijke studievoorlichting naar verantwoorde werving, Integratie van instroom-, doorstroom- en uitstroombeleid', *Tijdschrift voor Hoger Onderwijs en Management*, 4 (1996), pp. 30–4.

Jong, U. de, H. Oosterbeek, J. Roeleveld, C.N. Teunings and H.D. Webbink, *Wel of niet verder studeren?* Ministerie van Onderwijs en Wetenschappen, Beleidsgerichte studies Hoger onderwijs en Wetenschappelijk onderzoek, nr. 26 (Den Haag: DOP, 1991).

Jong, U. de, D. Webbink, H. Meulenbeek, M. Voorthuis,. F. Haanstra and F. Verbeek, *Uitstel of afstel? Een onderzoek naar de achtergronden en motieven om niet direct verder te studeren* (Amsterdam: Stichting voor Economisch Onderzoek (SEO) / SCO-Kohnstamm Instituut, Universiteit van Amsterdam, 1996).

Jong, U. de, M. van Leeuwen, J. Roeleveld en M. Zijl, *Deelname aan hoger onderwijs, Toegankelijkheid in beweging, Kiezen voor hoger onderwijs 1995–2000*, Ministerie van Onderwijs, Cultuur en Wetenschappen, Beleidsgerichte studies hoger onderwijs en wetenschappelijk onderzoek 81 (Den Haag: Sdu, 2001).

Jonge, J.F.M. de, L. Huvers, D.M. Ligtermoet and A. Ziegelaar, *Effectiviteit en efficientie van de Wet op de studiefinanciering* (Leiden: Research voor Beleid, 1991a).

Kaiser, F., H. Vossensteyn, F. Beerkens, P. Boezevooij, J. Huisman, A. Lub, P. Maassen, C. Salerno and H. Theissens, *Higher Education Policy Issues and Trends: An Update on Higher Education Policy Issues in 11 Western Countries*, Higher Education Monitor Update Report (Enschede: CHEPS, 2003).

Kerstens, L. and J. de Jonge, *De leenmotieven van studenten bij banken* (Leiden: Research voor Beleid, 1999).

Lugthart, E. and J.J. Vossensteyn, *Attractiveness, Profile and Occupational Content of the Teaching Profession. A Descriptive Report on the Position of Teachers in Lower Secondary Education in the Netherlands,* Report for the first phase of the Eurydice study, 'Key Topics in Education Volume III: The Attractiveness, Profile and Occupational Content of the Teaching Profession in Europe' (Enschede: CHEPS, 2001).

Ministerie van Onderwijs, Cultuur en Wetenschappen, *Flexibele studiefinanciering, Een stelsel dat past* (Den Haag: Sdu Grafisch Bedrijf, 1999).

Ministerie van Onderwijs, Cultuur en Wetenschappen, *Naar een open hoger onderwijs, Invoering van een bachelor-masterstructuur in het Nederlandse hoger onderwijs* (Den Haag: SDU, 2000).

Oosterbeek, H. and D. Webbink, 'Enrolment in higher education in the Netherlands', *De Economist*, 143, 3 (1995), pp. 367–80.

Ramaekers, G.W.M. and T.G. Huijgen, *HBO-Monitor, De arbeidsmarktpositie van afgestudeerden van het hoger beroepsonderwijs*, Researchcentrum voor Onderwijs en Arbeidsmarkt (ROA) (Den Haag: HBO-Raad, 2000).

Regt, A. de, *Geld en gezin: Financiële en emotionele relaties tussen gezinsleden* (Amsterdam: Boom, 1993).

Sterken, E., 'De collegegeld-gevoeligheid van deelname aan het WO', *Economisch Statistische Berichten*, 10 May 1995, pp. 454–6.

Tweede Kamer der Staten Generaal, Wet twee-fasenstructuur wetenschappelijk onderwijs, 16, 106, (Den Haag: SDU, 1980).

Tweede Kamer der Staten Generaal (1987), Wijziging van onder meer de W.W.O, W.H.B.O. en de W.S.F. (harmonisatie collegegelden h.o.; invoering één inschrijvingsduur eerste fase h.o.), 20469, nr. 3, Memorie van toelichting, Den Haag: SDU.

Tweede Kamer der Staten-Generaal, *Rijksbegroting, Begroting VIII, Onderwijs, Cultuur en Wetenschappen 2003* (Den Haag: Sdu Uitgevers, 2002).

Vos, K. de and P. Fontein, *Actualisering leengedrag en schuldopbouw in de WSF* (Tilburg: Economisch Instituut Tilburg (EIT), 1998).

Vossensteyn, H., *Student Financial Assistance in the Netherlands: A Contextual Report* (Enschede: CHEPS, 1997).

Vossensteyn, J.J., 'Shared interests, shared costs: student contributions in Dutch higher education', *Journal of Higher Education Policy and Management*, 24, 2 (2002), pp. 145–54.

Vossensteyn, J.J., 'Fiscal stress, worldwide trends in higher education finance and in policy responses to the condition of higher education austerity', (Prague: paper presented at the 'University Reform and Accessibility of Higher Education' conference, 15–17 June, 2003).

7   Access to higher education in the Nordic countries

Per Olaf Aamodt and Svein Kyvik

Introduction

The aim of this chapter is to explain the strong growth in enrolments in higher education since the 1960s in Denmark, Finland, Norway and Sweden with an emphasis on access policy. During this period the entry rate has increased from less than 10 per cent to more than 50 per cent. The expansion of higher education in these nations has generally followed the trend in most European countries, with two distinct waves of growth in the 1960s and the 1990s. According to *Education at a Glance* (OECD, 2002) the Nordic countries are among those having the highest enrolment rates of all OECD countries. In Finland, about 65 per cent of each age group now enter higher education. In Norway, the enrolment rate can be estimated to about 60 per cent. In Denmark, the number of new entrants seems to be about 55 per cent, while in Sweden this percentage is likely to be about 50 per cent. Even though there are methodological weaknesses in reaching these estimates, it seems fair to conclude that Finland now has the highest enrolment rate in higher education, followed by Norway, Denmark, and Sweden (Kim, 2002: 40).

A traditional way of explaining expansion in higher education is that it originates from new societal needs, mainly in the labour market, which generate a demand for education among young people. As a response to these needs and demands the government decides on the expansion of the higher education system and allocates the necessary funds. An additional explanation is the political objective of enhancing equality of educational opportunity irrespective of gender, social class, ethnic and regional background. These two factors are of course important explanations in a Nordic context. In these social-democratic countries, higher education is regarded as a right for all (though not in strict legal terms), equality of opportunity by gender, geography and socio-economic status is an important goal, and there are no tuition fees. These policy objectives do not conflict with a pragmatic and utilitarian attitude to the role of higher education as a tool for economic development. On the contrary, these links are perhaps even more visible in the Nordic countries than in most other European countries. Investment in higher education has been explicitly justified as a tool for the development of the economy and has also been linked to labour market policy. The relative emphasis on the different arguments for political initiatives in the education sector has varied. With reference to Norway, the belief in education as a tool for economic development was strong in the late 1950s and the early 1960s, became less visible in the late 1960s, and practically disappeared in the 1970s (Eide, 1995). However, in the 1990s, economic arguments for investment in education have re-emerged. It could be questioned whether these changes are linked to real changes in the importance of education for the economy or merely reflecting changes in what type of arguments policy-makers use.

However, in reality, the relations between needs, demands and political decisions are far more complex than the above explanations may indicate, and they also vary between countries. The enrolment rate may increase independently of the demands of the labour market if the number of available study places is expanded. Individual demand for higher education for a number of reasons is not directly reflecting changes in the demand from the labour market. First, entrants to higher education do not have full information about what jobs are most accessible and highly paid today, and even less at the time when they will enter the labour market after graduation. Second, the choice to enter higher education is based on a broader set of considerations than income and job security, values and interests also play an important role.

The main objective of this chapter is, accordingly, to achieve a better understanding of the growth processes that have taken place in the Nordic countries. In addition, we will discuss to what extent growth has led to more equitable access to higher education by gender and social class.

Commonalities and differences in system characteristics

These four countries all belong to a group of highly developed industrialised nations that have much in common – socially, culturally, economically and politically – but are in many respects also different from each other. Historically, there have been close connections between the four countries. Denmark and Norway were united for 400 years and share a common language and culture with Sweden. Finland's position is different with a totally distinctive language from the other Nordic countries, even though for 500 years it was a part of Sweden. They are all relatively small countries, three of them (Denmark, Finland and Norway) each having between 4.5 and 6 million inhabitants, while Sweden has about 9 million people. Situated close to each other, the four countries still differ considerably in geography and natural resources. Denmark has the best conditions for farming, while Sweden has the strongest industrial traditions. Norway's long coastline has historically been important for its strong position in fishery and shipping, while since the 1970s oil and gas have put Norway in a favourable economic situation. Finland has historically had a strong position in forestry, and during the last two decades has developed into one of the most successful high-tech countries in the world.

The concept of the Nordic countries is more than merely being a group of geographically close countries. It has also an important meaning in political terms. Especially since the Second World War, Nordic cooperation has developed in a wide range of fields, under the umbrellas of the Nordic Council and the Nordic Council of Ministers. In the 1950s and the 1960s, the idea of close Nordic cooperation was strong, but political efforts in establishing a Nordic economic union somewhat parallel to the European Union did not succeed. Denmark, Finland and Sweden later chose to become members of the European Union, while Norway has only an associate status. Still, Nordic cooperation has continued to be important in many fields.

The impression of Nordic unity within a larger European setting is strengthened by the fact that all Nordic countries during the second half of the twentieth century developed relatively similar welfare state policies based on social democratic values. These policies also included the field of higher education where the state plays an important role in the funding and coordination of the systems. In all countries, higher education is free of tuition, and there are comparatively generous financial support systems to cover students' cost of living. Moreover, all Nordic countries have had more or less similar traditions with regard to governance and funding of higher education. The general move towards more institutional autonomy, more incentive-based funding, and improved managerial steering of the institutions is also similar for these countries.

However, in spite of the strong similarities and cooperation between the Nordic countries the systems of higher education have been surprisingly different. For example, the degree structures, although now converging due to the Bologna process, have historically been quite distinctive from each other. Furthermore, the organisation of higher education has differed markedly but all four countries now have developed various kinds of binary systems with a distinction between traditional universities and colleges offering mainly short-term vocationally oriented programmes (Kyvik, 2004).

In *Sweden*, the present institutional system was introduced in 1977 by a comprehensive reform. Practically all post-upper-secondary non-university education was upgraded to higher education, and fourteen multidisciplinary state colleges were established through mergers of many small and specialised post-secondary institutions. Simultaneously, three of four university branches established in 1965 were converted to state colleges. In addition, two new colleges were established at the end of the 1980s. However, the distinction between universities and colleges has changed over time. In 1999, three large state colleges were given university status by the government (Bauer, 2000) and Sweden now has eleven general universities.

In *Norway*, a binary system developed gradually from the late 1960s with the establishment of district colleges as alternatives to the traditional universities and the existing institutions for teacher training, technical education, and health education. In the 1970s and 1980s, all the latter institutions were upgraded to higher education institutions and together with the district colleges constituted the regional college sector. In 1994, this sector underwent a major reorganisation through the merging of ninety-eight regional colleges into twenty-six state colleges (Kyvik, 2002). Norway also has four general universities and six institutions with university status.

In contrast to Sweden and Norway, *Finland* in the 1960s and 1970s focused on the development of higher education within the university sector through the establishment of several small regional universities and colleges with university status. This resulted in a marked imbalance in the Finish system with a clear dominance of student numbers following longer higher education programmes. Short-cycle vocational programmes were neither attractive to students nor were they sufficiently adapted to changes in the labour market. This gradually became a major problem, and from 1991, a number of polytechnic colleges were established on an experimental basis through the merging and upgrading of eighty-five vocational schools into twenty-two multidisciplinary colleges (Höllta, 2000). This experiment was considered to be successful and the college system was formalised in 1995. In 1996, all other vocational institutions were upgraded to higher education institutions through a number of mergers resulting in a total of twenty-nine such colleges. By comparison, twenty institutions have university status of which ten are general universities.

Officially, *Denmark* does not distinguish between a university and a college sector, but between long, medium and short higher education programmes. The long programmes are the prerogative of the university sector that consists of five general universities, and seven university-level colleges. Vocational education is assigned to two sectors: medium-cycle and short-cycle post-secondary institutions. Until recently the first group comprised about a hundred small, specialised institutions covering three- to four-year programmes in economics, teacher training, engineering, health and social work. The total number of such colleges is now in the process of being reduced to a smaller number of multidisciplinary institutions as a result of mergers. The second group generally offers one- to two-year programmes in technical and economic subjects. In an international context it is more appropriate to consider the medium-cycle programmes as higher education but offered in the colleges, and the short-cycle programmes as vocational training without the status of higher education (OECD, 1998; European Commission, 2000).

Differences in time between the countries with regard to the upgrading of vocational schools to higher education institutions, and differences in cultural traditions and economic development have thus led to important contrasts in growth rates between the countries. There have been large variations in the proportion of students enrolling in long university programmes and shorter vocationally oriented college programmes. The relative size of the university and non-university higher education sectors still varies between the four countries (Kyvik, 2004). The percentage of first-year students in the university sector in 1999–2000 was highest in Sweden (about 60 per cent) and Denmark (about 50 per cent), and lowest in Norway (about 45 per cent) and Finland (about 40 per cent).

In all four countries, a guiding policy principle has been to give access to those who are qualified for entry into higher education. However, access has always been restricted, but the degree of restrictions has varied over time according to the number of applicants relative to available places and also because of the employment situation of graduates. Furthermore, within each country there have been large differences between fields of study. In the universities, the number of new students in prestigious and professionally oriented studies such as medicine has always been restricted, while degree programmes in the humanities and social sciences have had more or less open access. For most non-university higher education programmes, the governments have traditionally decided the number of new students for the individual institutions and programmes.

A final observation is that access to higher education also has an international dimension. There are considerable student exchanges and student flows across borders, including amongst the Nordic countries. Norway, however, differs from the other three Nordic countries since the majority of Norwegians studying abroad do so for the whole of their degree programmes rather than for short periods as exchange students. Before 1960, the percentage of Norwegian students studying abroad was high, up to half of the students in fields with restricted access like medicine and technology graduated abroad. Most of them entered the Norwegian labour market after graduation, which means that studying abroad was an alternative policy to expanding national capacity, and this policy was supported by quite generous financial support from the state. The number of Norwegian students studying abroad stagnated after 1960, but post-1970 the ratio stabilised at about 6 per cent of the total number of students, and it has increased again in recent years. Today, there is a larger spread by both field of study and country, as well as a broader diversity of reasons to study abroad, among them the absence of equivalent domestic opportunities and expected positive outcomes from an international experience. The positive impacts of these international experiences, not only for the individual, but also for a small peripheral country, should not be underestimated. But the shortage of domestic supply in certain fields remains a major cause for students choosing to study abroad (Wiers-Jenssen, 2003), and therefore influences Norwegian access policy.

A model for the analysis of growth in student numbers

What are the reasons for the strong growth in student numbers? As a starting point for the discussion, we have for analytical purposes developed a model which indicates the relationship between important explanatory factors. This model indicates the interplay between the three important variables which have traditionally been applied in the analysis of the move towards mass higher education: *labour market needs, individual demands* and *access policy*.

The relations between these three variables are shown by the direction of effects indicated in Figure 7.1. The unbroken lines show the major

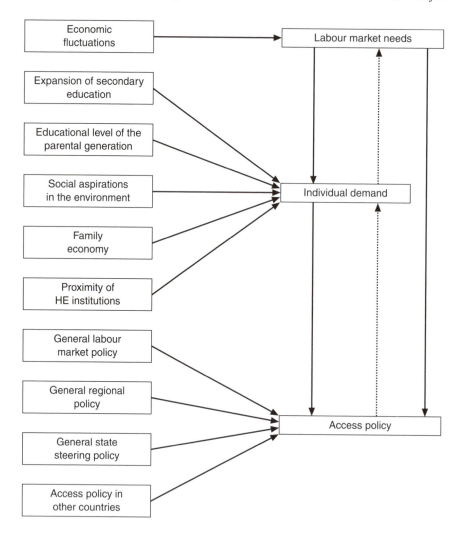

Figure 7.1 The interplay between factors causing expansion in higher education.

direction of effects, while the dotted lines indicate that the relations may also work in the opposite direction. The access policies in the various countries can be seen as the consequence of the interaction of the demands of young people for higher education and the needs of the labour market for highly skilled manpower. However, governments also impact upon access policy by intervening to enhance equality of educational opportunity by gender, social class and place of residence. In addition, the government may regard investment in higher education as a tool for economic, social and cultural development. Political decisions thus may lead to expansion in the number of available study places irrespective of needs in the labour market and the demands of young people.

In addition, a number of important contextual factors affect each of the three variables in the model. *Labour market needs* for highly trained manpower not only develop in line with the introduction of new technology, but are also affected by fluctuations in the economy. Furthermore, the attractiveness of highly educated manpower is affected by the rate of return, that is, the expected wage differences between university and college graduates and less trained job seekers. If there is a surplus of graduates compared to the demand from the labour market, the rate of return will tend to be reduced and vice versa.

Individual demands are not only affected by the demands of the labour market and the number of available study places, but are also heavily affected by contextual factors such as the expansion of upper secondary education, the educational level of the parental generation, social aspirations in the community, family financial circumstances and proximity to higher education institutions.

Access policy is not only affected by labour market needs, individual demands, equity policy and socio-economic political concerns, but also by contextual factors such as the general public policy in fields such as labour market policy and regional policy. Moreover, changes in the state steering of higher education may affect access policy. For example, if the state decentralises the decisions on student intake numbers to the individual institutions, the actual number of students who are admitted to various programmes might be quite different from the targets set by the government. In addition, the access policies of other countries may be used as a guide to governmental discussions on the number of available study places.

In the following section we will briefly describe the expansion of higher education as well as access policies with a specific focus on which factors have been the driving forces in the expansion of the higher education systems. The presentation is structured according to three periods: a first wave of expansion during the 1960s until the mid-1970s, a period characterised by stability in the late 1970s and the 1980s, and a second wave of expansion commencing in the first half of the 1990s. The timing of these waves has not been exactly identical in the four countries, but the deviations are small enough to justify this time frame.

Growth patterns in higher education

The 1960s and early 1970s – the first wave of expansion

From a level of less that 10 per cent of each age group entering higher education around 1960, the proportion of secondary school-leavers enrolling in higher education programmes increased dramatically in the late 1960s and early 1970s. The total number of students increased by a factor of between three and four during this period. To manage this rapid growth the Nordic countries launched comprehensive reform processes during the second half of the 1960s. However, different solutions to the expansion were developed in each country. In *Denmark* and *Finland*, growth was planned to take place within the existing universities and in a number of new universities, while *Sweden* and *Norway*, in addition to expanding the university sector, gradually developed a binary system through the establishment of many new non-university higher education institutions and the upgrading of existing post-secondary schools to the status of higher education institutions. The structural changes in the higher education systems of the four countries were responses to the rapid growth in enrolment in the 1960s, but at the same time these changes were preconditions for the further expansion that took place after 1970.

As in most other industrialised countries, the first wave of higher education expansion, starting around 1960, was based on the idea of investing in human capital for economic development. The expansion of higher education in this phase cannot, however, be regarded in isolation, but is closely related to wider educational reforms as well as increased access at lower levels in the system. Thanks to the inclusion of lower secondary education, compulsory schooling was prolonged from 7 to 9 years and upper secondary education was gradually changed from an academically selective system to one that also incorporated both general and vocational education. There were also demographic components since the large birth cohorts of the immediate post-Second World War years received their schooling in this period. This development led to an increasing number of applicants to higher education programmes, which in turn resulted in political concern about the capacity of higher education institutions to provide sufficient places of study.

In line with the welfare state policy of the Nordic countries, the expansion of the higher education systems was also seen as a policy that would enhance equity. The policy was not only based on social justice, but also on the argument in favour of 'utilising all the reserves of talent'. For this reason, schooling should be made more accessible for all young adults regardless of geography, gender and social background. All Nordic countries had established economic support systems of grants and loans for students before 1950, and the concern with equity is also one of the main reasons for keeping higher education free of tuition fees. Perhaps the most visible result of this policy is related to geographical accessibility, and in all countries higher education policies were closely linked to regional policy. For example, in Norway, the political climate changed remarkably in this period in favour of the regional decentralisation of higher education (Kyvik, 1983). While only 9 per cent of the Norwegian population considered regional policy to be one of the three most important political issues in 1957, this percentage increased to 27 per cent in 1965 and 59 per cent in 1969. The importance of viable local communities was stressed as a reaction against centralisation tendencies in the past years. As a result of these developments, new higher education institutions were established in all regions in the four countries.

In the early phase of educational expansion in the 1960s, several factors thus pulled in the direction of growth: an increasing need for qualified manpower, especially within a rapid expanding public sector and particularly within the educational sector itself (Williams, 1985), expanding individual demand arising from demographic trends, expansion in the access to upper secondary school, and increased interest in studying at universities and colleges. Last, but not least, this development was to a large extent stimulated by and made possible by political priorities.

Late 1970s and 1980s – stabilisation of student numbers

In the years between the mid-1970s and 1990, the growth in enrolments in higher education was weak in all four countries, partly because of economic recession and increasing unemployment among higher education graduates. The general belief in the value of university education turned towards the fear of over-supply. Further expansion in higher education was increasingly questioned, enhanced by a forecasted downturn in the relevant age groups in the 1990s. The demand for long-term university education stagnated, and shorter, more vocationally oriented studies attained increased popularity, particularly in those countries which had established an alternative sector. As in most other European countries, cuts in public expenditure also hit higher education. The demand for higher education to be more relevant to the needs of the economy became more visible in the 1980s, and the institutions were challenged to develop greater flexiblity in moving resources between different fields of study.

Even though the total number of students did not increase so much in this period, there were a number of important changes in the composition of the student population. While the number of male students stagnated, the number of female students continued to increase. In the mid-1980s, men and women had an equal share of the student population, but the percentage of women continued to increase, approaching 60 per cent by the turn of the century.

In addition to the trend towards diminishing trust in the role of higher education as a stimulus for economic growth in the 1970s, there were also attempts to reduce the expansion of public expenditure. These challenges hit higher education directly since reductions in public expenditure also included public spending on higher education, and also indirectly since the increase in the number of jobs in the public sector flattened out. There was a concern not only about the total number of students in higher education, but perhaps even more about the distribution by fields of study, and especially that there were too many students in the humanities and social sciences. In this respect, the situation in the Nordic countries did not differ from that in other OECD countries, and the problems hit the Nordic countries to different degrees. Denmark, in particular, was affected by graduate unemployment in the humanities and social sciences, and policies to help these graduates to gain access to jobs outside their traditional labour market within the public sector were implemented. Norway, on the other hand, escaped from most of these problems. First, the use of oil money softened the effects of the recession; second, enrolments in the humanities decreased rapidly during the second half of the 1970s; and third, the increase in enrolments took place in the college sector.

Early 1990s – the second wave of expansion

By the end of the 1980s, nobody expected any further expansion in higher education in the Nordic countries, mainly because of demographic trends and a subsequent decrease in secondary school-leavers. This decline was strongest and continued for the longest time in Denmark and Norway, with a 20–25 per cent decrease in both countries between 1990 and 2000. The downward trend was lower in Sweden, while in Finland the size of the age groups remained more stable throughout the decade.

However, in all four countries, the number of students increased very strongly in the first half of the 1990s, particularly in the college sector. This growth was most visible in Finland because of the upgrading of vocational education to higher education status and the establishment of a large number of new polytechnics. The changing balance of student enrolment between universities and colleges favouring the latter was in line with the national policies at least in Denmark, Finland and Norway, while the policy was less pronounced in Sweden. Moreover, this policy also seems to be understandable given the demand both from the students and from the labour market. In the Nordic countries, it is not necessarily the first priority of secondary school leavers to enter traditional university programmes, and the attractiveness of the alternative study programmes is generally high.

As in the 1960s, the political arguments that the expansion of higher education is important for the development of the society were applied. In Sweden and Finland, the increase in enrolments was politically directed, while in Norway and Denmark the development rather seemed just 'to happen'. Sweden, after the higher education reform of 1977, had a system of strict central regulation of access to each study programme, and this was probably the main reason why enrolment in higher education did not increase at all during this period. Around 1990, Swedish political authorities realised that enrolments in higher education had fallen behind most other OECD-countries, and a radical reform was launched to increase the number of available places. As a consequence of this supply-driven demand, the number of applicants increased strongly. Also in Finland the expanding access to higher education arose from a conscious policy after the severe economic problems that hit the country after the breakdown of the Soviet Union. Growth in higher education was given high priority, even though the universities did not escape the general budget cuts in the public sector. Still, the universities were encouraged to increase their enrolment. In addition, in 1991 a new sector of polytechnics based on former vocational schools was established, and these colleges experienced a very strong increase in student numbers in the 1990s.

In Norway, at the end of the 1980s, there was political concern at the stagnation of enrolments in higher education. Therefore, the increasing number of students came as a total surprise. However, several factors pulled in the same direction to expand student numbers. One explanation for the rapid growth in enrolments was that unemployment increased. When unemployment is high, especially among young people, entry into higher education may be an alternative to not having a job. While over time the enrolment rate may not be affected, at least those who otherwise would have postponed their entry into higher education chose to enter earlier. Studying is also a means of improving one's position in the competition for future jobs (Aamodt, 1995). Another explanation is that increased aspirations for higher education among secondary school leavers are closely related to the educational level of their parents, which on average had increased substantially as a result of the first wave of expansion in the 1960s (Aamodt, 1995). Individual decisions are also affected by those belonging to the same age cohort, and educational aspirations are influenced by friends. In addition, the demand for higher education increased particularly among women because of the general changes in women's role in society and increased female labour market participation. There was also a generation effect since most of the female school-leavers at that time had mothers who were working. Moreover, the general improvement in family income and the fact that higher education had become more accessible because of the establishment and expansion of many institutions in the various regions pulled in the same direction.

As in the early 1960s, the rapid increase in the number of applicants to higher education led to public concern about the large number being rejected, as there were few opportunities on the labour market. It therefore became a challenge to the government to expand the number of places of study to enable more applicants to be admitted. This again indicates that within the framework of welfare policy the conception of a right to access to higher education constitutes a quite strong political pressure, and indeed results in political action. Expansion in the number of study places to meet growing individual demands was an option to prevent unemployment. This policy was not necessarily openly addressed, but at least in Norway this was regarded as a practical solution to cut unemployment rates among young people. Some of the state funds to combat unemployment were transferred to fund the increase in study places, and this policy could be assessed as being reasonably successful (Try, 2000). There was some concern that this expansion in turn would lead to increasing graduate unemployment, but this did not happen because of a boom in the economy at the time when increasing numbers of graduates were ready to enter the labour market.

Has access become more equitable?

One of the main arguments behind the policy of expansion in higher education in the Nordic countries has been to include new groups in higher education and to reduce inequalities of gender, place of residence and social class. Since the proportion of the age groups enrolled in higher education has increased from less than 10 per cent to 50–60 per cent over four decades, it would seem almost self-evident that inequalities have diminished. In one sense, this is of course the case: under-represented groups – women, youth from remote places and from lower social strata – have increased their participation numerically. But this is not to say that these groups have obtained equal representation in higher education.

Hernes (1974) uses three concepts of equality: 'formal equality', 'equality of opportunity', and 'equality of results'. In modern societies, 'formal equality' has long been established, since no student could legally be discriminated against in terms of gender, place of residence, ethnicity or social origins. 'Equality of results' would imply the use of certain compensatory measures meaning that individuals are consciously treated differently. Such compensatory mechanisms can of course be found in the school system; for example, to help students with a broad range of learning problems. If such problems are found more frequently in lower social strata, these measures may also have an indirect compensatory effect on social patterns of access to higher education. For example, efforts to help students with language problems may enhance educational opportunities for ethnic minorities. There are also examples of quota-based access to higher education by gender to increase the enrolment of the under-represented sex, or to admit students who have not received an academic upper secondary education. However, compensatory measures consciously and openly targeted at young people *from specific social background as such* are rarely to be found. Therefore, it is the concept of 'equality of opportunity which has proven to be most relevant for both policy and research.

In all Nordic countries, enrolment by gender and by place of residence has become more equitable. In all four countries there is a majority of female students, ranging from 54 per cent in Finland to 57–58 per cent in Denmark, Norway and Sweden (*Nordic Statistical Yearbook*, 2001). In most former male-dominated fields of study, enrolment is today either gender neutral or even female-dominated. However, in technology there is still a strong majority of male students, and programmes like nursing and preschool-teaching are as female-dominated as ever. Also enrolment difference by place of residence has been reduced, but the number of students from rural regions is still relatively lower than those from urban areas.

Inequality by social origin, however, still seems to persist. In Sweden, a move towards more social equitable access to higher education took place between 1940 and 1970, but thereafter this trend levelled out (Erikson and Jonsson, 1993: 85). In Norway, Aamodt (1982) reported decreasing social differences in access patterns between 1960 and 1975, while Knudsen *et al.* (1993) found only a weak tendency towards decreasing social inequality of access to higher education between 1980 and 1990. However, even this weak tendency seems to have levelled out in the 1990s (Hansen, 1999). Also in Denmark and Finland, large inequalities in access to higher education by social origin still persist (Hansen, 1996; Kivinen *et al.*, 2001).

All in all, the overall conclusion is that the expanding access to higher education over the last decades has led to surprisingly small changes in the enrolment pattern by socio-economic background in the Nordic countries. The persisting inequality is a much more striking feature than the tendencies towards equity. However, as we move towards mass higher education, the differences in enrolment between sectors and programmes within higher education are becoming perhaps as interesting as the inequity in enrolment to higher education as a whole. Norwegian and Swedish data show that enrolment to universities has been far more socially biased than enrolment to the short-term college programmes, and that enrolment to the most prestigious study programmes like medicine, law and architecture is more socially biased than to other university programmes (Aamodt, 1982; Hansen, 1999; Statistics Sweden, 2002; Högskoleverket, 2003).

Conclusion

Was expansion in access to higher education driven by state policy, individual demands or labour market needs? The answer presented here has stressed the interplay between needs of the labour market, individual demands and state policy. Even though arguments about knowledge being important for the development of the economy have been put forward, our main conclusion is that the interaction between individual demands and political priorities has been the most important driving force behind the increased access. We have also argued that reforms and expansion in secondary education as well as access requirements have had a decisive impact on individual demand for higher education. In addition, the implementation of more diversified higher education systems supports our view that the expansion of higher education in the Nordic countries to a considerable degree has been driven by government policy. It can be argued that this is related to the welfare state policy of the Nordic countries, and that higher education is seen as a public good that should be made available to all citizens.

The needs of the labour market have accordingly been of less importance than state policy and individual demands. Of course the future job market is one of the factors influencing individual decisions to enter higher education, but direct interventions from the labour market on state policy have been limited. Labour market forecasts have had some impact on the regulation of study capacity, but mainly in certain professional fields. Labour market projections always have to be based on assessments of prevailing patterns of formal qualifications and the occupational structure, and hence tend to be rather conservative. It could be argued that if the capacity of higher education had been based on long-term labour market projections, then student numbers would have been considerably lower than the actual numbers in all Nordic countries.

In the 1960s there was still a strong belief in central planning in the Nordic countries, and future manpower demands were frequently used as arguments for educational investment in general, and for the distribution of resources and study places between fields of study. It could, however, be questioned whether manpower projections really played an important part at that time in the formation of the actual policy goals. For instance, the reforms that were initiated in Norwegian higher education in the second half of the 1960s were based on projections, but these were formulated on the basis of expected individual demand. One reason for the limited use of manpower forecasting may be that neither the methodologies nor the quality of statistical data have proven sufficiently robust. These aspects improved strongly during the 1970s through the improvement of the statistical databases and the marked increase in computing capacity. But, at the same time, there was a growing scepticism towards manpower projections for political and methodological reasons. In the 1980s, central planning became even less important because of trends towards market-oriented solutions and decentralisation of decision-making authority. Nevertheless, projections for future manpower needs have been made frequently, and have had an impact especially on the regulation of access to professional studies such as teacher training and health education. Sweden has probably been the most active country in this respect, but the actual use of the projections in determining policy goals has been rather limited (Aamodt, 1999). The question could therefore be raised whether manpower forecasting in general has played the relatively marginal role of establishing broad steering parameters. Nonetheless, its methodology and the projections have had a legitimating function in giving the impression of rational decision-making processes.

Based on our observations, we would argue that the expansion in higher education in the Nordic countries to a considerable degree has been supply-driven. The individual demand for higher education is strongly affected by the reforms and the expansion at all levels of the education system making higher education a far more realistic possibility for potential entrants. Also, there is a strong component of supply-driven development in the labour market. As more and new types of graduates became available, the employers took advantage of this, hiring new recruits with more formal qualifications than those who previously had been hired for the same positions, as well as creating new jobs requiring more qualifications.

A combination of many factors working in the same direction contributed to the expansion of higher education during the 1960s, including the demographic trend resulting from the rapid growth in the birth rate after the Second World War, and an increasing influx of women into secondary and higher education. But without a strong political belief in the value of education as an investment in the development of the economy – in human capital – the demographic trend alone would probably not have resulted in such a significant rate of expansion. This is true also for the second wave of expansion in the first half of the 1990s, even though both the policy arguments and the steering instruments changed.

Today, the policy on higher education in all Nordic countries is still aiming at further expansion. Official arguments for further growth may vary between countries, but both Swedish and Norwegian government documents see expansion as confirming that they are 'a leading nation in the production of knowledge', while Finnish documents use the expression 'the international competitiveness of Finnish higher education'. Statements about higher education policy are usually also linked to policy change. Although such policy statements are quite vague, nonetheless they are still translated into rather exact target figures on enrolment. Finland has aimed at enrolling 65 per cent of secondary school graduates, a target that has already been reached. In Sweden, the objective is that 50 per cent of an age cohort should have started in higher education by the age of twenty-five. In Denmark the target has been set that 50 per cent of an age group should pass a degree, which means that about two-thirds of the age group have to enter higher education. Only Norway has set no quantitative target. So far few objections have been raised towards these expansionist policies; for example, by pointing out the declining value of a degree in obtaining employment. Expansion in higher education is generally justified as an 'investment in the future', but at the same time the actual policy pursued is designed to solve immediate problems.

However, access policy is experiencing an important change. The general relationship between the state and higher education institutions is moving towards decentralisation and deregulation. In line with trends in the OECD countries, this policy change started in the late 1980s, and the steering of higher education institutions shifted from central regulation towards increasing institutional autonomy (Neave and van Vught, 1991). These shifts are clearly visible within the policy of access regulation that prevails in the Nordic countries. In all Nordic countries, and particularly in Sweden after the 1993 reform, there has been a move away from centrally determined student numbers and their distribution by degree programme, towards leaving these decisions to the institutions. The institutions of higher education in the Nordic countries are today relatively free to decide how many students to enrol and to distribute the intake between fields of study and individual programmes. They also have considerable freedom to establish new programmes or close down programmes. Under the 'old' regimes, the governments set target figures for student numbers and enrolment of new entrants for most study programmes in each institution. There were differences between fields of study and between institutions as to the degree of regulation, and there were variations over time, but, in principle, the number of places available was decided by the government, and funds allocated accordingly. The present policy implies that direct tools for the central regulation of student numbers is no longer in the hands of the government. Both the availability of courses as well as student numbers are decisions for the institutions.

The main question, therefore, is what will be the national aggregates resulting from the decisions of the individual institutions, and how will these aggregates relate to the actual needs or demands of the labour market. If an institution decides to increase the enrolment in, for example, nursery teacher training programmes, this decision is not made in a vacuum. Therefore there is a risk that other institutions will make the same decisions, leading to overcapacity at a national level. An even more severe risk is that several institutions may decide to close down small programmes. Unless it is accepted that access and enrolment should be left completely to the market, without any possibilities for the government intervention, this constitutes a dilemma. A related problem is how to impose national policies on access for social groups such as women, underrepresented groups, and mature students when the government has abandoned most of its direct steering tools. Ironically in Sweden, after the reform of 1993 which gave more autonomy to the institutions, the official funding allocation letters from the government to the institutions gradually became more detailed, giving instructions about their special responsibilities for small subjects, distribution by gender, etc. (Aamodt, 1999). However, the long-term effects of the changes towards deregulation and decentralisation in the Nordic countries remain to be seen.

References

Aamodt, P.O., *'Utdanning og sosial bakgrunn'*, Samfunnsøkonomiske studier 51, (Oslo-Kongsvinger: Statistics Norway, 1982).

Aamodt, P.O., 'Floods, bottlenecks, and backwaters: an analysis of expansion in higher education in Norway', *Higher Education*, 30 (1995), pp. 63–80.

Aamodt, P.O., *Dimensjonering av høyere utdanning. Et komparativt perspektiv med særlig vekt på Storbritannia, Sverige og USA* (Oslo: NIFU, Report 3/1999).

Bauer, M. 'Higher education reform in Sweden: consolidation, transformation and renewal', in File, J. and L. Goedegebuure (eds) *Thinking About the South African Higher Education Institutional Landscape. An International Comparative Perspective on Institutional Differentiation and Restructuring* (Pretoria: The Council on Higher Education, 2000), pp. 157–66.

Eide, K., *Økonomi og utdanningspolitikk* (Oslo: NIFU, 1995).

Erikson, R. and J.O. Jonsson, *Ursprung och utbildning. Social snedrekrytering til högre studier* (Stockholm: Utbildningsdepartementet, Statens offentliga utredningar, 1993).

European Commission, *Two Decades of Reform in Higher Education in Europe: 1980 onwards* (Brussels: European Commission/EURYDICE, 2000).

Hansen, E.J., *The First Generation in the Welfare State* (Copenhagen: The Danish Institute of Social Research, Report 1996).

Hansen, M., 'Utdanningspolitikk og ulikhet', *Tidsskrift for samfunnsforskning*, 40 (1999), pp. 173–203.

Hernes, G., 'Om ulikhetens reproduksjon', in *Forskningens lys* (Oslo: NAVF, 1974).

Högskoleverket, *Universitet og Högskoler* (Stockholm: Högskoleverkets Årsrapport, 2003).

Hölttä, S., 'Higher education in the service of society: the structural reforms of the finnish higher education system', in File, J. and L. Goedegebuure (eds) *Thinking About the South African Higher Education Institutional Landscape. An International Comparative Perspective on Institutional Differentiation and Restructuring* (Pretoria: The Council on Higher Education, 2000), pp. 77–90.

Kim, L., *Lika olika* (Stockholm: Högskoleverket, Report 2002).

Kivinen, O., S. Ahola and J. Hedman, 'Expanding education and improving odds in higher education in Finland', *Acta Sociologica* 44, 2 (2001), pp. 171–81.

Knudsen, K., A.B. Sørensen and P.O. Aamodt, *Endringer i den sosiale rekrutteringen til høyere utdanning etter 1980* (Oslo, NAVFs utredningsinstitutt, 1993).

Kyvik, S., 'Decentralisation of higher education and research in Norway', *Comparative Education*, 19 (1983), pp. 21–9.

Kyvik, S., 'The merger of non-university colleges in Norway', *Higher Education*, 44 (2002), pp. 53–72.

Kyvik, S., 'Structural changes in higher education systems in Western Europe' (unpublished paper, 2004).

Neave, G. and F. van Vught (eds), *Prometheus Bound. The Changing Relationship Between Government and Higher Education is Western Europe* (Oxford: Pergamon Press, 1991).

Nordic Statistical Yearbook 2001 (Copenhagen: Nordic Council of Ministers, 2001).

OECD, *Redefining Tertiary Education* (Paris: OECD, 1998).

OECD, *Education at a Glance* (Paris: OECD, 2002).

Statistics Sweden, *Higher Education, Social Background among University Entrants 2001/02 and First Time Postgraduate Students 2000/01*(Stockholm: SCB Statistiska meddelanden UF 20 SM 0202, 2002).

Try, S., *Veksten i høyere utdanning: et vellykket arbeidsmarkedstiltak?* (Oslo: NIFU, Report 2, 2000).

Wiers-Jenssen, J., 'Norwegian students abroad: experiences of students from a linguistically and geographically peripheral European country', *Studies in Higher Education*, 28 (2003), pp. 391–411.

Williams, G., 'Graduate employment and vocationalism in higher education', *European Journal of Education*, 20 (1985), pp. 181–92.

8 Mass higher education in Poland

Coping with the 'Spanish Collar'

Clare McManus-Czubińska

Introduction

Poland is the only former communist country examined in this book and, as such, it has a markedly different pattern of higher educational development than the other countries under consideration. Cut-off from mainstream European political and economic developments, Poland languished under the iron fist of communist dictatorship for over forty years. Higher education, like all spheres of life, was transformed by communist rule and the imposition of Marxist–Leninist ideology. Education, in general, as a vehicle of political socialisation, had a specific role to fulfil within communist societies. But higher education, in particular, was targeted by the communist authorities who hoped to produce a new generation of intelligentsia that was ideologically supportive of the communist regime. And despite an expansion of the system of higher education, certain barriers in access to education were created during the communist period.

Access to higher education in Poland has increased dramatically since the collapse of communism. One of the very first acts of the new Solidarity government in 1989 was to bring about the reform and expansion of the system of higher education. Under communism, higher educational institutions[1] had suffered from a lack of autonomy and this rigid system of centralised control even extended to determining admissions numbers for each institution and even every faculty. Although the number of students in Polish higher education has increased fourfold, some barriers still to higher education exist. Since 1989 the increase in widespread poverty in Poland has been the most serious barrier and young people living in rural areas have been most badly affected. Moreover, the decrease in funding for education and science has exacerbated the difficulties faced by those from low income backgrounds who want to enter university. The lack of government funding for the higher educational system has led to the issue of tuition fees being hotly debated in the Polish parliament.

This chapter examines the nature of the political discourse that has driven the expansion of higher education in Poland since 1990 and the continuing existence of barriers to access. Before doing so it is necessary to examine the nature of the higher educational system which developed in Poland and how access to higher education was restricted even under communism.

The European roots of Polish higher education

Polish higher education has a long tradition stretching back to at least 1364 with the founding of the Kraków Academy. This was only the second university founded in Central Europe.[2] By the sixteenth century, Poland had four universities. In addition to the Jagiellonian University there were universities in Poznań (founded in 1519), Wilno also known as Vilnius (founded in 1578) and Zamość (founded in 1578) (Niezgoda and Kosiarz-Stolarska, 1997: 3). These universities fostered the establishment of new scientific fields of enquiry such as the socio-political sciences, economics, philology and pedagogy. Great Polish thinkers like Nicolaus Copernicus (1473–1543), Jan Kochanowski (1530–84) and Jan Zamoyski (1542–1605) led this 'Golden Age' (Markiewicz, 1979: 45; Davies, 1982a: 148–52). Polish universities were renowned centres of learning which attracted scholars from across the European continent. The importance of an educated society for the well-being of the Polish state had long been accepted. For example, the first public library in Europe was established in Warsaw in 1748 by Bishop Józef Andrzej (1702–74) and contained over 400,000 volumes (Davies, 1982: 509). Furthermore, Poland may claim the distinction of having been the first state to have a Ministry of Education. The formation of the Commission of National Education (which in effect was the first Ministry of Education in the world) on 14 October 1773 by the Polish parliament was championed by Stanisław August, the last King of Poland (Wroczynski, 1987; Suchodolski, 1973).

Historically, the fortunes of the Polish state and higher education have been closely connected. After a period of stagnation in the seventeenth and first half of the eighteenth centuries,

> The rebirth of the Polish humanities took place in the second half of the 18th Century, [in] parallel with the great reform of the State which culminated in the passage of the Constitution of May 3, 1791, and the reform of the educational and university systems. During this period Warsaw became the main scientific center, and a scientific infrastructure of laboratories, libraries, scientific collections, and publishing houses developed there.
>
> (Markiewicz, 1979: 46)

Political actors of the time recognised that the attempt to reform the Polish political system (by achieving greater democratisation and autonomy for the Polish state) would not succeed unless a corresponding reform took place within the educational systems, especially higher education. And it was for this end the Commission of National Education was established. The Commission achieved the following:

• The creation of a unified system of elementary schools and provision of standardised school textbooks.
• The modernisation of secondary schooling.
• Modernisation of higher education.
• The creation of a coherent national educational system with unified curricula and efficient management.

Reforms within higher education included replacing Latin with Polish as the language of instruction, devoting more attention to the study of the sciences as opposed to the previous emphasis on theology, and the secularisation of the educational system. Previously the Roman Catholic Church had controlled the majority of educational institutions (and all four of the Polish universities). Following the Commission's reforms, the educational system was brought under the control of the state. The foundations of the modern Polish system of education were laid with the enactment of the reforms of the Commission of National Education.

The three-level schools were to provide, apart from mass education for everybody (which was the source of many controversies), specialists and experts. Their job was to educate the elites and form a new individual (a member of this elite) according to the Enlightenment ideal. It is difficult to overestimate the influence of the Commission on the Polish educational system. It was easily seen after Poland's collapse when the institutions created by it survived the destruction of the Polish state in 1795 and continued to operate in the different partitioned areas of the nation. Their characteristics were:

1 Education for everybody (very often questioned by the conservative gentry).
2 Care about teaching standards.
3 Modern knowledge transmitted to pupils and students.
4 Modern ideas in teaching and education (Niezgoda and Kosiarz-Stolarska, 1997: 4).

Higher education suffered when Poland was wiped off the map of Europe in 1795 as a consequence of the third and final partition of the state by its three great neighbouring powers: Austria-Hungary, Prussia and Russia.[3] The partitioning powers sought to 'Germanise' and 'Russify' Polish centres of learning and many leading Polish intellectuals, especially in the humanities, were persecuted. After carving up the Polish state amongst themselves, the victors sought to destroy Polish nationhood by forbidding the use of Polish as the language of instruction in both schools and universities. The teaching of Polish history and literature was also forbidden. It was the universities at Krakow and Wilno which played the most prominent role in ensuring the continuance of Polish culture. In 1867 while the authorities in the Russian partition were trying to obliterate all traces of Polish culture through the educational system, the Austrian authorities in Galicia – Kraków was brought into Galicia in 1846 – granted limited autonomy to its Polish inhabitants, which allowed the repolonisation of the region's two universities and the entire school system that had been Germanised. But in the Russian and German partitions the process of 'Russification' and 'Germanisation' continued. Ultimately, the attempts to extinguish *Polishness* in the Prussian and Russian partition failed principally because of the many underground centres of learning established by Polish patriots. The most famous of these was the Flying University in Warsaw, which had an even more famous pupil who went on to win two Nobel Prizes – for physics and chemistry – Maria Skłodowska-Curie (better known as Marie Curie). The real turning point came in 1914 with the outbreak of the First World War when all the partitioning powers sought to gain Polish support in the War. It prompted Russia to decolonise all schools and universities within its partition area following a similar action by the Austrians in 1867.

At the end of the First World War, Poland regained its independence for a brief period until the Nazi invasion on 1 September 1939. During this short period of independence, the Polish authorities were confronted with many problems, including the high illiteracy rate and scarce resources. By 1939, the former problem had been addressed and considerable success had been achieved but the problem of scarce resources meant that '[o]nly the most exceptional peasant children could hope to obtain higher education' (Davies, 1982a: 418). The most immediate problem confronting the Polish government led by Józef Piłsudski[4] with regard to education was that an entirely new national system of education had to be built from scratch. Furthermore, the new state was afflicted by a severe shortage of qualified people, so the political authorities laid much stress upon the necessity of expanding the Polish educational system quickly. Considerable success was achieved at the tertiary level. In 1918 Poland had only two universities but by 1939 this figure had risen to thirteen (Zarnowski, 1990: 231).

The Polish model of higher education developed within the circle of the European continental medieval tradition and later of the tradition of the liberal, autonomous German university (Jabłecka-Gębka, 1994: 11–24). The traditional organisational structure of the Humboldtian German university was based upon a group of faculties, usually the four traditional faculties of law, theology, philosophy and medicine. Faculties were subdivided into professorial chairs. In 1920 a law was passed by the newly independent state which affirmed the liberal tradition of Polish universities by guaranteeing the dominance of the collegial decision-making model within universities. The university senate, faculty councils and the general assembly of professors were bestowed with the 'greatest authority' (Jabłecka-Gębka, 1994: 12). Other provisions contained within this law included the legal guarantee of freedom to learn, freedom to teach and freedom to pursue academic research. The law stipulated that faculty councils were to be responsible for the coordination of lectures and accordingly empowered faculty councils to review the 'scope of individual lectures and exercises in order to adapt them to the general programme of studies' (Jabłecka-Gębka, 1994: 13).

The legal framework for the construction of an entire new school system was established with the passage of the 1932 Education Law and the 1933 Higher Education Law. These reforms were known as the Jedrze-jowicz Reforms after the Minister of Religious Beliefs and Public Enlight-enment who had drafted the Acts. Seven year of compulsory elementary schooling for children who were not going to proceed to secondary schools, while only six years of elementary education were compulsory for those children who were going on to obtain a secondary education. Several types of secondary schools were established. First, there was the general secondary school which included the four-year gymnasium and the two-year liceum. At the end of this students who passed the matura (university qualifying examinations) could proceed to apply to universities. Second, the pedagogical liceum replaced the former teacher training colleges and educated students who wished to become elementary school teachers. Third, there was the vocational secondary school. Other vocational schools, known as vocational retraining schools, also existed. These schools were not recognised as secondary schools and prepared qualified workers and sales assistants, among others, on the basis of the seven-year elementary school. The Jedrzejowicz Reforms unified and modernised the Polish educational system, which remained almost unaltered until the post-communist reforms of the 1990s. But the interwar system of educa-tion was highly selective with only 20 per cent of society forming the social base of 75 per cent of students of secondary schools which led to a univer-sity education (Niezgoda and Kosiarz-Stolarska, 1997: 10–13). Peasant and workers' children as well as children from ethnic minority backgrounds were under-represented. Nevertheless the achievements of the Second Republic were considerable: the eradication of illiteracy; the introduction of vocational secondary schools and the expansion of the higher educa-tional system. All of this took place while the Polish state was recovering from the devastation of the First World War and subsequent civil wars, and also engaged in state-building. In addition, it was a time with an extremely difficult international climate with seemingly insurmountable obstacles (Davies, 1982a).

The Nazi occupation (1939–45)

The Nazi occupation of Poland during the Second World War had a devastating impact on every area of Polish life, including Polish intellectual life. Polish intellectuals were viewed as a threat by the Nazi regime, which planned eventually to exterminate all those Poles who had held positions of political, intellectual and even religious authority within the Polish state. During the Extraordinary Pacification Campaign (1939–40) over 10,000 Polish intellectuals, including university teachers, were interned in the concentration camps at Dachau, Buchenwald and Sachsenhausen and more than 3,500 political leaders were executed in the Palmiry Forest on the outskirts of Warsaw (Davies, 1982a: 447).

Poland was once again partitioned by an occupying power and its system of national education broken up and virtually eradicated. Polish education in those territories which were incorporated into the Reich was abolished on all levels. Only very limited Polish education remained (elementary and lower vocational schools) in the area of German-occupied Poland. The German occupants sought to exterminate the Polish intelligentsia and to prevent its reproduction since they were aware of the crucial role played by educated elites in preserving political culture and national identity. During the War, 40 per cent of all Polish university professors were killed, most of Poland's thirty-two institutions of higher education were destroyed (either totally or partially) and two-thirds of all library collections perished at the hands of the Nazis (Markiewicz, 1979: 48).

Recognition by Polish partisans that the preservation of the Polish state and identity lay in the intellectual development of its youth led to the organisation of two underground universities and other higher education institutions in the immediate aftermath of the Nazi invasion. According to one estimate, in German-occupied Poland there were 20,000 teachers involved in underground education (26,000 teachers were employed prior to the War) teaching around one million pupils and students (Niezgoda and Kosiarz-Stolarska, 1997: 14).

The communist years of dictatorship (1945–89)

At the end of the Second War World, the Yalta division of Europe by the leaders of the victorious powers put Poland firmly within the Soviet sphere of influence. Out of all the states which found themselves under Soviet control, Poland was the one in which the Soviets found it hardest to impose communism. Stalin was quoted as saying, 'introducing communism into Poland was "like fitting a cow with a saddle"' (Davies, 1982: 3). One of the first actions which the communist authorities took was to re-organise Polish higher education on the basis of the Soviet model (Szczepanski, 1978). Certain faculties were separated from universities and set up as separate academies and put under the control of ministries other than the Ministry of Science, Technology and Higher Education.[5] Access to higher education was restricted because the Ministry controlled not only the overall number of students which could be admitted to higher educational institutions in a given academic year but also admission levels for every institution and even for each faculty. There was also a state-wide university selection procedure determined by the centre (Ministry of National Education (MEN), 1996: 141). A core plank of communist policy was to encourage young people from rural and working-class backgrounds to enter university. To this end, they were given preferential points in the university entrance examinations. By allowing young people from such backgrounds to have access to higher education, the communist authorities hoped to produce a new class of intelligentsia that was sympathetic to the regime. The widening of access to higher education to young people from rural and working-class backgrounds who previously would never have had the opportunity of going to university was also promoted by the existence of a generous scheme of scholarships and subsidies to support them throughout their university studies. There were no financial barriers to higher education because of the communist government's policy of cheap books, scholarships and grants (United Nations Development Programme, 1998). Another positive aspect of the period of communist rule,[6] was the equal right to education for both sexes.

So despite this centralised control of students admitted to HEIs, the number of students in HEIs did increase overall during the post-Second World War period. This expansion began from an extremely low starting point after the devastation of the Second World War as well as from the inherited elitist interwar university system. During the academic year 1949/50, there were 4.6 students per 1,000 population. By 1980, this figure had risen to 16.6 students per 1,000 population, only to decrease slightly in 1987 to 12.2 students per 1,000 population (Lewis, 1994: 132). In 1977, there were 491,400 students attending institutions of higher education. This was the highest number during the entire communist period. By 1986, the total number of students attending institutions of higher education had fallen to 334,500 but rose slightly to 356,000 by 1988. In other words, in 1988 only 10 per cent of all 19-year-olds entered higher education as opposed to 14 per cent in the late 1970s. Also, by 1986 the total state expenditure on higher education in real terms was only 80.9 per cent of that in 1978. Even so, despite this significant expansion, by the end of the communist period, access to higher education remained tightly restricted by the Ministry of Education and the system of higher education still retained its elitist character.

Democratising the higher educational system

An examination of the political discourse of the post-communist elites in 1989 reveals that higher education reform was regarded as extremely important for the successful consolidation of democracy and establishment of a market economy in Poland. For example, a report published by the Polish Ministry of National Education stated that it is the higher educational system which helps to create the 'the political, economic and social' environment in a given country (MEN, 1996a: 9). It was recognised that universities are institutions specifically designed for the development and dissemination of ideas and values. Political leaders recognised universities' potentials as agents of political and social change. Higher education reform was also vital to help Poland achieve its most important foreign policy objective: membership of the European Union. Polish society needed to acquire certain skills if Poland was to become a modern European democracy. Promoting access to higher education for all sectors of the population would contribute to the strengthening of democracy and the economic 'intellectual' capacity of the state.

Therefore, increasing access to higher education has been one of the core elements of higher education policy since 1989 and is seen as an integral part of the process of democratising the system of higher education in Poland. In 1989 for every 100,000 people there were 1,101 students in Poland compared with 2,700 students in the UK, 2,995 students in France and 1,927 students in Greece. But by 2002 the number of students per 100,000 inhabitants in Poland had increased to 4,000, thus making Poland comparable with other European countries (MEN, 2004). Similarly, the percentage of young people in the 19–24 age group in higher education increased from 13.1 per cent in the academic year 1990/91 to 43.7 per cent in 2001/02. Comparable rates for the 2001/02 academic year in other countries are: the USA (81 per cent), Australia (80 per cent), New Zealand (63 per cent) and Norway (62 per cent) (MEN, 2004).

Other policy aims included granting considerable autonomy to universities, broadening the educational curricula and the diversification of higher education. This latter aspect of the reform involved the introduction of shorter-cycle professional degree courses as an alternative to the five-year Masters degree courses which had been the only undergraduate degree course available. And the broadening of the educational curricula, counter-intuitively, included reducing the number of officially recognised fields of study in which degrees could be awarded from around 194 to 96. Under communism, fields of study were very narrow and circumscribed and once you had embarked upon a particular course you had to follow a set curriculum and it was very difficult to change subjects within a given faculty and virtually impossible to move between faculties. Fields of study which were adopted were much broader and were adapted to the needs of the new market economy and political system. New courses of study such as marketing, business studies, European Union law and politics were introduced. Curricula was internationalised and flexible study systems, which allowed students a greater choice of subjects within a particular course, were introduced (Przybysz, 1996).

Despite the difficulties of the simultaneous transformations of the political, economic and social systems as well as the challenges presented by European integration, the new Polish elites undertook the reform of the higher educational system almost immediately. It was recognised that higher education reform was an integral part of the processes of democratic consolidation and European integration.

Three Acts designed to facilitate the expansion and democratisation of higher education, countermanding the influence of the communist legacy, were passed by the post-communist parliament. These were the Act of 12 September 1990 on Schools of Higher Education; the Act of 12 September 1990 on the Academic Title and Academic Degrees; and the Act of 12 January 1991 setting up the Committee for Scientific Research (MEN, 1994).

Only the 1990 Act on Schools of Higher Education[7] will be examined in this chapter. It was the most important of these Acts since it provided the framework for the expansion and reform of the system of higher education. Among other things this meant that the number of students entering university was no longer restricted by central government. The 1990 Act also permitted the establishment of private schools of higher education, and allowed universities to operate extra-mural or evening classes for which students had to pay. According to the 1990 Act, one of the tasks of schools of higher education is to educate its students 'in the spirit of respect for human rights, patriotism, democracy and responsibility for the future of society and the State' (MEN, 1994).[8] Academic freedom was enshrined in this new legislation so that academics were free to pursue research and publish their findings – even if these criticised the government – without fear of state retribution. Furthermore, the Act introduced a new system of university financing based upon the principle of competitive funding. Thus the decentralisation of the Polish higher educational system paralleled that of the political system with the liberal democratic ideology of the state being imposed upon higher education. Finally, the 1990 Act on Higher Education established the General Council for Higher Education, which is an elected academic body which partly oversees the activities of the Ministry of Education.

The current autonomy of institutions of higher education is reflected in the fact that the Act granted them the right to pass their own statutes (the Ministry of Education must approve the statutes of non-state institutions). Other powers which have been awarded under the 1990 Act include:

- The right to establish and close down particular programmes on the suggestion of the faculty council.
- The right to open, close, or reorganise faculties or parts of an institution.
- The right to determine the principles and practice of admissions procedures.
- The form of entrance examination and regulations for students.

The dramatic increase in university autonomy during the 1990s led to greater unpredictability in the numbers of students being admitted. Admission policies and entrance requirements may vary between faculties in a given university, and may vary widely for the same academic discipline in different universities. This would not be a serious problem were it not for the fact that rules governing admission requirements, the number of students entering HEIs and programmes of studies' requirements are in a state of flux by being incessantly altered by individual university senates and faculty councils whenever they believe it is required.

A related problem is that of equality of access to education, the attainment of which is, on the surface, at least only possible by the democratisation of Polish higher education. But there are several dimensions to the process of democratisation of Polish higher education including those related to equality of access to higher education; the internationalisation/Europeanisation of teaching and research methods; and freedom of research and teaching. Arguably, in many states which are widely regarded as having consolidated democracies, such as the United Kingdom, higher education is fully democratised in only the latter two senses. But as the other chapters in this book have shown equality of access has very rarely been achieved and remains problematic for even the longest established democracies.

Equality of access to higher education has been a particularly important issue in the context not just of higher educational reform but also has significant implications for democratic consolidation in Poland. There was a concern that if only a small proportion of the Polish population were able to avail themselves of higher education, this would have a deleterious affect upon the nascent democracy and, for that matter, the new market economy. But since 1990 Poland has moved from an elite to a mass system of higher education: the number of students attending HEIs has more than quadrupled. Approximately 400,000 students were enrolled in HEIs in 1990 and by 1998 that figure had risen to over 850,000 (Drozdowicz, 1998). And by 2003 that figure stood at 1,800,500 (GUS, 2003: 146). Also in the 1990/91 academic year the age participation rate was 13.1 per cent and by the 2001/2002 academic year it had risen to 43.7 per cent (MEN, 2003a: 2). Unfortunately there has been practically no new investments in university buildings during this period. Partly, the rapid expansion of the higher educational system was aided by the establishment of private universities, or, more accurately, non-state institutions of higher education. Prior to 1990 non-state HEIs did not exist in Poland. Private universities reflected the individualism of the new liberal, political order in Poland and were further evidence of the democratisation underway within the system of higher education. The first privately owned HEI was founded in 1991 (on the basis of the Act of 12 September 1990). Another eleven non-state HEIs were registered in 1992 and by 1993 there was a total of thirty-two non-state HEIs (MEN, 1996a: 171). By 2002 there were 123 state and 241 non-state HEIs established in Poland (Eurydice, 2003). Moreover, many of these non-state HEIs cannot operate without lecturers from state universities. At the beginning of 1993/94, approximately 10,000 students were enrolled in non-state HEIs and by 2002 there were over 500,000 students attending private HEIs accounting for 27 per cent of the total number of students in higher education (MEN, 1996: 173; MEN, 2004: 2)

Although non-state institutions of higher education usually operate in big cities, some of them, unlike the state institutions, are also located in small towns. The size of non-public higher education institutions varies a lot: from several dozen to several thousand students. The only admission requirements are the *matura* certificate and usually an interview. Most non-state HEIs offer three-year professional training courses leading to the *licencjat* or Bachelor's degree (BA). Previously, higher education had consisted of a five-year course of study leading to the professional title of *magister* or Master's (MA). The majority of non-state HEIs offer vocational courses with a business slant such as management and marketing, economics, finance and banking. Other less popular courses include administration, education, political and social sciences, tourism and recreation and computing. Payment of tuition fees is, of course, mandatory at such institutions.

The expansion of the higher educational system was further stimulated by the 1997 Act which allowed Schools of Higher Vocational Education to be established. Unlike the larger traditional state universities, these new Vocational HEIs are usually established in smaller towns, thus offering easier access to youth from rural and farming backgrounds. Such young people are more badly affected by the funding crisis in Polish higher education than their counterparts in the city. Indeed the funding crisis is a major obstacle for youth from the countryside wishing to obtain higher education. The increasingly prohibitive accommodation costs in Polish towns and cities prevents many young people from the countryside from pursuing higher education. For example, in 1998 only 1 per cent of those working on family farms had completed tertiary education while 58 per cent had only an elementary education or less (United Nations Development Programme, 1998). Reductions in the number and value of university scholarships, the introduction of charges by state universities for certain educational services (tuition fees by the back door), and the increased costs of books all represent financial burdens once borne by the Polish government but now being carried by students and their parents. Many students from villages or small towns are forced to commute long distances daily while attending university because they cannot afford to pay for accommodation in the city where the university is situated.

In an attempt to address this problem the 1997 Act on Schools of Higher Vocational Education was passed. Vocational HEIs also offer short three-year Bachelor degree courses and some of these institutions give students the option of completing a Masters degree in two stages. In the first stage, which lasts three years, students would complete the Bachelor's degree and then, if they wanted to, could continue studying for a further two years in order to complete the MA. Not all students are capable of or inclined to complete a five-year degree course, and so the introduction of the three-year Bachelor's degree allows such students the chance of completing higher education and obtaining a first degree. Another added advantage of the Vocational HEIs is that the connection between the type of higher education offered and future employment is more visible. The vocational nature of the degree courses offered persuades many students of the value of higher education and of the existence of a direct link between having a higher education and gaining employment. Students from farming backgrounds who intended to work on their parents' farms once they had left school in particular had to be persuaded of the value of having a higher education. Now higher vocational schools offer courses which will equip students with the desirable skills for working in rural locations. And the link between possessing a higher education and finding employment is discernible even to those students from rural areas who intend to seek work within their own village or small town. There are 102 Schools of Higher Vocational Education in Poland attended by 99,800 students (Eurydice, 2003).

In a ranking of institutions of higher education based upon the criterion of which of them best prepared their students for the job market, the strengthening position of private HEIs and all types of HEIs based in Warsaw in comparison with state HEIs and those based outside of Warsaw was noticeable (Jaroszewicz, 2004: 78–9). But this survey has been heavily criticised for being flawed by academics from large university centres in Gdańsk, Lublin, Wrocław, Kraków, Katowice and Poznań. This is the third such ranking of universities undertaken by *Newsweek Polska*. Several weekly Polish current affairs magazines have since the late 1990s provided regular rankings of higher education institutions and produced special educational supplements devoted to higher education containing advice for students on the following: finding a job; writing a good Masters thesis; looking for sponsors; looking for work experience and studying abroad. This practice is in response to the soaring demand for information

Table 8.1 The rate of unemployment by level of education in 2002 (%)

The unemployed by level of education	
Higher	3.9
Post-secondary and secondary vocational	21.2
Secondary general	6.2
Basic vocational	36.2
Primary and below	32.5

Source: The Information Database on Education Systems in Europe.

on higher education by young people who are increasingly aware of the connection between having a 'good' degree and getting a 'good' job (see Table 8.1). Given that currently in Poland unemployment is 20 per cent, it is not surprising that the demand for higher education has soared.[9]

And while it is true that a university degree is still the best defence against being jobless, a recent survey shows that in this area there have also been many negative changes. For instance in the Polish provinces of Lublin and Kielce, every third graduate with a Masters degree is unemployed. Graduates living in the south eastern and in the north eastern parts of Poland are more likely to be jobless than elsewhere. The main cause of such high unemployment among graduates in these areas is the inappropriate links between the local economies and the higher education institutions. For instance in the Kielce and Lublin regions there are too many schools which offer degrees in marketing and managing when the economy in these regions is based mainly on agriculture and the food industry.

A very interesting situation has occurred in Warsaw, which is the centre of higher education in Poland, containing the largest number of state and non-state HEIs producing increasing numbers of graduates. As a result of this, the percentage of graduates amongst the unemployed is increasing. Warsaw is based in the Mazowsze region and the following figures for the whole of this region illustrate this point. In 2000 some 10 per cent of the unemployed in Mazowsze were university graduates. By 2002 this figure had risen to 20 per cent and rose yet again in 2003 to 24 per cent (Sadłowska, 2004: 4). Such discourse in the Polish media, which emphasises the negative aspects of increasing access to higher education, namely greater graduate unemployment, has been counterbalanced by other more positive articles on the expansion of the system of higher education. For example, a recent article in *Rzeczpospolita* (the Polish equivalent of the *Financial Times*) argues that Poland requires even more educated young graduates (Kryńska, 2004: 2). It observes that there are many HEIs in Poland which do not offer students a good education. And argues that the outlook for young graduates is not so bad as long as the Polish government makes effective use of the predicted high economic growth (predicted at 5 per cent for 2004) and its membership of the European Union. It also warns that Poland is at the end of its second population boom. The generation of post-Second World War baby boomers (1946–56) produced another wave of baby boomers (1978–88) but the birth rate has decreased drastically since 1992. The number of graduates will probably not continue to increase at the same rate and so the job market should become much easier for them.

Increasing access: the draft of the new Polish higher educational law

Unfortunately, the mass expansion of the Polish higher educational system has not been accompanied by an increase in government spending. Instead there has been a lack of government funding for the higher educational system resulting in calls to impose tuition fees, a topic which has been hotly debated in the Polish parliament. The ongoing crisis in public finances is largely responsible for this lack of funding but it does reflect the re-evaluations of how to finance higher educational provision taking place in other European countries.

One widely respected Polish academic likened the constant squeezing of university funding by the Polish government to the torture instrument known as the 'Spanish Collar'. Moreover, the fact that most government ministers were former university professors did not help the educational system to secure more funding. The introduction of university tuition fees by a British Labour government, traditionally viewed as upholding egalitarian principles of free access for all, has not escaped the attention of Polish politicians. Currently, Polish universities may charge students tuition fees only for evening or extramural studies. Regular day studies continue to be free.

As Article 70, paragraphs 1 and 4 of the Polish Constitution state:

> Everyone shall have the right to education. Education to 18 years of age shall be compulsory. The manner of fulfilment of schooling obligations shall be specified by statute.

(paragraph 1)

Table 8.2 Government expenditure on Polish higher education, 1991–2002

Year	Budgetary expenditure (in million PLZ)	Baseline year (1991 = 100%)	Real rate of growth of expenditure (in %)	Spending on higher education (% of GDP)
1991	665.0	100.0	–	0.82
1992	1,011.0	152.6	6.3	0.88
1993	1,270.0	125.6	−7.2	0.82
1994	1,626.4	128.1	−3.1	0.72
1995	2,174.7	133.7	4.6	0.71
1996	3,011.3	138.5	15.1	0.77
1997	3,752.2	124.6	8.8	0.79
1998	4,272.3	113.9	1.8	0.77
1999	5,084.7	119.0	10.9	0.82
2000	5,326.7	104.8	−4.9	0.78
2001	6,370.7	119.6	3.5	0.88
2002	6,827.0	107.2	2.6	0.89

Source: 'Strategia rozwoju szkolnictwa wyższego w Polsce do roku (2010: 4).

Public authorities shall ensure universal and equal access to education for citizens. To this end, they shall establish and support systems for individual financial and organisational assistance to pupils and students. The conditions for providing of such assistance shall be specified by statute.

(paragraph 4)

However, the Polish Constitution, whilst stipulating that education is free, does seem to leave open the possibility that some sort of tuition fee could be introduced indirectly by recognising that charges may be imposed on some higher education services:

Education in public schools shall be without payment. Statutes may allow for payments for certain services provided by public institutions of higher education.

(Article 70, paragraph 2)

The issue of higher education reform, in particular how to finance a system of mass education, is one that preoccupies the current Polish government. A draft of the new Polish Higher Educational Law was submitted to the Polish parliament on 19 March 2004. Apart from some cosmetic changes to the existing 1990 Act, the draft deals with the issue of improving access to higher education by outlining the circumstances under which financial assistance may be offered to students to help them study at university. First, a student may take a loan of up to 600 PLZ (about £87) monthly and start to pay it back two years after graduation. Previously it was only 460 PLZ (£67) monthly, which the student had to begin repaying one year after graduation. Furthermore, it is not only regular day students attending state HEIs who are eligible for the loan, students attending private HEIs as well as evening (non-regular, fee-paying) students at state HEIs are also eligible. In fact, all types of students will be covered under this system, including doctoral students. However, the special income tax refund previously available for the sum of money spent on higher education has been eliminated.

In 2004, the government reserved 1.5 billion PLZ (£145 million) for students' financial assistance, which is much more than the 800 million PLZ (£116 million) spent in the previous year. Apart from loans, students may apply for a special social scholarship (MEN, 2003: art. 162(1)). Each university determines the amount and decides upon the award of social scholarships which may be granted if income per capita in a student's family is lower than 569 PLZ (£82.50) per month. For instance, at the Jagiellonian University in Kraków, the social scholarship is worth about 200 PLZ (£29) monthly, while social scholarships offered by the Academy of Economics and by the Academy of Mining and Metallurgy also in Kraków are worth 300 PLZ (£43) monthly. Apart from that students may have subsidised meals – about 5 PLZ (£0.70) per meal – and also a place in the university halls of residence for a monthly rate of about 150 PLZ (£22).

However, students who are unable to find a place in the student dormitory have to rent a room privately and the price for this varies from between 300 PLZ (£43) to 400 PLZ (£58) monthly per person in the room (there are usually two people per room) in large cities like Kraków. Renting accommodation outside the city centre in smaller towns like Nowa Huta on the outskirts of Kraków is much cheaper and prices range from 150 PLZ (£22) up to 200 PLZ (£29) per person each month. In case of an emergency, once a year students may receive up to 500 PLZ (£72) in financial aid (MEN, 2003: art. 162(3)). Under the draft Law, a special stipend is also available for disabled students (MEN, 2003: art. 162(2)). Finally, in some extraordinary cases there is a special stipend from the Minister of National Education and Sport available for the best undergraduate students and for young talented PhD students – 900 PLZ (£130) monthly (MEN, 2003: art. 162(4)). At the Jagiellonian University in Kraków (Poland's oldest university) there are altogether about 30,000 students and 3,000 of these receive some form of scholarship. Very few students can afford to study without having some additional income. In Poland about every third student has a job. It is much easier for students attending HEIs in Warsaw, Kraków, Gdańsk and Poznań to find employment and much more difficult in Katowice and Łódź.[10] And under the draft Law students will continue to have a special reduction (50 per cent) for public transport in each city and on the railways (MEN, 2003: art. 166).

The draft Law on Higher Education states that regular studies in state universities are free of charge but that state universities may impose and collect fees for special educational services such as:

- non-regular studies;
- evening doctoral studies;
- repeating regular studies;
- additional studies not covered by the regular programme such as the study of a foreign language (MEN, 2003: art. 93).

It is up to the rector of the university to determine the level of such fees. And even more remarkably, given the current financial crisis, regular (day) doctoral studies are free of charge (MEN, 2003: art. 171(7))! But irregular (evening) doctoral studies are paid for and the fee for this type of doctoral studies is determined by the rector of the university (MEN, 2003: art. 171(8)). Furthermore a PhD student may obtain a stipend which cannot be lower than 60 per cent of the salary of the assistant of a professor. It is up to the director of the institute to determine whether or not the stipend will be awarded. And PhD students may only work if this job does not harm their doctoral studies (MEN, 2003: art. 177).

The role of the European Union in promoting access to higher education

The influential role of the European Union in Polish higher educational reform, first of all through the TEMPUS programme[11] and later through ERASMUS-Socrates, facilitated increased access to higher education through their support for the development of diversified study systems. TEMPUS was adopted by the Council of Ministers of the European Community on 7 May 1990 and was part of the PHARE programme designed to support economic, political and social reform in Central and Eastern Europe. It was funded from the Union's overall PHARE budget. TEMPUS 1 started on 1 July 1990 and was due to operate for an initial pilot phase of three years. It was, however, extended further for one year and ended in June 1994. The second phase of the TEMPUS programme (TEMPUS II) was agreed in the Council decision of 29 April 1993 and was implemented at the start of the 1993/94 academic year. TEMPUS II, known as the 'Trans-European Cooperation Scheme for Higher Educa-tion', originally envisaged to run for four years until 1997/98, TEMPUS but was again extended until 2003 (although the last TEMPUS applica-tions took place in 2000). TEMPUS helped provide support for the imple-mentation of the Ministry of National Education's higher educational reforms such as the diversification of higher education by establishing new units and new types of courses within existing schools of higher education, including vocational degree courses. Over 13,000 Polish students were granted scholarships to various HEIs in EU member states under TEMPUS (MEN, 2003a: 4).

TEMPUS was replaced by the Socrates programme, which Poland joined in March 1998. Unlike TEMPUS where the assistance granted was 'free', Socrates contains a reciprocity requirement between the participating HEIs. This means that Poland must match the funding provided by the EU. As well as supporting the diversification of the university system, Socrates pro-motes the establishment of the European Credit Transfer System (ECTS) which currently facilitates exchanges between Polish and other European students and the introduction of a more flexible system of study within Poland. After only four years of operation, over 12,000 students had partici-pated in the Socrates exchange programme (MEN, 2003a: 4).

On 19 June 1999, Poland along with twenty-nine other countries signed the Bologna Declaration which aimed to create a European Area of Higher Education. The Bologna Process (Declaration of European Educa-tion Ministers) has focused upon harmonising educational systems within Europe. Such harmonisation is to be achieved by the introduction of a system of comparable degrees, by the further development of the two-stage degree system, by widening the use of the European Credit Transfer System (ECTS) in European universities, and by removing barriers which limit student and teacher mobility.

Conclusion

Poland has been successful in moving in a very short space of time from an elite to a mass system of higher education but new barriers in access to higher education have appeared with the ending of communist rule. Under communism there were no financial barriers to higher education because of the policy of cheap books, scholarships and grants. And access to higher education was widened to young people from rural and working-class backgrounds who previously would never have had the opportunity of going to university. Nevertheless, the overall number of students admitted to higher education was rigidly controlled by the communist state. Since 1990 the system of higher education in Poland has undergone tremendous changes. Access to higher education has been both positively and negatively affected by these changes. On the positive side the rapid expansion of the higher educational system partly facilitated by the establishment of non-state HEIs and schools of higher vocational education has allowed more young people than ever before to avail themselves of a university education. More than four times as many students are enrolled in tertiary education than in 1990. European Union funding for higher education in Poland especially through TEMPUS injected much-needed finance into the system for the restructuring of university departments and the introduction of new courses. And through its student–staff mobility programme, TEMPUS also promotes the sharing of experiences and ideas between Polish staff and students and their EU counterparts. But it was the EU's support for the development of diversified study systems firstly through TEMPUS, later under the Socrates programme and then through the Bologna Process, that promoted increased access to higher education in Poland. The introduction of the two-stage degree (three-year Bachelors + two-year Masters) allowed many young people to gain a higher education degree by completing the three-year Bachelors' degree. Many students find the costs of studying for five years at university prohibitive, while others are more academically inclined towards vocational three-year degrees.

Fundamental problems, however, remain over how the system of higher education is to be financed in future. Government funding remains inadequate and increasingly state HEIs are charging fees for 'special educational services' such as extramural studies. Poverty is now the greatest barrier in access to higher education faced by Polish students. The new draft Law on Higher Education tries to overcome this barrier by offering some limited social scholarships to students from families in low income brackets and reductions, for example, in the cost of public transport. In reality this is just a drop in the ocean as only a relatively small number of students will be eligible for social scholarships and the rapidly rising cost of public transport still makes it relatively expensive for students even with the 50 per cent reduction. The draft Law's commitment to free higher education not only for regular day students but also for doctoral students, while perhaps promoting access, appears to be rather unrealistic. Is it possible that Poland can maintain a system of free higher education at a time when states with much higher levels of GNP are introducing tuition fees?

Notes

1 The terms 'higher educational institution' and 'university' are used interchangeably in this chapter, although a subtle difference in meaning does exist. Typically, a university offers a widespread selection of courses ranging from engineering and medicine to the arts and social sciences. A higher educational institution may only offer a narrow range of closely related subjects at the tertiary level; for example, only those subjects related to mining and metallurgy.
2 Charles University in Prague (founded in 1347) was the first university in Central Europe. It preceded the Kraków Academy (renamed the Jagiellonian University in 1400) by seventeen years. The university which was founded in Bologna in 1088 is recognised as the first university in Europe. And when the Jagiellonian University was established only thirty-six other universities existed in the entire world (see Davies, 1996: 1248).
3 The Polish state was partitioned in three stages by its neighbouring powers, Austria–Hungary, Prussia and Russia. After the first partition in 1793, the Kingdom of Poland was left with only 70 per cent of its original territory, reduced to 30 per cent after the second partition and Poland was disappeared from the map of Europe for 123 years after the third partition in 1795.
4 Józef Piłsudski (1867–1935) was instrumental in Poland regaining its independence in 1918. Between 1918–21 he led Polish forces in their successful campaign to establish the frontiers of the state. He served as Chief of State and Commander-in-Chief from 1918 until 1923. He staged the May Coup of 1926 and from then until his death on 12 May 1935 ruled Poland as a pseudo-dictatorship (see Davies, 1982b: 53–6, 393–434).
5 The Ministry of Science, Technology and Higher Education controlled universities, economics academies, agricultural academies, higher schools of pedagogy, technical universities and theological academies. Medical academies were governed by the Ministry of Health and Social Welfare, while the Ministry of Culture was responsible for the academies of music, academies of fine arts and academies of theatre and cinematography. Additionally, there were other ministries which controlled physical education academies, military academies and maritime academies (see Ministry of National Education (MEN), 1996a: 131).
6 Interview with Professor Edmund Wnuk-Lipiński, Director of the Institute of Political Studies, Polish Academy of Sciences, Warsaw on 20 May 1998.
7 The 1990 Higher Educational Act applies both to state schools of higher education with the exception of military schools of higher education and to non-state (i.e. private) schools of higher education. It does not, however, apply to schools of higher education or theological seminaries run by the Catholic Church, with the exception of the Catholic University of Lublin.
8 From the 1990 Act on Schools of Higher Education, art. 3, para. 3(1).
9 The unemployment rate in Poland at the beginning of 2004 was 20.6 per cent (see GUS, 2004).
10 The figures contained in this paragraph were taken from 'Dyploma zardarno' ('Diplomas for free'), *Dziennik Polski* (20 March 2004), pp. 1, 4. For more technical details regarding the stipends available to students under the draft Law on Higher Education see *Projekt z dnia 31 października 2003* Art. 163.

11 TEMPUS is the 'Trans-European Mobility Programme for University Staff and Students'.

References

The Constitution of the Republic of Poland (as adopted by the National Assembly on 2 April 1997) (Warsaw: Chancellory of the Sejm).

Davies, Norman, *God's Playground. A History of Poland.* Volume 1 (New York: Columbia, 1982).

Davies, Norman, *God's Playground. A History of Poland.* Volume 2 (New York: Columbia, 1982a).

Davies, Norman, *Europe: A History* (Oxford: Oxford University Press, 1996).

Drozdowicz, Zbigniew, 'Polskie Uczelnie w Okresie Przemian Lat 90-Tych' ('Polish Academies during the 1990s Period of Transition') (Poznań: Instytut Filozofii, UAM, 1998), unpublished manuscript.

Dziennik Polski, 'Dyploma zardano' ('Diplomas for free') (20 March 2004), pp. 1, 4.

Eurydice European Unit, *The Information Database on Education Systems in Europe: The Education System in Poland, 2001/02.* (Brussels: Eurydice European Unit, 2003). www.eurydice.org/Eurybase/Application/frameset.asp?country=PL&language=EN (18 March 04).

GUS (Polish Government's Main Statistical Office), 'Stopa bezrobocia w latach 1990–2004' ('Unemployment rate, 1990–2004) at http://www.stat.gov.pl/ (22 March 2004).

GUS, 'Higher Education Institutions', *Mały Rocznik Statystyczny* (GUS: Warsaw, 2003, Table 14, 146). www.stat.gov.pl

Jabłecka-Gębka, J., 'Reflections on the Polish higher education', in I. Białecki *et al.* (eds) *Changes in Higher Education in Central European Countries* (Warsaw: IfiS, 1994).

Jaroszewicz, Karolina, 'Dyplom, który daje pracę' ('The degree which gives you a job'), *Newsweek Polska,*(21 March 2004), pp. 78–9.

Kryńska, Elżbieta, 'Młodzi nie wejda do Unii' ('Young people will not enter the Union'), *Rzeczpospolita* (9 March 2004), p. 2.

Lewis, Paul G., *Central Europe Since 1945* (London: Longman, 1994).

Markiewicz, Wladysław, 'Achievements of the humanities and social sciences in Poland', in H. Bargiel (ed.) *Research Guide to Polish Sciences and Humanities* (Warsaw: National Centre for Scientific and Technical Information, 1979).

Ministry of National Education and Sport (MEN), *Projekt z Dnia 22 Stycznia 2004 R. Prawo o szkolnictwie wyższym.* Article 93. www.men.waw.pl/ (1 March 2004).

Ministry of National Education and Sport (MEN), *Projekt z dnia 31 października 2003 roku ustawy. Prawo o szkolnictwie wyższym* (Warsaw: MEN, 2003). http://www.men.waw.pl/ (26 March 2004).

Ministry of National Education and Sport (MEN), 'Higher Education in Poland . . .', See also 'Strategia rozwoju szkolnictwa wyższego w Polsce do roku 2010' ('Strategy for the expansion of higher education to the year 2010') (Warsaw: MEN, 2004). www.men.waw.pl (26 March 2004).

Ministry of National Education and Sport (MEN), 'Higher Education in Poland. Implementing the Assumptions of the Bologna Declaration in 2000–2002', (MEN: Warsaw 2003a), p. 2. www.men.waw.pl/english/bologna/bologna_4.htm (18 March 2004).

Ministry of National Education (MEN), *Education in a Changing Society* (Warsaw: MEN, 1996).

Ministry of National Education (MEN), *Development of Education in Poland* (Warsaw: MEN, 1996a).

Ministry of National Education (MEN), *Acts on Schools of Higher Education, the Academic Title and Academic Degrees* (Warsaw: MEN, 1994).

Niezgoda, Marian and Anna Kosiarz-Stolarska, 'Education and educational policy in Poland. A sociological perspective' (Krakow: Jagiellonian University, 1997), unpublished manuscript.

Piasek, Ryszard and Michalina Vaughan, 'The crisis of Polish higher education', *Higher Education*, 16, pp. 53–61.

Przybysz, K., 'Introduction by Ministry of National Education'. Document sent to author by the Polish Ministry of National Education (Warsaw: MEN, 1996) p. XIV.

Sadłowska, Katarzyna, 'Nie każdy dyplom Pomaga' ('Not every diploma may help you [to find a job]'), *Rzeczpospolita,* (9 March 2004).

Suchodolski, B., *Komisja Edukacji Narodowej [National Commission of Education]* (Warsaw, 1973).

Szczepanski, J., *System of Higher Education in Poland.* (New York: International Council for Educational Development, 1978).

United Nations Development Programme, *National Human Development Report: Access to Education in Poland* (Warsaw: UNDP, 1998).

Wroczynski, R., *Dzieje oswiaty polskiej do roku 1795 (History of Polish education until 1795)* (Warsaw, 1987).

Zarnowski, Janusz 'The evolution of polish society since 1918', *East European Quarterly*, 24, 2 (1990) pp. 227–35.

9   British higher education and the prism of devolution

Gareth Parry

Introduction

> All those who have the potential to benefit from higher education should have the opportunity to do so. This is a fundamental principle which lies at the heart of building a more socially just society, because education is the best and most reliable route out of poverty and disadvantage.
>
> (Department for Education and Skills, 2003: 68)

At no other point in its history has access to British higher education assumed such policy and political proportions. With much of the system still coming to terms with the shift to mass higher education, a new phase of expansion is under way that will see participation approach near-universal levels by the end of the decade. Unlike the policies driving the spectacular growth of the late 1980s and early 1990s, the new phase of expansion is accompanied by specific measures to close the 'social class gap' in entry to higher education and address the 'skills deficit' at higher levels in the knowledge economy. While deregulation of undergraduate fees and university titles are expected to create a more competitive climate for recruitment, another set of proposals will extend the reach of the state into the previously insulated zones of student admissions and course curricula.

The radical nature of these access and funding proposals, at least for British audiences, is one reason why higher education policy is a source of unprecedented media coverage and political turbulence. The relative democratisation of access brought about by the last major expansion drew young people into undergraduate education who were often the first in their families to attend a university or college. It also attracted large numbers of adult students, many of whom had left school with few formal qualifications. This, alongside improved performance in upper secondary examinations and increased emphasis on the economic returns to degree qualifications, have signalled a larger interest among voters and other 'stakeholders' in the future of higher education. In short, higher education in the United Kingdom has become a popular undertaking.

As in other mass systems, expansion and democratisation have created pressures for more differentiation: in the missions of academic establishments as well as in the costs and standards of their courses. For 'selecting' institutions, this has meant sharper competition for places, with the fairness of selection procedures coming under increasing scrutiny. For 'recruiting' institutions, this has meant aggressive marketing of their programmes as well as collaboration with schools and further education establishments to encourage students in their direction. At one end of the system, the highest performing school-leavers compete for places at the most prestigious and most research-intensive universities. At the other end, the teaching-intensive colleges of further education provide short-cycle vocational higher education to mainly local students. In between, the great majority of students – young and mature – exchange their qualifications and experience for entry to undergraduate courses at universities and higher education colleges that differ markedly in size, mission, history and subject mix.

The result is a social class gradient and age profile in the student population that is strongly related to the reputational range of institutions. Since 1997, the UK government and its funding bodies have launched a series of widening participation initiatives aimed at tackling the under-representation of working-class students in higher education and challenging the selective universities to do more to attract applications from candidates with less advantaged backgrounds. In making admissions decisions, institutions are expected to assess the potential of applicants as much as their achievement, with targeted funding to meet the extra costs of reaching out and supporting students from less traditional backgrounds. In monitoring access strategies, information is now published on how well each establishment has recruited from low participation groups and how successful they have been in maintaining high rates of course completion. More controversially, there is to be an 'access regulator' whose 'office for fair access' will have the power to impose financial penalties on institutions in England that fail to meet their access benchmarks; and, if necessary, to withdraw approval for those wishing to charge variable fees.

For universities and higher education colleges in the British system, formally independent yet publicly funded, these were unwelcome incursions. Although preserving the long-established policy of leaving to institutions the decisions on which individuals to admit, the new proposals promised to change the terms on which funding was offered by the state and access was operated by the individual university or college. Institutional responsibility for admissions was a 'freedom' that survived the passage to mass higher education and, for that reason alone, was not to be surrendered lightly. Governments had ventured into admissions before, but rarely directly and usually only when the policies or practices of individual institutions had been called into question. The new access measures were of a different order and they reflected the strategic importance that a New Labour government accorded to its elite and mass institutions of higher education. Ministers were not persuaded that all institutions were even-handed in their selection and admission of students and, in England, an independent review will report on the principles that should underpin the conduct of 'fair admissions' (Admissions to Higher Education Review, 2003).

Convinced of the need for a 'high-skills' solution to improved productivity and global competitiveness, the expansion of higher education and the provision of work-focused education at the higher levels have been declared key government priorities for the first decade of the new century. Aligned to these economic imperatives are expectations about the social contribution of higher education, including a belief that wide access will promote social mobility and cohesion. In this, as in other spheres, the requirement on institutions to demonstrate their access commitments was but one outcome of a determined attempt by government to bring higher education behind a twin strategy for wealth creation and social inclusion.

There is, however, an additional dynamic and distinctive dimension to these developments. The arrival of mass higher education has coincided with administrative and political devolution in the four parts of Great Britain and Northern Ireland. In 1999, a parliament was restored in Scotland and separate national assemblies were introduced in Wales and, until it was suspended, in Northern Ireland. The coming together of these two movements – a democratisation of higher education and a democratisation of government – serve to highlight similarities and differences in the evolution and character of the tertiary systems in each country. Much less expected, these intersecting developments have made higher education policy the main contemporary battleground of devolution. The fee and regulatory policies of the first Blair government and, more immediately, the funding and access measures proposed during the second Blair premiership have transformed the domestic politics of higher education. The reform of higher education is simultaneously a critical stage in the 'modernisation' agenda of a New Labour government and an early test of the policy powers and party allegiances brought about by political devolution.

Equally contentious, the UK government has a headline target to increase participation in higher education 'towards' 50 per cent of those aged eighteen to thirty by the year 2010. The target has its origin, not in the policy work of a government department, but in the New Labour manifesto for the previous general election. Essentially, it is a target for England, where the participation figure based on this new definition is currently 43 per cent. What some regarded as an ambitious target for England had already been reached and overtaken in Scotland.

In the long-awaited White Paper that announced its proposals on deregulated fees and regulated access, the Blair government reaffirmed the importance of the 50 per cent target (Department for Education and

Skills, 2003). Straight after, the Scottish Executive published its own goals for expanding participation. Pointedly, the Executive was 'proud' to release figures for 2002 that showed 50 per cent of young people in Scotland had undertaken some kind of higher education by the time they were aged twenty-one (Scottish Executive, 2003a). Not only was this proportion calculated using the conventional measure for participation, but it had also been attained nine years ahead of the date set for England. Such were the ways that access and higher education played into post-devolution politics and policy-making.

An understanding of these changing contexts has benefited from a new wave of academic studies that examine the 'Britishness' of the education systems in England, Scotland, Wales and Northern Ireland, their dimensions of difference, and their relations of interdependence. Foremost amongst these are 'home international' comparative studies that analyse patterns of change within and between the four systems, including their post-compulsory frameworks (Raffe, 1998; Raffe *et al.*, 1999; Raffe, 2000; Canning and Cloonan, 2002). Complementing this work, theoretically and empirically, have been 'home nation' studies concerned with how English-based and London-centred policy-making is interpreted and 'recontextualised' at the territorial level (Daugherty *et al.*, 2000). In Scotland, in particular, devolution has stimulated scholarly reviews of the whole field of Scottish education (Bryce and Humes, 2003).

On a broader front, the model of elite–mass–universal higher education, originally outlined by Trow in the 1970s (Trow, 1974) and widely adopted as a standard account of how higher education systems develop, has been subject to critical assessment. As a framework for interpreting the experience of British higher education in the 1980s and 1990s, it was seen to underestimate the pluralism of the system and the diversity of its institutions (Scott, 1995; Watson, 1998). On the other hand, it provided a common language to describe its development and that of analogous systems. In a comparative context, the same model was able to consider claims to 'British exceptionalism' as well as expressions and assertions of difference among the four countries. As with school education, the Scottish and Welsh systems were mature enough to have generated their own 'myths' about the distinctive identity of higher education in each country.

Devolved government and the interest in home international comparisons have prompted questions about how mass levels of participation were achieved in each country and how this experience shaped the development of their access strategies. In this chapter, the territorial patterns in each country are reviewed, their growth trajectories are compared, and the nature of their access policies and discourses are examined. As a backdrop to these comparisons, general features of the present-day organisation of British higher education are reviewed, especially those that bear on conditions of access at the national, institutional and local levels.

In what follows, the Trow typology is used as a convenient heuristic. In short, elite systems were those that enrolled up to 15 to 20 per cent of an age grade; mass systems attracted up to 50 per cent of the age grade; and universal systems enrolled even larger numbers and proportions. Although these were somewhat arbitrary markers, they focus attention on the points of transition between one phase and another. Problems arose at these points because different aspects of higher education changed at different times and at different rates. Moreover, national systems did not shift completely from one to another. Elite institutions might survive (and flourish) even as the system as a whole expanded to provide mass higher education. Similarly, both elite and mass institutions might survive into a period of near universal access.

Finally, by way of clarification, all the participation figures produced in the remainder of this chapter follow the conventional definition applied to the four countries of the UK. Although this is a narrow measure, based on the number of young entrants to full-time undergraduate education, it has the merit of consistency and comparability. By contrast, the definition adopted for the 50 per cent target is used by government for England and figures have only been published for the three most recent years. The non-comparability of this measure has not passed unnoticed and a review of its rigour and transparency has been instituted.

Conditions of access: across and within four countries

Participation in British higher education attained its mass dimensions as a result of the surge in growth that occurred between 1988, when the participation rate for young people stood at 15 per cent, and 1994, when it more than doubled to 32 per cent. Following a policy of consolidation and a period of renewed expansion, the level of participation has since risen to 35 per cent. To achieve this level required a twofold increase in the number of students, with over two million young people and adults now studying courses leading to higher education and higher level qualifications.

Although transforming opportunities for individuals to gain access to higher education, even to participate on more than one occasion, the British encounter with mass higher education involved the creation of no new or alternative institutions and, until recently, no major reform of its standard entry and exit qualifications. The present number of higher education establishments is actually lower than that at the beginning of the expansion period, mainly the result of the merger or amalgamation of smaller colleges. It was therefore left to existing establishments to absorb the bulk of demand and, as before, graduate them in the minimum time, at the required standard and with minimal attrition.

What did change was the level of resource to underpin this growth and the separation made between the polytechnics and other major institutions on the one side and the universities on the other. The first involved a year-by-year reduction in the unit of funding: a consequence of the introduction of quasi-markets in higher education and the allocation of public funds on a more competitive basis. The second, implemented during the peak years of expansion, ended the binary divide in higher education: an acknowledgement that non-university institutions – the polytechnics in particular – were at a disadvantage in competing for funds and students. They had led the 'efficient expansion' required of all higher education establishments but they did not enjoy parity of esteem with the universities, especially among intending students:

> The title of polytechnic has never been widely understood. The British academic world realises that the polytechnics are higher education institutions achieving the same academic standards of education as most universities. Many able school-leavers and their parents still tend, however, to regard the title as a reason for making them a second choice to a university when seeking a place in higher education.
>
> (Department for Education and Science, 1991: 32)

All the same, it was essential that:

> the distinctive emphasis on vocational studies and widening access developed by polytechnics and colleges is maintained and extended.
>
> (Department for Education and Science, 1991: 14)

Accordingly, in 1992, degree-awarding powers were granted to the polytechnics and some other establishments in England and Wales, along with the corresponding institutions in Scotland. The same institutions were allowed to adopt university titles and these 'new' universities joined the 'old' universities in a unitary system of higher education for the UK. Higher education in Northern Ireland, where the only polytechnic had merged in 1984 with one of the two universities in the province, was already largely constituted as a unitary system.

As a result of the elimination of the binary line, the number of universities increased from seventy-four to the present 114 and, together with more than fifty other higher education colleges, they are administered and funded in a single higher education sector. At the same time, separate funding councils for higher education were created in England, Scotland and Wales. To ensure 'fair competition' across territorial boundaries, the funding allocations made by each territorial Secretary of State were to reflect the general policy of the Westminster government, subject to adjustments for particular circumstances, such as the different structure and duration of degree courses in Scotland. Over and above these territorial arrangements, the funding councils were required to collaborate in the assessment of quality for both teaching and research 'so as to achieve UK-wide standards'.

When, at the end of the 1990s, devolved administrations were established in Scotland, Wales and Northern Ireland, the funds for higher education were channelled through the relevant minister in each jurisdiction. Subject review, institutional audit and research assessment remained a UK-wide responsibility, albeit with country variations in respect of how the inspection of courses and institutions was conducted. The periodic assessment of research is an exercise conducted jointly by the funding councils, with the same rules applied to all higher education establishments in the UK. Unlike the grading of teaching, the ratings given for research have major implications for the volume and distribution of institutional funding, with each funding council deciding how to reward the performance of its own universities and colleges. This side of the dual support system for research is complemented by UK-wide arrangements for the award of grants on a competitive basis for specific projects approved by the research councils.

The concentration of research funding on a small number of research-intensive 'old' universities, together with the publication of teaching and research assessment scores for individual departments and institutions, have become increasingly important in student (and parent) decisions about where to apply for courses, at undergraduate and postgraduate levels. Students, as customers and consumers, now have a wide range of information to guide their choices, some of which is regularly used by national newspapers to construct league tables.

Like the quality regimes introduced to monitor teaching and research, the admission arrangements for full-time undergraduate education are another UK-wide system little disturbed, as yet, by the processes of devolution in Scotland, Wales and Northern Ireland. More than that, these arrangements have their origin in the small university system of the 1960s and they have continued, with only minor modifications, into the post-binary, mass era. Its principles and processes convey key messages about the relative positions of students and providers in the access system as well as the status and selectivity of different courses and institutions.

First, and pivotally, the decision about which individual to admit to a course is a matter for the institution. In the British system, the student has no right of access to higher education. Rather, each and every applicant must provide evidence of eligibility for admission. Through the centralised admissions service operated on behalf of the universities and colleges (Universities and Colleges Admissions – UCAS), students can apply for entry to named courses at establishments of higher education anywhere in the United Kingdom. Except in a few subjects, up to six courses can be chosen. Where previously these were ranked in order of preference by the applicant, each is now considered on equal terms and without the course provider knowing which other programmes and institutions have been chosen.

Application forms include information about past and forthcoming examinations, and a personal statement. For students taking qualifying examinations or completing qualifying programmes, the school or college will usually supply references and predict the likely grades and perform-ance of candidates. In their turn, universities and colleges will reject appli-cations or offer places to individual students based on the general and specific requirements for each course. These standard requirements (and their equivalents) are published by the central admissions body. Over time, institutions have come to recognise a wider set of entry routes and the application form has been revised to accommodate 'non-standard' qualifications and other forms of experience.

Second, the offer of a place is normally made before the results of exami-nations are known. For the majority of young people, the offer is condi-tional upon the achievement of specified grades in the main upper secondary qualifications undertaken in schools or further education institu-tions: the A-level examinations sat by eighteen-year-olds in England, Wales and Northern Ireland; and the Higher examinations sat by seventeen- and eighteen-year-olds in Scotland. Both are long-standing qualifications and both have been the object of recent reform. A-level qualifications (including the Advanced Subsidiary), together with advanced general vocational quali-fications and occupationally specific vocational qualifications, represent three qualification tracks available to young people. By contrast, Higher qualifications (including the Advanced Higher) are part of a unified and uni-tised system spanning academic and vocational studies.

Whatever the scope of their reform, the A-level and Higher qualifica-tions remain the dominant pathways into higher education: the A-level track providing a specialist subject preparation for the three-year (some-times four-year) degree in the English, Welsh and Northern Irish systems; and the Higher offering a broader pattern of studies consistent with entry to the Scottish four-year degree. In Scotland, undergraduate programmes are offered both on a three-year basis, leading to a general degree, and on a four-year basis, leading to an honours degree. One consequence of these different qualification frameworks and degree structures is that Scottish students have the opportunity to enter higher education one year earlier than their counterparts in other parts of the UK.

A third feature of this elaborate system is that decisions about which applications to accept are still largely undertaken by academic staff who teach on the courses concerned. Moreover, in their role as admissions tutors these gatekeepers have the discretion to vary the offer they make to individual students. Although the interviewing of applicants is less common under mass conditions, some institutions and some courses will do this more than others. At some of the most selective institutions, the admissions procedure might include interviews and additional assess-ments.

In an earlier period, the conduct of interviews and the range of offers made to candidates were aspects of the private life of higher education. Today, they are frequently the target of high-profile media stories, especially when schools, parents or politicians report examples of 'unfairness'. In 2003, one 'selecting' university (Bristol) was threatened with a boycott by the leading private schools following allegations that applicants from state schools were treated more favourably than those from fee-paying establishments. The practices of some 'recruiting' universities have also attracted publicity, especially those institutions enrolling large numbers of their students during 'clearing': the late stage in the admissions process when students who have not met the conditions of an offer can apply for unfilled places on other courses.

A fourth and final feature of the central admissions system is its exclusive focus on full-time undergraduate education, not just the Bachelors degree but two-year short-cycle vocational qualifications such as the higher national diploma and the newly created 'Foundation degree'. However, entry to the higher national certificate, which in Scotland is a one-year full-time qualification, is only marginally included in the national admissions arrangements. Since higher diplomas and certificates are offered predominantly by further education colleges in Scotland, and because many such courses recruit locally and regionally, few colleges have chosen to join the national admissions scheme. This is also the situation in England, Wales and Northern Ireland, although in these countries such qualifications are also provided in sizeable numbers by higher education establishments and, for this reason, come within the central machinery for admissions.

Admission to part-time higher education, along with postgraduate education, is by direct application to the institution. Although the distinction between full-time and part-time higher education has begun to blur or break down, largely as a result of more flexible modes of study and the need for many fee-paying full-time students to combine academic study with part-time employment, the role and reach of the UK-wide admissions system is a reminder of two enduring features of higher education as a whole: the primacy of the full-time first degree; and the mobility of students in search of this qualification.

Territorial patterns and cross-border flows

For all the growth and greater accessibility achieved over the last fifteen years, the core territory of British higher education and the focal point for its access debates and struggles is still the full-time honours degree. In the UK, the Bachelors degree is the first degree and it is studied mostly on a full-time basis. It is the main qualification taught at nearly all higher education establishments, the source of the strongest demand from students and, at the undergraduate level, the most selective part of the system. Access to postgraduate education, whether for taught (mainly Masters) or for research (mainly Doctoral) degrees, has normally required the completion of a first degree, often at a specified level. Since only a minority of undergraduate students proceed directly to postgraduate education on graduation, entry to higher degree programmes has not attracted the interest reserved for admission to the first degree.

Similarly, access to courses offering qualifications below the level of the first degree has rarely featured in media reporting or mainstream policy development. These courses do not carry the title of degree and, in the English-cum-British manner, they do not share its status. As such, they find themselves styled variously as 'non-degree', 'sub-degree' or 'other undergraduate' programmes. Their vocational orientation, their shorter duration, their lower entry requirements, and their frequent location in further education colleges have reinforced a view – in some quarters – about their lower standing. In England, in particular, vocationally-oriented sub-degree courses might be well-regarded by individual employers but find themselves displaced or disregarded in the larger competition for undergraduate places.

Nevertheless, these programmes have long provided an access and second-chance route into higher education for local students, especially those holding non-traditional qualifications. In earlier years, the higher national diploma and certificate were free-standing awards serving local, regional and, sometimes, national labour markets. Today, these same courses function as both end-qualifications and staged-awards, with an increasing number of students completing their studies at degree level. Since 2001, a new short-cycle, work-focused qualification has begun to augment and replace some of this provision in England and Wales. The Foundation degree is the first major addition to British higher education qualifications since the invention of the Diploma of Higher Education in 1970s. It is also the first qualification of this kind to be designated a 'degree'.

Whatever else it signalled, the designation was testimony to the hegemony and continuing popularity of full-time first degree in a mass system. Notwithstanding the decline in the value of maintenance grants during the 1980s, their gradual replacement by loans after 1990 and, more recently, the introduction of fees for full-time undergraduate education, the attractiveness of the first degree has not diminished. Across the whole of higher education in the UK, including the Open University, more than half of the student population – over one million students – are currently engaged in studies leading to the first degree. At the undergraduate levels, those studying for the first degree account for four out of five enrolled, the vast majority taught as full-time students in establishments of higher education (Table 9.1).

However, there are variations in the size and shape of higher education in the four countries, with important consequences for patterns of access and movements of students. The English system is by far the largest, enrolling close to 80 per cent of the UK student population in its eighty-eight universities, forty-three higher education colleges, and over 300 further education colleges offering courses of higher education. Scottish institutions, on the other hand, recruit around one in seven of this total,

Table 9.1 Students undertaking higher education and higher level qualifications by country, type of institution and qualification aim, 2000–01 (thousands)

	England	Scotland	Wales	Northern Ireland	United Kingdom
Higher education institutions					
Postgraduate	290.0	47.3	18.4	8.6	364.3
First degree	761.9	113.7	54.0	26.8	956.4
Other undergraduate	275.5	28.9	21.2	7.5	333.1
Total	1,327.4	190.0	93.6	42.8	1,653.8
Further education colleges					
Postgraduate	8.0	0.5	0.8	0.1	9.4
First degree	24.9	2.3	0.6	0.8	28.6
Other undergraduate	154.4	70.1	7.5	11.1	243.1
Total	187.3	72.9	8.9	12.0	281.1
Open University					
Postgraduate	16.1	1.5	0.6	0.6	18.8
Undergraduate	139.2	12.3	5.0	3.3	159.8
Total	155.3	13.8	5.7	3.9	178.7
All institutions	*1,670.0*	*276.7*	*108.1*	*58.7*	*2,113.5*

Sources: Education and Learning Wales, Further Education Funding Council, Higher Education Funding Council for England, Higher Education Statistics Agency, Open University and Scottish Executive.

Notes
Figures for further education colleges in England and Wales include students registered in higher education institutions but taught in further education colleges (franchise students). The numbers of franchise students in Scotland and Northern Ireland are small and not collected by the relevant national bodies.
Qualification aims include students studying for institutional credit and higher level vocational qualifications.

and those in Wales (5 per cent) and Northern Ireland (3 per cent) take a smaller share. These proportions hardly change if students studying at a distance with the Open University are included. Although most, if not all, universities draw students from different parts of the United Kingdom, the Open University has regional offices in each of the four countries and can claim to be called a national university. In terms of access, it is still the only higher education institution in the British system to operate a policy of open entry to all its undergraduate programmes.

The scale of provision in each country is a key element in the access equation, especially if students are unable to study in their home country or where the cross-border movement of students is likely to affect the social class profile of institutions. Whether by choice or constraint, the most mobile category of students are those on full-time first degree programmes. The rates and directions of exchange between the four countries differ widely (Table 9.2), and not always to the advantage of the access and equity ambitions of the sender or receiver country.

This is uniquely so in Northern Ireland where, by the 1990s, approximately one-third of entrants came from working-class backgrounds and where the high rate of participation in higher education in that country was achieved by large numbers leaving to study in Scotland and England (as well as the Republic of Ireland). Compared to England, Scotland and Wales, access to undergraduate education is severely constricted by an under-supply of places. The result has been increasing pressure on available places at the two Northern Irish universities and a driving-up of

Table 9.2 Full-time higher education students in establishments of higher education in United Kingdom by country of domicile, 2000–01 (thousands)

	Total	Percentage
English higher education institutions		
England	816.1	80
Scotland	7.7	1
Wales	20.6	2
Northern Ireland	7.0	1
EU	65.9	6
Non-EU overseas	97.6	10
Total	1,014.9	100
Scottish higher education institutions		
Scotland	95.1	71
England	17.0	13
Wales	0.5	0
Northern Ireland	5.5	4
EU	7.2	5
Non-EU overseas	8.8	7
Total	134.1	100
Welsh higher education institutions		
Wales	31.9	47
England	26.9	40
Scotland	0.3	0
Northern Ireland	0.4	1
EU	4.3	6
Non-EU overseas	3.8	6
Total	67.7	100
Northern Irish higher education institutions		
Northern Ireland	26.7	89
England		
Scotland		
Wales		
EU	2.5	8
Non-EU overseas	0.9	3
Total	30.1	100

Source: Higher Education Statistics Agency.

Note
Excludes unknown, Channel Islands and Isle of Man.

A-level entry requirements. With many students forced to leave the province to study elsewhere or not to study in higher education, concerns have been raised about 'the negative differential impact on students from disadvantaged backgrounds and students from the Catholic community' (Osborne, 1996; Cormack *et al.*, 1997).

The character of participation in Wales is also regarded as unique amongst the home countries. Not only do a large proportion of Welsh students register at institutions in England, but also the nine constituent colleges and universities of the University of Wales, together with the one 'new' university in Wales, serve very substantial numbers of students from England. Founded at the end of the nineteenth century as part of a wider political 'project' to assert a distinctive Welsh identity, the University of Wales developed as a national university and recruited nearly all of its students locally. By the beginning of the 1970s, this situation had reversed and the pattern of recruitment and participation had become increasingly and overwhelmingly integrated into what Rees and Istance describe as an 'England and Wales' system:

> Only during the expansion of the 1990s was there any indication that recruitment to HEIs [higher education institutions] in Wales was assuming a greater degree of 'Welshness', but with some parts of the university sector most readily associated with Welsh curriculum culture, continuing to draw only a quarter to a third of their students from Wales itself.
>
> (1997: 64)

Despite the recent trend towards a greater recruitment of Welsh students to their national system, there was little to suggest that the social class character of recruits to Welsh higher education establishments was significantly different from that of entrants to English institutions.

In Scotland, where nineteenth-century debates over the Anglicisation of universities find expression in late twentieth century worries about the rising proportion of non-Scottish students, a decline in localism has been linked in part to the relatively low and falling proportions of working-class students in the older universities. Not only were Scottish universities taking fewer school-leavers from their local region but, by the 1980s, some had also started to recruit large proportions from outside Scotland altogether. During the 1990s it had reached more than half at one of the 'ancient' universities (Edinburgh), although the proportion varied a great deal from institution to institution (Paterson, 1997).

Since most non-Scots came from England, there were then accusations that the universities were designing their first-year classes to suit entrants with A-levels, rather than for people who followed the less specialised upper secondary curriculum in Scotland. By the end of the century, the proportion of all undergraduate students from outside the UK at the thirteen Scottish universities remained at under one in ten: the same as it had been during the binary era and throughout the century. Despite the decline in choosing a local university, only around 6 to 7 per cent of entrants to full-time undergraduate courses left Scotland to study else-where and, from the 1970s onwards, 70 per cent or more of graduates who were originally from Scotland stayed in that country for their first job or for a postgraduate course. Indeed:

Scots themselves preferred to remain in their own country

and

Whatever else they may have been, the higher education institutions remained the training ground of new generations of the Scottish middle class.

(Paterson, 2003: 169)

Another probable reason for the weaker and declining representation of working-class students in the older universities was the sheer scale of higher education in the further education colleges in Scotland (Osborne, 1999). In matters of access and accessibility, the shape of provision can be as important as the size of the system. Compared to a broadly similar dis-tribution in England, Wales and Northern Ireland, Scotland is the only country where less than half of its students are enrolled at the first-degree level and where a much larger proportion (38 per cent) are taught at the other undergraduate levels. This pattern is all the more significant given the longer Scottish degree and the minor role of higher education estab-lishments in providing courses below the first degree. Northern Ireland also has more of its sub-degree higher education in the further education sector, but in Scotland this proportion is considerably higher (70 per cent) and the overall contribution of the colleges is immeasurably greater. Not only are Scottish further education colleges by far the largest providers of part-time undergraduate education, but they also account for more than one-third of the new entrants to full-time undergraduate education.

The academic and institutional division of labour accomplished in the Scottish system, whereby further education colleges have primary respons-ibility for higher diplomas or certificates and higher education institutions for first degree and postgraduate programmes, can be viewed as 'two par-allel systems of higher education' (Gallacher, 2002). Within the frame-works provided by the Scottish Qualifications Authority and its predecessor bodies, the colleges have been able to develop independently of the institutions of higher education and evolve 'a strong and distinctive tradition of higher education'. While part-time provision in colleges has remained dominant, continuing a long and well-established pattern of stu-dents studying while in employment, the more recent growth has seen a new focus on full-time courses at the higher national levels. As a result, the majority of new undergraduate level entrants to Scottish higher education now begin their studies in further education settings.

As in all regions of the UK, the opportunity to study in a college which is locally accessible is particularly important in providing a route back into education for adult students, both at the stage of initial entry to further education and then into higher level programmes. Scottish further education institutions do not just bring an older range of students into undergraduate studies than other face-to-face establishments. There is evidence as well that, compared to the higher education sector, they have been successful in attracting a much higher percentage of students from disadvantaged areas (Raab, 1998). Participation rates in the colleges for those from the most disadvantaged areas are about twice as high as those in the higher education sector and, in the Scottish system at least, the further education colleges 'appear to have a key role in widening access to higher education' (Gallacher, 2003).

Growth trajectories and the English

To an extent not found elsewhere, though creating its own tensions, the further education colleges are the main location for expansion in Scottish higher education as well as the main means of broadening its social base. In many respects, the Scottish road to mass higher education took a shape and direction that Trow, writing in the 1980s, posed for the whole of British higher education (Trow, 1987, 1989). In this scenario, the bulk of any increase in student numbers was to be taken by institutions for mass higher education that stood alongside – and connected to – the elite, selective and degree-awarding system. Such institutions, he averred, would form a 'genuine' part of higher education, accepting their role as mass institutions functioning at lower costs and lower standards, and thereby relieving pressure on the universities, polytechnics and central institutions to surrender their elite standards. How much of this applied to the Scottish case is less important here than pointing to differences in the trajectories taken by the four countries and relating these to the access debates and discourses that followed.

In proclaiming 'the limits of expansion' of British higher education, Trow was not alone in failing to give sufficient attention to the big differences that existed in the participation rates in the four territories. For most of the 1980s, the age participation index for Great Britain barely moved and showed little sign of approaching the levels associated with mass or semi-mass higher education. This arrested development was attributed by Trow to the enduring attachment and commitment to an English idea of the university and a consequent reluctance or refusal to come to terms with diversity.

However, participation levels in Scotland and Northern Ireland were much higher than in England and, at the beginning of the expansion period, these two countries already had participation rates in excess of 20 per cent (Table 9.3). By the end of the growth phase, participation levels in Scotland were 25 per cent higher than in England, with Northern Ireland and Wales located between the two. Although its increase was faster than for other territories, England was the only country not to have passed the 30 per cent mark by 1993.

The scale and rapidity of this expansion surprised most observers and, when it came, went way beyond that identified in official projections. In a break with the retrenchment policies applied under the early Thatcher governments, the White Paper of 1987 announced plans for a 'revised' policy on access to higher education and a modest increase in student numbers. Where previously a predicted fall in the size of the school-leaver population had been used to justify restraint and rationalisation, demographic decline was now a reason for permitting a measure of growth. It would also require a widening of access. Concerned to meet future requirements for highly qualified people, the White Paper expected institutions to accommodate students with a wider range of academic and practical experience than before, 'many of whom will not have the traditional qualifications for entry'. Entry requirements and procedures would need to change and institutions would have to adapt the design and teaching of their courses. On the other hand, some things were not to change:

> The Government attaches no less importance than previously to its policy of maintaining and raising standards. It believes that increased participation in higher education need not be at the expense of academic excellence; indeed the stimulus of change should help to sharpen awareness of the different types of achievement that properly form part of the output of higher education.
>
> (Department of Education and Science, 1987: 9)

Table 9.3 Age participation indices for the countries of the United Kingdom

	1989	1990	1991	1992	1993	2000
England	16	18	22	26	28	32
Scotland	23	24	28	32	35	45
Wales	19	19	21	29	32	28
Northern Ireland	24	26	28	32	33	45
Great Britain	17	19	23	28	30	33

Source: Department for Education and Skills.

Notes
The API for England is the number of English domiciled initial entrants to full-time and sandwich undergraduate higher education aged under 21 expressed as a percentage of the average number of 18- and 19-year-olds in the England population. Similarly, for Scotland, Wales and Northern Ireland.
The API for Great Britain is the number of UK domiciled initial entrants to full-time and sandwich undergraduate higher education aged under 21 expressed as a percentage of the average number of 18- and 19-year-olds in the population of Great Britain.

The decision about which individual students to admit, including discretion to modify or waive the formal entry requirements for adult applicants, remained the responsibility of individual institutions. For establishments that did not award their own degrees, this freedom was sometimes a qualified one, as when establishments were enjoined to limit the percentage of older students admitted to a course without the conventional qualifications (Council for National Academic Awards, 1983; Department of Education and Science, 1985). Access courses that prepared adults for entry to higher education were now to be recognised as a third route into higher education, alongside traditional A-level (and Higher) examinations and vocational qualifications. Nevertheless, the White Paper insisted that institutions receiving access students must select them responsibly and support them appropriately 'if risk to quality and waste of talent are to be avoided'.

The majority of young students in higher education would continue to gain entry to higher education through 'traditional sixth form examinations' and, outside Scotland, the introduction of a new examination for 16-year-olds (the General Certificate of Secondary Education, or GCSE) was expected to encourage more people to continue their education beyond the compulsory years. However, A-level examinations remained as they were, despite the major recommendations of a government-appointed inquiry to broaden their nature (Department of Education and Science, 1988). A growing number of students would also enter higher education with vocational qualifications. According to the White Paper, the particular value of these qualifications was that they helped maintain the shift in the balance of higher education provision 'towards subjects for which future employer demand is strongest – those with a technical, numerical or other vocational content'.

Rather than look to a unified system of education and training that would bridge or dissolve the divide between academic and vocational education, the government chose instead to establish a national framework of competence-based vocational qualifications and to introduce the General National Vocational Qualification (GNVQ) as a 'separate but equal' track to the A-level. Intended as a broad preparation for employment as well as a route to higher qualifications, GNVQs in England and Wales were soon dubbed 'vocational A levels', yet without the status of 'academic A-levels' and with many higher education establishments sceptical about their suitability as a preparation for undergraduate education.

By the time these new vocational qualifications found their way into further education colleges and secondary schools, participation in higher education had climbed to mass levels throughout the UK. The mainspring of this expansion was the introduction of new funding and governance arrangements and, more especially, the use of market mechanisms to expand student numbers while reducing the unit of resource. Following the Education Reform Act of 1988, new and separate higher education funding bodies were established for all the universities in the UK and for the polytechnics and higher education colleges in England. The English polytechnics and larger colleges were thereby removed from the control of local government and established as independent corporations. In their own sector and funded through their own funding council, these former local authority institutions embarked on a phase of growth that increased their share of higher education in England to more than half of the total student population.

In Wales, because the polytechnic and colleges sector of higher education was 'small', these institutions continued to be planned and developed through the Wales Advisory Body. This was the sister organisation to the National Advisory Body for Local Authority Higher Education in England, which was replaced by one of the two new funding councils for higher education. Similarly, in Scotland, the central institutions and colleges of education continued to be funded directly by the Scottish Office. Only in England did these changes impinge on the further education colleges, where some of their higher education courses were now funded through the funding council for the polytechnics and colleges sector and others remained the responsibility of the local authorities.

Territorial variations – new and old, structural and cultural – were also reflected in different levels and patterns of growth in each country (Table 9.4). Rates of increase were considerably higher in Wales and England, where total student numbers rose by 56 per cent and 47 per cent respectively, and lower in Scotland and Northern Ireland, where both rose by under 40 per cent. In all countries, institutions in the non-university sector of higher education (including those becoming universities after 1992) grew faster than the established universities. However, the gap between these two sectors was smaller in Scotland, mainly because of further education colleges securing the most rapid growth in higher education enrolments (a feature it shared with Northern Ireland). By contrast, the further education sector in England was a source of much slower growth and in Wales the numbers of college-based enrolments actually declined.

As already noted in the case of Scotland, the delivery of higher education in further education institutions can play a potentially significant role in widening access and participation, especially where provision is large and long-established. Equally important, the teaching of higher education programmes in further education colleges is a way that institutions of higher education can make some of their courses more accessible to a local or regional population. Franchising – the arrangement by which students registered in higher education establishments are taught (in whole or part) in further education colleges – pre-dated the expansion period but in England, and to a lesser degree in Wales, it proved a distinctive feature of the shift to mass higher education.

In England, it was a means by which some of the fastest-growing polytechnics were able to increase their numbers when capacity constraints

Table 9.4 Higher education students by country, type of institution (excluding Open University) and qualification aim, 1989/90–1993/94 (thousands)

	1989/90	1993/94	(% change)
England			
Higher education institutions			
UFC and former UFC	299.0	409.3	(+37)
PCFC and former PCFC	389.4	634.9	(+63)
Total	688.4	1,044.2	(+52)
Further education colleges	119.2	146.4	(+23)
All institutions	807.6	1,190.6	(+47)
Scotland			
Higher education institutions			
UFC and former UFC	52.4	68.0	(+30)
SED and former SED	46.1	64.5	(+40)
Total	98.5	132.5	(+35)
Further education colleges	33.1	47.3	(+43)
All institutions	131.6	179.7	(+37)
Wales			
Higher education institutions			
UFC and former UFC	24.6	36.4	(+48)
WAB and former WAB	21.0	36.1	(+72)
Total	45.6	72.5	(+59)
Further education colleges	1.6	1.1	(−31)
All institutions	47.2	73.6	(+56)
Northern Ireland			
Higher education institutions	23.8	32.6	(+37)
Further education colleges	3.4	5.1	(+50)
All institutions	27.3	37.7	(+38)
United Kingdom			
Higher education institutions	856.3	1,281.8	(+50)
Further education colleges	157.3	199.9	(+27)
All institutions	1,013.7	1,481.6	(+46)

Sources: Further Education Statistical Record, Scottish Office, Universities Statistical Record and Welsh Office.

Notes
Figures for franchise students were not collected for these years.
Figures for SED and former SED institutions include colleges of education.

had otherwise been reached. The further education colleges were equally keen to enter into franchise arrangements, especially if this enhanced progression opportunities for their students and diversified their sources of income. Again, it was the polytechnics rather than the universities that were most active in establishing such arrangements, with some individual polytechnics operating franchises with over twenty colleges of further education. When the Conservative government brought a halt to expansion in 1994 it was estimated that over 40,000 students in England were engaged on franchised or collaborative programmes, just over half on sub-degree courses and another third on first-degree programmes. If this number is added to the population of higher education students registered at further education colleges, then something like one in eight (13 per cent) of all higher education students in England were studying in the further education sector. Without franchising, the proportion of higher education students in English further education colleges would actually have fallen over the growth years (Parry and Thompson, 2002).

Like the competition for funded student numbers, franchising in England was a largely unplanned phenomenon, with polytechnics and further education colleges seeing financial as well as educational benefits in their partnership relationships. In Wales, on the other hand, franchising was a result of planning and funding decisions taken by the Wales Advisory Body. What looked like a decrease in numbers studying in Welsh further education colleges was offset therefore by students studying on franchise and 'outreach' schemes sponsored by the planning body.

Another distinctive feature of the English experience of mass higher education was a higher rate of participation for older entrants, across all levels of full-time higher education, including the first degree. Mainly because of the efforts of the polytechnics and higher education colleges, England was the first to record a majority of its full-time student population as 'mature', the official categorisation applied to those aged twenty-one and over. Not only did England exhibit an older age profile than in other territories, but there was also evidence to suggest that a wider range of qualifications and qualifying pathways were used to achieve admission to its first-degree programmes (Parry, 1995, 1997).

Before the take-off to growth at the end of the 1980s, many of the large urban local authorities used their control of polytechnics and further education colleges to enhance opportunities for adults to return to study and prepare for higher education. These included access courses taught in further education colleges and linked to one or more neighbouring polytechnics. In some Labour-controlled local authorities these courses were designed as positive action programmes that targeted those who had benefited least from the existing system, including women, working-class, and black and other minority ethnic groups. At a time when admission to most full-time degree courses involved a rationing of places, the guaranteed entry arrangements operated by some of the partner polytechnics provoked strong government disapproval and an accompanying 'discourse of derision' (Parry, 1996).

Access alliances of this kind were the nearest the British came to affirmative action. Always a small part of the 'second chance' provision available to adults, the discomfort and hostility they elicited were an illustration of the powerful discourses of autonomy, eligibility and selectivity governing the admissions process (Williams, 1997). They were an indication too of the worsening relationship between local and central government. When the government eventually removed the English polytechnics from the local authorities, the funding link with further education colleges and access courses was broken.

By recognising access courses as a third entry route, the government was able to bring them under the regulatory control of the central authorities. After 1989, access courses in England, Wales and Northern Ireland were validated and approved within a common framework of national recognition. In Scotland, access courses were a later development and they took a different form than elsewhere. In addition to being launched and funded nationally, they were organised through regional consortia and they drew on the modules of qualifications already offered through the Scottish vocational education system. From the beginning, the integration of this provision into 'a strong national system' was a notable feature of Scottish arrangements (Osborne and Gallacher, 1995).

The regulatory architecture for access courses was maintained as the pace of expansion accelerated, encouraging institutions to look again at the openness and flexibility of their own programmes rather than waiting for pre-higher education programmes to provide them with well-prepared students. Alongside the modularisation of their provision, one way that institutions were able to admit students with lower or different qualifications than normally required was to enrol them on sub-degree programmes run jointly with the early years of first-degree programmes, with the prospect of progression and transfer at appropriate points. In this way, short-cycle studies – provided by a higher education establishment or a further education college – came to function more and more as pathways into degree-level provision.

The capping of full-time undergraduate places from 1994 and the deepening financial crisis that followed saw some drawing-back from access and franchise arrangements. As conditions deteriorated, those institutions that had been most active in extending participation looked to the funding councils to recognise the additional costs of attracting and supporting students from non-traditional backgrounds. At the same time, the English funding council sought to develop a funding approach for the 'complex and diverse framework of relationships' that had arisen between higher education establishments and further education colleges.

High policy and political devolution

How countries responded to the arrival of mass higher education was not unrelated to the growth patterns and trajectories each had experienced. The velocity, volatility and runaway nature of English expansion, with the first degree at higher education institutions as the primary destination of 'new' students, were sources of unease and ambivalence. Concerns about quality and the spread of franchising were particularly acute in England, although these anxieties were generalised by the government for the whole system. The under-funding of expansion and the more crowded conditions for teaching and learning were shared features of the British mass system but, for the English, the idea of mass higher education and the democratisation of access it entailed were not easily accommodated. Elsewhere, arguably, the transition was less encumbered and fractured. While the democratic and national traditions represented in the Scottish and Welsh systems provided one kind of explanation, there were also specific features of their tertiary arrangements which smoothed the passage to mass levels of participation.

In Scotland, the large and leading role of the further education colleges meant that the pressure of numbers was spread across a broad range of institutions and qualifications. Furthermore, a mass level of participation had already been recorded by the time that the major expansion began and, despite a slower growth in numbers than in England, still enabled Scotland to maintain the gap in participation rates between the two countries. In Wales, where student numbers grew the fastest and where only a small part of this increase was taken by the further education colleges, the expansion was shared more evenly between the University of Wales and the local authority higher education establishments, including the one polytechnic. In contrast to the dominance of the polytechnics and higher education colleges in the English system, the university and non-university sectors in Wales and Scotland were roughly equal in their student numbers by the end of the expansion period.

In dealing with the consequences of mass expansion, Scotland and Wales already had operational experience of running a 'separate' higher education system. Following the establishment of their own higher education funding councils in 1992, both countries acquired a capacity to manage and coordinate the impact of expansion, during the final years of growth and into the period of consolidation. As Scott (1998) observed, although nationalist (or devolutionist) sentiment played little part in the 'repatriation' of the Scottish and Welsh universities, the very existence of these systems highlighted their distinctiveness and, especially in the Scottish case, 'enhanced the potential for its separate development'.

Because of the size and connective capability of their systems, Scotland and Wales have been able to embrace or at least identify with a tertiary concept of post-secondary education. Even though its higher education resembled two parallel systems, Scotland has developed its own cross-sector framework of qualifications and has unified its curriculum and assessment systems. Similarly, Wales has seen early collaboration between its higher and further education bodies in the formation of an all-Wales access unit and a credit framework for Wales. These were examples of what Griffiths (2003) has called 'policy-practice proximity': the translation of local and bottom-up initiatives into national and cross-sector developments. In both countries, the two funding bodies have joint executives and, significantly, Scotland has chosen to merge these two organisations. Prior to the suspension of the Northern Ireland assembly, a tertiary funding council had been proposed for the province, with separate standing committees for higher and further education.

The need for sector-specific funding councils in each jurisdiction was one of the many issues considered by the national committee of inquiry set up with bipartisan support to consider the future of higher education in the UK (the Dearing committee, 1996–97). Its recommendations on growth and participation, and their acceptance by a newly elected Blair government, elevated access and access-related matters into the realm of 'high' policy. Thereafter, widening participation was always 'at the heart' of its higher and further education policies for creating 'a learning society':

> The Government is committed to the principle that anyone who has the capability for higher education should have the opportunity to benefit from it and we will therefore lift the cap on student plans [sic] imposed by the last government. Our priority is to reach out and include those who have been under-represented in higher education, including young people from semi-skilled or unskilled family backgrounds and from disadvantaged localities, and people with disabilities.
>
> (Department for Education and Employment, 1998: 11)

The forms taken by these policies and the positions and priorities pursued in the four countries owed much to their individual experience of mass higher education. Where differences were most marked, as between England and Scotland, it was also because Westminster policies on higher education were strongly contested and sometimes rejected by the devolved governments elected into office for the first time in 1999.

Between the Dearing report and the 2003 White Paper on higher education, UK-wide and country policies on widening access have been elaborated along three main fronts: actions to address the under-representation and distribution of working class students; measures to alter the supply of places to steer and stimulate demand in line with the 50 per cent target; and reform of the fee and student support regimes to fund future expansion. The compatibility of these policies on the one side and their acceptability or applicability in all parts of the UK on the other have given access debates a profile and complexity not seen before in the British context.

The Dearing inquiry concluded that, while overall participation for women and most ethnic minority groups was in line with (or better than) their demographic representation, the ratio of participation between higher and lower socio-economic groups had remained largely unchanged. There were pronounced differences as well in the participation of students from different groups in different types of institution. Pre-1992 universities had a much higher proportion of students with A-level qualifications whilst mature, ethnic minority and working-class students were most likely to be found in the new universities. The inquiry wished to see the differentials between groups 'reduced significantly over the coming years'. In recommending a return to growth, priority in funding expansion was to be given to:

> those institutions which can demonstrate a commitment to widening participation, and have in place a participation strategy, a mechanism for monitoring progress, and provision for review by the governing body of achievement.
>
> (National Committee of Inquiry, 1997: 107)

As already begun in Wales, and as the English funding body had done in respect of mature and part-time students, the funding authorities were asked to allocate a funding premium for the recruitment and retention of students from disadvantaged backgrounds (as measured by geodemographic data) and for students with disabilities. The coupling of access and retention was a feature of widening participation policies in all four countries. In addition, the bodies responsible for funding further and higher education in each part of the UK were to collaborate and fund projects designed to tackle low expectations and achievement among young people and to promote progression to higher education.

The implementation of these proposals coincided with political devolution in Scotland, Wales and, for a short time, Northern Ireland. Under Scottish devolution arrangements, policy on further and higher education is made by the Scottish parliament in Edinburgh, which has powers to make and repeal laws as well as vary the basic rate of income tax by up to three pence in the pound. The Secretary of State for Scotland is a member of the UK government and the funding of the total Scottish budget is influenced by a formula (the Barnett formula) devised to share out changes in public expenditure. In Wales, the Welsh assembly in Cardiff does not have law making or tax varying powers. It has the power to make orders and regulations through secondary legislation and the Secretary of State for Wales is also a member of the Westminster government. The assembly also has the power to allocate the budget of the Welsh higher education funding council and thereby determine the total number of students and other policy priorities, including access and participation.

At the same time, legislation was enacted to establish nine regional development agencies in England. These are government-sponsored public bodies with boards that are business-led and some of which have representation from higher education. Among their core functions are exercising leadership in developing and implementing regional economic strategies and improving the skills base. Together with the sector skills councils and the local learning and skills councils, they are involved in identifying priorities for tackling 'skills gaps' at the regional level, including higher level skills (Department for Education and Skills *et al.*, 2003). Furthermore, regional elected assemblies, similar to that created for London, are to be introduced in three northern regions in England planned by 2006, subject to their approval in forthcoming referendums. Although these assemblies will have no powers over higher education, they will be expected to reinforce regional concerns about access to tertiary education for local people.

The higher education funding council responded to the emerging regional agenda in England through its encouragement of widening participation partnerships between higher education institutions, colleges and schools. The funding of collaboration at the regional and sub-regional levels has been central to its widening participation strategy and a national coordination team – Action on Access – now has responsibility for a unified outreach programme in England ('Aim Higher') targeted at the most disadvantaged areas. Some partnerships were also the result of more further education colleges being funded indirectly for their higher education courses, through franchise or consortia arrangements.

Unsurprisingly, one of the first actions of the Scottish parliament and the Welsh assembly was to set up their own policy reviews of higher education and lifelong learning. In Scotland, these reviews also built on the report of a separate Scottish committee (the Garrick committee) established within the Dearing inquiry in recognition of 'the distinctive Scottish context'. On the important matter of access and articulation arrangements between further education colleges and higher education institutions, the Garrick committee emphasised the need for progression to be 'as smooth as possible for reasons of both equity and cost-effectiveness'. The committee believed more could be done to ensure 'a better fit' and to make information about progression pathways more available to prospective students (National Committee of Inquiry, 1997a).

Like the appearance of the lifelong learning strategy for Scotland, the report on the review of Scottish higher education was published immediately after the 2003 UK White Paper (Scottish Executive, 2003a). Given the controversies surrounding the White Paper, the Scottish variant studiously avoided any response to its proposals on access and funding: 'that document now becomes part of the context of the implementation of the proposals here'. Although Scotland had a higher proportion of students coming from low participation neighbourhoods than in other parts of the UK, the proportion of these students in higher education institutions remained 'fairly static' and the number of formal articulation agreements between higher education establishments and further education colleges remained 'relatively small' (Scottish Executive, 2002).

Alongside the setting of new sector-wide targets for improvement in access from the most economically disadvantaged groups and an expectation that all higher education institutions should build links with schools and further education colleges, the review placed a strong emphasis on increasing opportunities for articulation and progression. However, Scotland was not to follow England in creating a new flagship qualification for this purpose:

There are no plans in Scotland to go down the route of Foundation Degrees. For many students HNC/Ds [higher national certificates and diplomas] will rightly remain an end in themselves. In developing more progression and articulation routes – which will be critical to opening up our HEIs to a wider mix of students – it is in the long-term interests of Scotland that we still maintain the integrity of HND/Cs and their equivalents as free-standing qualifications, characterised by a strong vocational focus.

(Scottish Executive, 2003: 35)

In Wales, on the other hand, the direction of development was likely to follow the English pattern. In the tradition of 'for Wales, see England', the decision to adopt the English prototype for the Foundation degree was taken before the Welsh Assembly came into being and was subsequently endorsed as a focus for much of the future growth in Wales. Nevertheless, like the Scottish report, the review of higher education in Wales stressed the need for more progress in widening access, given that only a quarter of its intakes to higher education establishments were from disadvantaged groups. That said, such establishments had been 'particularly successful in delivering the aims of the widening access agenda' and had 'outperformed those in England and Scotland in terms of widening access'. Underpinning this conclusion was the claim that:

Wales has traditionally displayed greater egalitarianism than most parts of the UK in respect of the extent to which its people, across all social classes, have aspired to enter higher education.

(National Assembly for Wales, 2001: 111)

Wales also committed itself to build new access routes with schools and colleges, but the most radical part of their review was directed at 'reconfiguration and collaboration' to support 'clusters' of institutions with a shared mission. Given the presence of sizeable institutions close to Wales and the disproportionately large number of small establishments in Wales, there was a need to bring together individual universities and colleges to create networks of excellence in research and teaching. Besides reconfiguration, widening participation was identified as the other key priority for higher education in Wales, although the relationship between these two objectives was less clear (Welsh Assembly Government, 2002).

In England, the success of the Foundation degree experiment is central to achieving the 50 per cent target and changing the social composition of higher education. The Dearing inquiry had dismissed suggestions for a new 'degree' but, alarmed at the weak demand for existing qualifications, the Foundation degree was subsequently created to lead the renewed expansion that both Dearing and the UK government expected to be expressed at the sub-degree levels. In a proposal that surprised some observers, the Dearing committee borrowed from the example of Scotland and recommended that priority in future growth should be accorded to further education colleges. Given the trend for students to attend institutions closer to their home and the evidence that working-class students were the least geographically mobile, the college-delivered Foundation degree was positioned to meet the requirements of both the 'access' and the 'skills' agendas.

To ensure 'employability' was inscribed into their curricula, core design features were expected of all Foundation degrees. To safeguard the 'quality' of the qualification, most further education colleges were to be funded indirectly (through franchising or consortia working) for the teaching of these degrees. This reflected the low-trust relationship between further education colleges and the government in England, as well as the continuance of sub-degree higher education in the new universities. With further education institutions accounting for around one in nine students in English higher education, the colleges had still to be accepted as normal and necessary settings for undergraduate education, even though they were now recruited to help drive the expansion to near universal participation.

Having moved to mass higher education largely by expanding the first degree, the English and Welsh were to borrow from the Scottish example if not from the work of Trow, to inform their next phase of growth. In England, in particular, the difficulties surrounding this idea, together with the disappointments experienced in trying to 'break' the traditional pattern of demand for higher education, were indicators of how uneven, uncomfortable and unfinished had been the transition to mass higher education (Parry, 2003). The Foundation degree is also one element in a larger policy push to establish 'a new vocational ladder' spanning the English compulsory and post-compulsory systems. If, in England, the access problem is still mainly a front-end question of demand, achievement and selection, then in Scotland it is also an issue of progression between the colleges and the universities, new and old. There is a risk as well that, if working-class students become the main audience for the Foundation degree, then England might follow Scotland in allowing two relatively disconnected systems to conceal new patterns of inequality in 'a new learning divide' (Morgan-Klein, 2003).

From the Dearing inquiry onwards, the policies of widening participation in all four home nations have attracted less notice than the debates and divergences that have occurred over undergraduate fees and student support. One of the major services performed for the UK government by the Dearing report was to make the 'breakthrough' on acceptance of a private contribution to the costs of full-time higher education. Rather than adopt the funding option proposed by the Dearing committee, the Blair government favoured the introduction of a flat-rate, up-front fee and the use of loans rather than grants to provide for student support.

Whereas the Dearing model was designed to be neutral in respect of future social demand for higher education, the government proposals were widely criticised as likely to depress demand and deter applications from working-class students. The immediate response of the Scottish parliament was to launch its own independent inquiry into student finance, the Cubie committee (Independent Committee of Inquiry, 1999). The Scottish government rejected the Westminster policy and, consistent with its devolved powers, adopted a graduate repayment scheme. In Wales, where no such powers were available to the assembly, the Welsh government introduced 'learning grants' to support students in higher and further education.

Seven years on, the UK government acknowledged the shortcomings in the original scheme and used its White Paper to propose a partial deregulation of fees in undergraduate education, the adoption of a graduate repayment model and the re-introduction of grants. Even more than in 1997, the new proposals have ignited passions and caused major divisions in the governing party, with issues of funding, access and equity at the centre of these arguments. In advance of the White Paper, both the Scottish and Welsh governments announced their opposition to 'top-up' fees. Their next moves will be watched with interest.

References

Admissions to Higher Education Review, *Consultation on Key Issues Relating to Fair Admissions to Higher Education* (London: Department for Education and Skills, 2003).

Bryce, T.G.K. and W.M. Humes, *Scottish Education* (Edinburgh: Edinburgh University Press, 2003).

Canning, R. and M. Cloonan, 'The "home international" comparisons of vocational qualifications', *Comparative Education*, 38, 2 (2002), pp. 189–209.

Cormack, R., A. Gallagher and R. Osborne, 'Higher education participation in Northern Ireland', *Higher Education Quarterly*, 51, 1 (1997), pp. 68–85.

Council for National Academic Awards, *Opportunities in Higher Education for Mature Students* (London: CNAA, 1983).

Daugherty, R., R. Phillips and G. Rees, *Education Policy-Making in Wales. Explorations in Devolved Governance* (Cardiff: University of Wales Press, 2000).

Department of Education and Science, *Academic Validation in Public Sector Higher Education*, Cm 9524 (London: Her Majesty's Stationery Office, 1985).

Department of Education and Science, *Higher Education. Meeting the Challenge*, Cm 114 (London: Her Majesty's Stationery Office, 1987).

Department of Education and Science, *Advancing A levels* (London: Her Majesty's Stationery Office, 1988).

Department for Education and Science, *Higher Education: A New Framework*, Cm 1541 (London: Her Majesty's Stationery Office, 1991).

Department for Education and Employment, *Higher Education for the 21st Century. Response to the Dearing Report* (London: Department for Education and Employment, 1998).

Department for Education and Skills, *The Future of Higher Education*, Cm 5735 (London: The Stationery Office, 2003).

Department for Education and Skills, Department of Trade and Industry, Department for Work and Pensions and HM Treasury, *21st Century Skills. Realising Our Potential. Individuals, Employers, Nation*, Cm 5810 (London: The Stationery Office, 2003).

Gallacher, J., 'Parallel lines? Higher education in Scotland's colleges and higher education institutions', *Scottish Affairs*, 40 (2002), pp. 123–39.

Gallacher, J., *Higher Education in Further Education Colleges. The Scottish Experience* (London: Council for Industry and Higher Education, 2003).

Griffiths, M., 'Policy-practice proximity: the scope for college-based higher education and cross-sector collaboration in Wales', *Higher Education Quarterly*, 57, 4 (2003), pp. 355–75.

Independent Committee of Inquiry into Student Finance, *Student Finance. Fairness for the Future* (Edinburgh: Independent Committee of Inquiry into Student Finance, 1999).

Morgan-Klein, B., 'Scottish higher education and the FE-HE nexus', *Higher Education Quarterly*, 57, 4 (2003), pp. 338–54.

National Assembly for Wales, *Policy Review of Higher Education* (Cardiff: National Assembly for Wales, 2001).

National Committee of Inquiry into Higher Education, *Higher Education in the Learning Society. Main Report* (London: National Committee of Inquiry into Higher Education, 1997).

National Committee of Inquiry into Higher Education, *Higher Education in the Learning Society. Report of the Scottish Committee* (London: National Committee of Inquiry into Higher Education, 1997a).

Osborne, M. and J. Gallacher, 'Scotland', in P. Davies (ed.) *Adults in Higher Education. International Perspectives in Access and Participation* (London: Jessica Kingsley Publishers, 1995), pp. 224–51.

Osborne, R.D., *Higher Education in Ireland. North and South* (London: Jessica Kingsley Publications, 1996).

Osborne, R.D., 'Wider access in Scotland?', *Scottish Affairs*, 26 (1999), pp. 36–46.

Parry, G., 'England, Wales and Northern Ireland', in P. Davies (ed.) *Adults in Higher Education. International Perspectives in Access and Participation* (London: Jessica Kingsley Publishers, 1995), pp. 102–33.

Parry, G., 'Access education 1973–1994: from second chance to third wave', *Journal of Access Studies*, 11, 1 (1996), pp. 10–33.

Parry, G., 'Patterns of participation in higher education in England: a statistical summary and commentary', *Higher Education Quarterly*, 51, 1 (1997), pp. 6–28.

Parry, G., 'Mass higher education and the English: wherein the colleges?', *Higher Education Quarterly*, 57, 4 (2003), pp. 308–37.

Parry, G. and A. Thompson, *Closer by Degrees. The Past, Present and Future of Higher Education in Further Education Colleges* (London: Learning and Skills Development Agency, 2002).

Paterson, L., 'Trends in higher education participation in Scotland', *Higher Education Quarterly*, 51, 1 (1997), pp. 29–48.

Paterson, L., *Scottish Education in the Twentieth Century* (Edinburgh: Edinburgh University Press, 2003).

Raab, G., *Participation in Higher Education in Scotland* (Edinburgh: Scottish Higher Education Funding Council, 1998).

Raffe, D., 'Does learning begin at home? The use of 'home international' comparisons in UK policy-making', *Journal of Education Policy*, 13 (1998), pp. 591–602.

Raffe, D., 'Investigating the education systems of the United Kingdom', in D. Phillips (ed.) *The Education Systems of the United Kingdom* (Wallingford: Symposium Books, 2000), pp. 9–28.

Raffe, D., K. Brannen, L. Croxford and C. Martin, 'Comparing England, Scotland, Wales and Northern Ireland: the case for 'home internationals' in comparative research', *Comparative Education*, 35, 1 (1999), pp. 9–25.

Rees, G. and D. Istance, 'Higher education in Wales: the (re)emergence of a national system?', *Higher Education Quarterly*, 51, 1 (1997), pp. 49–67.

Scott, P., *The Meanings of Mass Higher Education* (Buckingham: Open University Press and Society for Research into Higher Education, 1995).

Scott, P., 'The higher education system that Scotland needs', *Scottish Affairs*, 22 (1998), pp. 85–98.

Scottish Executive, *Shaping Our Future. Scottish Higher Education Review. Second Consultation Paper* (Edinburgh: Scottish Executive, 2002).

Scottish Executive, *A Framework for Higher Education in Scotland. Higher Education Review: Phase 2* (Edinburgh: Scottish Executive, 2003).

Scottish Executive, *Life through Learning, Learning through Life. The Lifelong Learning Strategy for Scotland* (Edinburgh: Scottish Executive, 2003a).

Trow, M., 'Problems in the Transition from Elite to Mass Higher Education', *Policies for Higher Education* (London: OECD, 1974), pp. 51–101.

Trow, M., 'Academic standards and mass higher education', *Higher Education Quarterly*, 41, 3 (1987), pp. 268–92.

Trow, M., 'The Robbins Trap: British attitudes and the limits of expansion', *Higher Education Quarterly*, 43, 1 (1989), pp. 55–75.

Watson, D., 'The Limits to Diversity', in D. Jary and M. Parker (eds) *The New Higher Education: Issues and Directions for the Post-Dearing University* (Stoke-on-Trent: Staffordshire University Press, 1998).

Welsh Assembly Government, *Reaching Higher. Higher Education and the Learning Country. A Strategy for the Higher Education Sector in Wales* (Cardiff: Welsh Assembly Government, 2002).

Williams, J. (ed.), *Negotiating Access to Higher Education. The Discourse of Selectivity and Equity* (Buckingham: Society for Research into Higher Education and Open University, 1997).

10 Access to higher education in England

Who is in control?

Ted Tapper

> Our guiding principle here is that all young persons qualified by ability and attainment to pursue a full-time course in higher education should have the opportunity to do so.
>
> (Committee on Higher Education, 1965: 49)

> Repeated studies have shown that Britain's workforce is under-educated, under-trained and under-qualified ... The case for widening access to higher education rests equally on the proposition that in the past we have failed to meet the needs of the nation, or to match the performance of our competitors, and upon the prediction that changes in society and work will in future require an increasingly higher level of initial and continuing education, if we are to achieve our national objectives and compete effectively in a learning world.
>
> (Royal Society of Arts, 1989: 14)

Introduction

The one glaring exception to the relative political obscurity of the affairs of higher education is the question of university access: who goes to university, and perhaps more significantly, who fails to win a place. Currently the issue is at the very forefront of the political agenda intimately entwined with the debate on how the costs of a university education are to be met. Historically there has been broad academic and political support for both expanding and widening access (Morgan-Klein and Murphy, 2002: 64–78). And, although there is some scepticism about the current government's pledge 'to increase participation in higher education towards 50 per cent of those aged 18–30' by 2010 (DfES, 2003: 57), and even more division on how to pay for it, the historical commitment remains substantially intact.

The question of access to higher education is not simply important in its own right, for the ramifications of expansion and greater social inclusiveness are wide-ranging. Whilst for the state the key issue may be how the costs of a mass system of education are to be underwritten, for the universities there is the question of how to manage its impact upon the teaching and learning process, and for the undergraduates how it shapes the quality of the student experience – academically, socially and culturally. To expand and diversify access to higher education means much more than offering the same product to a larger student body.

The British debate on access to higher education is in flux. Consequently it is very difficult to construct an accurate up-to-date picture of the state of play. Even if this were not so, this chapter would aspire to do more than present a descriptive overview of how access to English higher education is structured. The chapter's central goal is to place the current political struggles within the broader context of the changing relationship between the state and the universities, and in particular to evaluate their likely impact upon the role of the state in the governance of English higher education.

Undoubtedly the most developed social science understanding of the purposes of higher education (and, indeed, of education at large) is to be found within sociology. The theoretical thrust of the sociological literature is invariably based on interpretations of the part that education plays in the social reproduction process. Not surprisingly, it would be easy for an analysis of the politics of access to higher education to slip into this theoretical mould. The intention, however, is to avoid the temptation by relating the access struggles to how the system of higher education in England is governed. The question of access therefore provides an empirical focus for understanding the changing relationship between the state and the universities. It is hoped thereby to create a viable politics of education: one that looks more to the political science literature embedded in the analysis of policy networks and the new public management rather than to the macro-sociological traditions of social reproduction, ideological struggle and bureaucratisation (Archer, 1979; Deer, 2002; Salter and Tapper, 1994). In reality, of course, the intellectual division is not as sharp as implied, for much of the political debate on access has been driven by social reproduction themes: differential class patterns of access, the failure to secure equality of educational opportunity and cultural conflict.

The chapter will pursue its approach to the politics of access by organising the argument into a number of interrelated segments. First, it will analyse the main themes that have driven the political discourse whilst presenting reflectively some of the empirical evidence that has underwritten that discourse. Second, it will argue that the state's intervention has become increasingly intrusive: moving from exhortation and the offer of pragmatic assistance, through the setting of targets and the construction of incentives, and onto a more prescriptive stage marked by 'access agreements' and the definition of what constitutes good practice. The consequence is a process that places increasing pressure upon the current funding council model of governance, squeezed by a more demanding state. The politics of access is illustrative therefore of the more general turbulence in state–university relations, enhanced by the fact that who goes to university and who will pay are issues with potential electoral significance. Third, the chapter will conclude in a reflective vein: by reviewing the extent to which the analysis has aided the construction of a viable politics of education, and by outlining a scenario for the development of higher education in England that encompasses the question of access.

From elite to mass to universal participation: discourse and data

The contemporary themes in the access discourse are clearly defined and have a long pedigree. It is the current government's intention both to expand access to higher education and to take measures that ensure it is more socially diverse. Likewise, the reasons for these commitments have been well rehearsed: diversification enhances equality of opportunity as well as improving individual earning power whilst expansion strengthens Britain's knowledge-based economy within a competitive global market. Therefore, what is good for the individual is also good for the economy and society at large.

The 1960s Robbins Report, which has been widely interpreted as establishing official support for the expansion of the then elite university system, argued for 'a greatly increased stock of highly educated people' as a critical necessity 'if this country is to hold its own in the modern world' (Committee on Higher Education, 1965: 48). The recent Dearing Report, introducing the spectre of the global economy, urged support for investment in people so that the nation would be equipped 'to compete at the leading edge of economic activity'. And to galvanise us into action we were informed that, 'In the future, competitive advantage for advanced economies will lie in the quality, effectiveness and relevance of their provision for education and training, and the extent of their shared commitment to learning for life' (National Committee of Inquiry into Higher Education (NCIHE), 1997: Summary Report, 13). And one of the Prime Minister's leading academic gurus has claimed that Blair's commitment to '50 per cent participation by 2001' is more than a 'philanthropic preference' for 'the funding of schools, colleges and individuals to make it possible, are a national economic necessity' (Robertson, 19 July 2002: 12).

Perhaps the strongest political embracing of the link between economic prosperity and higher education, and more particularly to its capacity for expansion and social inclusion, is to be found in the Memoranda of Guidance that the Secretary of State issues annually to the Chairman of the Higher Education Funding Council for England. These are constant themes in the memoranda but were mostly strongly expressed in the statements issued in 2000 (29 November) and 1999 (23 November). In 2000 David Blunkett, the then Secretary of State, wrote:

In today's knowledge economy, higher education is one of the main drivers of national prosperity. This will be increasingly true as the 21st century unfolds. Higher education generates the research, knowledge and skills that underpin innovation and change in the economy and wider society.

(Department for Education and Skills, 29 November 2000: 1)

And what was the first priority of the Secretary of State?

I attach particular importance to the following: widening participation in higher education is the *main* priority and I look to the Council to help the sector work towards social inclusion both nationally and in the local community.

(Department for Education and Skills, 29 November 2000: 1 – stress added)

In the previous year's memorandum almost the precise words are used: there were references to 'developments in higher education' as the key to 'developments in the economy', with economic growth as dependent upon 'the generation and exploitation of knowledge'. And, of course, it was deemed important for higher education institutions to broaden access by recruiting more students from under-represented groups (Department for Education and Skills, 23 November 1999: 1).

Whilst socially inclusive access to higher education may serve the needs of the economy more effectively, the discourse has also incorporated the claim that individuals secure a positive economic return if they invest in education (a claim which also conveniently supports the argument that those with degrees should make a larger personal contribution to the payment of their fees!). The bald claim is evidently not as secure as its political advocates would seem to believe (Aston and Bekhradnia, 2003) but a recent OECD study shows that UK graduates gain a larger dividend than students in other OECD countries – in part a consequence of three-year degree programmes with comparatively low drop-out rates (as reported by Owen, 30 October 2002: 4). If the evidence is to be trusted, then it would suggest that middle-class students have used higher education to ensure their social class reproduction, and the longer they succeed in sustaining their disproportionate advantage the more it is a resource that works to their comparative advantage. A good reason therefore for diversifying the social pattern of access.

Although contemporarily the more prominent themes in the access discourse may be of an economic character – the need to enhance individual opportunities as well as the nation's long-term prosperity – the long-term political commitment to expanding equality of educational opportunity as a worthwhile goal in its own right should not be forgotten. The current government's advocacy of this principle establishes a politically convenient link between New Labour and the traditional Labour party. There is a certain irony in the fact that the opposition of backbench Labour Members of Parliament to the Higher Education Bill of 2004 is frequently expressed in terms that suggest top-up fees will make it more difficult for those social groups who are under-represented in higher education to gain access.

The dominant discourse has assumed a particular form but what does the evidence demonstrate? It has become fashionable to genuflect to Trow's taxonomy of elite, mass and universal access even if we are no nearer to resolving how to define the conceptual boundaries (Trow, 1974). But, regardless of what labels we may wish to use, it is evident that access to British higher education has changed dramatically, and that is not to overstate the case, in a comparatively short space of time. The Robbins Report recorded 61,000 home and overseas students in full-time education at British universities in 1924/25, a figure that had risen to 216,000 in 1962/63 (Committee on Higher Education, 1965: 69). In 1996 the Dearing Report, in the context of a total student population of some 1,650,000 (including part-time students), refers to an Age Participation Index (API – 'the principal measure of participation by the standard 18-year-old cohort') for the United Kingdom that expanded from 1.8 per cent in 1940 to 5.4 per cent by 1960 (immediately prior to the Robbins era) to 32.0 per cent by 1995 (NCIHE, 1997: Report 6, 39–40).

Before tempering somewhat the extent of this change by considering who precisely has benefited from expansion, it is informative to reflect a little upon the gross figures. The really dramatic increases in access, at least as measured by sheer numbers, are a comparatively recent occurrence: the API triples in the twenty-year period from 1940 to 1960, and more than doubles in each of the two following twenty-year periods with subsequently a more than 50 per cent increase in the years from 1990 (19.3 per cent) to 1995 (32 per cent). Although Wolf somewhat overstates the case, she expresses the point powerfully: 'The change in higher education has been dramatic and also sudden. This has been no slow, steady expansion – quite the contrary' (Wolf, 2002: 171). For Wolf it is as if the process of expansion is self-generating, once it reaches a certain speed it gains a momentum of its own:

> Rather, enrolments take-off because and when things reach a point of no return: at a certain level of participation potential students are destined – or doomed – to join in.
>
> (2002: 174)

However, the gross trend data, with the inevitable presentation of statistics at somewhat lengthy intervals, does disguise some important short-term variations. Indeed, the much-respected observer of developments in British higher education, Michael Shattock, once wrote an article on 'the *fluctuating* demand for higher education in Britain' (Shattock, 1981 – stress added). Besides the expected decline in demand during the war years there has also been the occasional loss of political nerve as well as outright opposition to growth. Thus, after rapid expansion in the first part of the 1990s, the then Conservative government used the language of 'consolidation', and an earlier Conservative Secretary of State, Sir Keith Joseph, openly questioned the worth of some degree programmes. Subsequently higher education would expand but 'the unit of resource' (the income per student that the HEIs received from the Treasury) was to be cut. Currently we are back on the expansionist track but the universities continue to plead poverty and 'the 50 per cent by 2010 goal' has generated conflict about the meaning of higher education and precisely what its value would be if such a target were to be met.

In spite of the uneven rate of expansion, and equivocation as to its merits and significance, it is impossible to deny that it has taken place. And yet scepticism remains: first, increased participation has failed to benefit all social groups equally; second, expansion has led to the creation of a hierarchical access model with the more and less privileged social groups attending different HEIs; and, third, the experience of higher education means something different from what it used to mean – to put it brutally, there has been an alleged 'dumbing down'. To interrelate the threads: it is those who come from families not traditionally encapsulated within the experience of higher education who are the biggest losers for they attend the universities and/or follow the courses with the least prestige.

The key social variables that have dominated the access debate in Britain are: social class, gender, ethnicity, schooling, mature student participation (variously defined but usually meaning those aged twenty-one and over at the point of entry) and disability. Given the paucity, as well as the unreliability, of the evidence on disability it is difficult to arrive at sensible conclusions on the inclusion or exclusion of the disabled in higher education except to say that it is now an issue on the political agenda and universities are under pressure to demonstrate that they are taking it seriously. The chapter, therefore, will offer no further reflections on this topic. Of the other variables it is 'participation by lower socio-economic groups' that has – rightly – commanded most attention. In spite of the alleged poor quality of the data (NCIHE, 1997: Report 6, 39) the research points consistently in one direction. However, because it is possible to make comparisons using different points of reference interpretations of the consistent direction soon deviate. Robertson has collated probably the best concise body of evidence. His Age Participation Index (API) reveals the percentage changes shown in Table 10.1 below.

In his commentary Robertson notes that, in spite of the increases in participation for all the socio-economic groups, the overall effect of the changes is 'to maintain nearly constant ratios of participation between

Table 10.1 API by social class[1]

Socio-economic group	1940	1960	1980	1995
l, ll, llln	8.4	26.7	33.1	45.0
lllm, IV, V	1.5	3.6	6.5	15.1
API (UK)	1.8	5.4	12.4	32.0

Source: The National Committee of Inquiry into Higher Education, 1997: Report 6, Section 1, 40.

Note
1 The data in the Dearing report covers UK higher education rather than specifically England. The limited impact this may have upon the interpretations I have made should be clear from both the text of this chapter and the previous chapter written by Professor Gareth Parry.

higher and lower socio-economic groups, by volume, at approximately 75:25 for the pre-1992 universities and 68:32 for the 1992 universities' and, with reference to a wide range of source material maintains that, 'These ratios have remained broadly unchanged over a long period'.

What the evidence on class representation demonstrates is that claims about changing class opportunities in higher education depend very much upon what are considered to be the important benchmarks. The contrasting pictures that emerge when presenting changes in terms of gross numbers, percentage increases, age participation rates or the overall social class profiles of student populations permit different evaluations. Robertson's relatively pessimistic conclusion is dependent upon comparing the class composition of undergraduate populations over time: working-class participation has increased but not as rapidly as middle-class participation and certainly not to the extent that the initial middle-class advantage has evaporated. But Robertson's own API data shows a narrowing of class differences, which has led the Higher Education Policy Institute to conclude:

> Although an oft-quoted statistic is that the gap between social classes in HE has not narrowed, the reality is that it has narrowed enormously: from the higher social groups being six times more likely to participate three decades ago to three time now.
>
> (Bekhradnia, 2003: 1)

Evidently Bekhradnia is comparing age participation rates over time as opposed to the class distribution patterns of undergraduate populations. It will be interesting to see whether working-class representation in higher education is now sufficiently large that it has reached, to quote Wolf, the point of take-off.

In terms of the other critical social variables, if one accepts the commitment that increased participation in higher education is a good thing, then it is possible to be more optimistic. The Robbins Report shows an almost unchanged representation of women in the full-time university student population from 1938/39 (23.3 per cent) to 1961/62 by when it had risen to 25.4 per cent (Committee on Higher Education, 1965: 24). Thereafter the percentage continues to rise steadily to over 50 per cent as the composite table drawn from Robertson's work for the Dearing Committee illustrates (Table 10.2).

In an interpretation of the changes, Coffield (NCIHE, 1997: Report 5) notes: the better representation of ethnic minorities in higher education than whites (although there are very significant differences between ethnic minorities – see Madood, 1993: 167–82), the equal proportions of women and men studying for first degrees (although female participation is concentrated in certain subject areas and they continue to be under-represented at the post-graduate level as well as in the academic profession), and the fact that some one-third of entrants into higher education are now older than twenty-one (although the differences between the pre- and post-1992 universities are stark).

The apparent advantages of an independent school education in securing university entry, especially entry to the elite universities and even more particularly to Oxford and Cambridge, has provided politicians, journalists and social scientists with much ammunition over the years. It is surprising, therefore, that the Dearing Committee did not consider it warranted a separate report. One can only surmise that this was too narrow an issue for the Committee to consider; a recognition of the fact that if the concern was to broaden access to higher education in Britain then it was critical to realise, in the reported words of a former Minister for Higher Education (Margaret Hodges), that 'you are *all* too elitist':

> There is an institutional elitism, which pervades the higher education system. I am not suggesting deliberate discrimination but what I think is embodied in the sector is that the criteria employed to select students deliberately exclude many young people from higher education.
>
> (as reported by Thomson and Tysome, 28 June, 2002: 1)

However, the elite universities have not been slow to recognise the pressures to which they are exposed, and politically it is always advisable

Table 10.2 Student intake by gender, age and ethnicity

	1986	*1995*
Women	42.4	51.5
Age 21+	14.5	29.0
Ethnic minorities	10.7	13.0

Source: The National Committee of Inquiry into Higher Education, 1997: Report 6, Section 1, 42.

to be ahead of the game. And Halsey and McCrum's research informs us that, at least on this front, Oxford is apparently ahead of the game: 'the deficit [that is in entry from state schools] declines from 1994–95 systematically in subsequent years. If this decline continues, the state school deficit will be eliminated by 2000–01. Good news indeed' (Halsey and McCrum, 17 November, 2000: 23).

The 'good news' of Halsey and McCrum is based on the fact that the Oxford colleges are moving rapidly towards accepting proportionate numbers of state and privately educated applicants who obtain 30 points in the A-level examinations. In other words the admissions procedures are discriminating progressively less in favour of the privately educated applicants. But if entry is to be determined by this definition of merit then for the foreseeable future there will continue to be a large wedge of privately educated students at Oxford for the simple reason that proportionately they have the better A-level scores. What Halsey and McCrum fear is the return of entrance examinations and 'psychometric tests' as part of the selection process should all Oxbridge applicants score thirty points. However, there is no evidence that interviews have to be biased against applicants from working-class families (indeed in a context that suggests it is politically correct to encourage their entry quite the reverse may be true), and whether A-levels are less class-biased than 'psychometric tests' (presumably the Scholastic Aptitude Tests – SATs – so widely employed by the elite American universities) is a moot point.

But Halsey and McCrum in fact conclude by accepting the essential marginality of schooling as an issue in the struggle to make access to higher education fairer for 'even if equalisation by A-level score is attained, the problem of a high correlation between class origin and university attendance would remain'. So we are back to the central issue of class and for politicians, journalists and social scientists alike it does not appear to be much of a step forward to replace privately educated middle-class boys with state-educated girls and boys who are also middle class (Tapper and Palfreyman, 2000: 72–95).

Therefore, the far-from-surprising conclusion is that expansion has not benefited all social groups equally but, nonetheless, it has led to a considerable change in the overall social character of the British undergraduate population. The one critical continuity is that its social class profile has to date remained relatively stable over time: whilst those from poorer families have entered higher education in increasing numbers, the participation of middle-class children, and especially of girls, has expanded at a rate to sustain their dominant representation and, importantly, this remains true even when changes in the class structure are taken into account. However, this stability should not detract from the evidence of very significant social class changes in the Age Participation Index (API) as revealed in the statistics of the Dearing Report.

There is an argument which runs that as the size of the undergraduate population has expanded and become more socially diverse, so patterns of institutional access have become more differentiated. Wolf presents data from the Universities and Colleges Admissions Service (UCAS) to illustrate the point for the 1998 first-year, full-time undergraduate cohort: the most 'exclusive' university is Cambridge recruiting 80 per cent of its undergraduates from social classes I and II, towards the middle of her list we find Leeds drawing 69 per cent of its students from the same social backgrounds, while at the bottom there is the University of Central Lancashire with 21 per cent. She concludes, 'There are no surprises. Middle-class teenagers are most over-represented in the selective universities, and least in evidence in the large-city ex-polytechnics and in the colleges of education that lack full university status' (Wolf, 2002: 213). While accepting the general thrust of Wolf's argument, some important qualifications need to be made. First, the significant comparisons are those made over time rather than at a chosen date and the question is whether these distributions have changed or remained stable. Second, what is the basis for selecting these particular institutional comparisons? The latter is an especially important consideration given the conclusion of Robertson's research for the Dearing Committee: 'Despite the significant attempts being made by the post-1992 universities to achieve higher levels of participation amongst students from lower socio-economic groups, the impact remains very modest' (NCIHE, 1997: Report 6, Section 1, 43). In other words, whilst some may be more elitist than others, 'the problem' is – to paraphrase the Minister – that across the board *nearly all* HEIs are too elitist.

But, nonetheless, in spite of these caveats, there is evidence to show that there are important differences in the social make-up of undergraduate populations. The Dearing Report reveals huge contrasts in the ages of the student population by university sector and, very significantly, many of the mature students are studying part-time: '63 per cent of first degree students studying part-time are over the age of 30' (NCIHE, 1997: Report 5, Section 3, 12). So, whilst the internal pecking order may be about class hierarchies it is also about age differentiation, part-time versus full-time study, and attending the local university rather than deciding to study away from home. Moreover, the point can be made that to describe institutions in general as elitist because they are disproportionately middle-class is to give far too much weight to broad class categories – the middle-class incorporates modesty and frugality as well as wealth and waste. Moreover, as Wolf's presentation of the evidence shows, there are clearly very different intensities of elitism, that is, some are more elitist than others!

What the differential patterns of access may be revealing is the emergence of a greater variety of university subcultures, especially if a link can be made to the degree programmes that are studied. To paraphrase Bourdieu, the universities become an increasingly significant part of the process by which different packages of cultural capital are transmitted, or more prosaically, there will be 'degrees of difference' (Bourdieu and Passeron, 1970; Ainley, 1994; Deer, 2002: 45–79). If such subcultures are emerging within and between universities, then it questions the validity of making comparisons over time – the product has so changed that we are not comparing like with like. There are two major responses to this development. First, to argue that the differentiation is a defence mechanism on the part of the established order: the most sophisticated strategy for continuing the status quo is to create alternative (and less-valued) models of the product so, whilst retaining the traditional labels, the products are acquired at HEIs with very different reputations. Second, perhaps the increasing variety within higher education may be a manifestation of the fact that it indeed encompasses a very different meaning. In other words we are not talking about mechanisms for upholding the status quo but rather we are illustrating the manner in which product and process have evolved within the universities in response to a rapidly changing societal context. Those who argue that we are experiencing more hierarchy and differentiation within the university system as the mass model of higher education develops are, therefore, simply missing the point. The mass model has to be judged in its own terms rather than by irrelevant comparisons with previous models. And note, what has status in the university and value in the marketplace is not immutable as the changing fortunes of 'theology' and 'business studies' would reveal.

The changing modes of state intervention

Certain of the sharper, and more interesting, critics of the British system of higher education have described it – with heavy irony – as our last nationalised industry. Whilst this perspective misses – purposefully – the subtlety in the state-university axis, nonetheless it is impossible to examine access to higher education in Britain without being struck by the state's current pervasive role. But this is a role that has evolved over time and, although it has become persistently more intrusive, it would be unwise to interpret its expansion as either unproblematic or inexorable. The evidence presented in this chapter has pointed to an uneven record on both expansion and the move towards greater social diversity. Therefore we need to know what further measures the current government is prepared to take to achieve its designated goals, and what impact these will have upon the governance of higher education.

Although it unduly simplifies historical reality, state intervention falls broadly into three historical stages:

1   The quiescent state: exhortation and pragmatic assistance.
2   The regulatory state: target setting and incentives.
3   The prescriptive state: defining good practice and access agreements.

The quiescent state

For much of the period (1919 to 1989) when the University Grants Committee (UGC) was responsible for distributing the Treasury's annual grant, the state occupied an essentially indirect supportive role. Indeed, it can be argued that prior to 1964 (when responsibility for the UGC was transferred from the Treasury to the then Department of Education and Science – DES), there was what can best be described as official, rather than state, pressure upon access to higher education. That pressure would be expressed by the UGC itself through its quinquennial reports on university development, and in the recommendations of officially appointed enquires of which the Robbins Committee was undoubtedly the most influential.

Certainly there was relatively consistent support for expansion and social diversification but not without a reoccurring hint of caution. For example, in its report for 1952–57 the UGC laid down three markers: expansion should not occur in those disciplines whose graduates experienced difficulties in finding satisfactory employment, additional student numbers should be matched by the requisite accommodation and equipment, and expansion should not lead to a decline in academic standards (UGC, 1958: 19–20). The Robbins Report famously promoted the idea of 'the pool of ability' and, whilst the universities had a long way to go before the pool was drained, access to higher education should be dependent upon the capacity of would-be students to meet prerequisite standards as defined by the universities (Committee on Higher Education, 1965: 49–66). Thus the universities would remain in control of the admissions process. Moreover, it can be reasonably argued that much of the interest (especially in the Robbins Report) is directed not so much at expansion and social diversity but rather at the academic balance of the student population. If higher education was to have a significant impact upon economic development, then it was recruitment to the sciences, and more especially the applied sciences, that needed to expand.

The concrete expressions of early state intervention were humble: the creation of state scholarships for the academically gifted, the instigation of grants to assist the training of worthy professionals who were in short supply (for example teachers), and selective support for those who had served their country on the battlefield – support for the talented, the worthy and the heroic. Over time the local education authorities could demonstrate their progressive leanings by offering various forms of financial support to residents lucky enough to win a place in higher education. The outcome was a patch quilt of variable support creating the impression of ad hoc responses to very specific interests and needs. They certainly do not suggest principled state support for expanding access to higher education in the name of social justice. And there was a price to be paid: in return for supporting the costs of professional training access was regulated and as student financial aid expanded so the controls on the number of would-be entrants were extended.

One of the great, if barely recognised, landmarks in the history of British higher education was the Anderson Report (Ministry of Education/Scottish Education Department, 1960), which swept away these quirky arrangements to replace them with the rationalising impulse of the central state. The consequence was that the state, with minor exceptions, committed itself to paying the fees of home-based undergraduates and supporting them with means-tested grants. Whereas the initiatives on behalf of particular interests were innocuous – costing small amounts of money, spreading goodwill, and perhaps doing some good – the acceptance of the recommendations of the Anderson Report suggests a quantum leap in government thinking about its relationship to higher education. However, the leap has to be set within its historical context. The system of higher education was small and even the expansion anticipated by the Robbins Report (which was to come later) would not jeopardise the elite model. The Anderson Report made its financial estimates and the predicted expenditure did not appear exorbitant. Clearly this was a policy initiative that the Conservative government of the day felt it could afford.

The first explanatory thrust to explaining the state's involvement is therefore essentially political in nature: a series of small measures accumulate to make the Anderson breakthrough possible, which – although driven by principle as much as by pragmatism – seemed at the time a relatively modest step. But the acceptance of the recommendations of the Anderson Report, such as the earlier forms of financial support, are essentially indirect inputs into the admissions process. Whilst restriction on the number of entrants is direct intrusion, there was no attempt to shape how universities conducted their admissions procedures, and certainly no strictures as to who should gain access. During this phase there was also considerable official support for the creation of a central admissions process that led to the formation of the Universities Central Council on Admissions (UCCA) although a central regulatory admissions framework was created, the aim was to enable the timetable to function more efficiently rather than to dictate to the institutions how they should conduct their affairs.

The regulatory state

Two critical changes mark the transition from the quiescent to the regulatory state. First, there is the change in the mode of governance. The funding councils, created by the 1988 Education Reform Act and modified by the 1992 Further and Education Act (when the funding councils for the universities, and polytechnics/colleges were combined but given separate national identities) are a manifestation of the new public management model of governance (Rhodes, 1997; Bleiklie, 1998; Marsh, 1998). Ironically, however, given the peculiar historical relationship between the state and the British universities, the consequence has been more government rowing and less steering – quite the reverse of the model's intended effect in other policy areas. The funding councils have a clear statutory basis, which bestows upon government the right to establish policy goals while requiring the funding councils to determine how these should be implemented. The role of the institutions of higher education is to fulfil the policy goals within the parameters established by the funding councils, and thus the increasing stress on the need for positive leadership and competent management.

Second, although the current system may not, in the government's judgement, be either sufficiently large or socially diverse, we have moved steadily into the age of mass higher education. Inevitably the state has sought to lessen its financial support for students: the value of maintenance grants steadily declined in real terms, students became ineligible for a range of benefits, loans replaced grants, at present most students are required to pay 'up-front' fees, and now we are moving towards 'top-up' fees, although these and other costs would be repaid after graduation as an income-contingent loan.

As the system of higher education expanded it continued to be dominated by the middle classes. So what was a relatively inexpensive measure in the context of an elite model of higher education became more costly, and it was obvious to all but the blind that the universities aided middle-class social reproduction more than working-class social mobility. State support for university students was a subsidy from the Exchequer to the middle classes and, not surprisingly, the middle classes sought to hold on to the largesse. Whilst it may be true that, 'In the medium, never mind the long term, no democratic government will hold out against the combination of voters' and potential voters' demand for higher education' (Wolf, 2002: 178), it also evident that governments are prepared to transfer the costs of expansion and risk the electorate's wrath. Muddle and timidity, borne out of the necessity to compromise politically, prevails at present but the way forward is clear.

Within the funding council model of governance the decisions on expansion and social diversification, as well as the financial support to underwrite those decisions, have been politically determined. Naturally, we have witnessed a wide input from the myriad of interests within the higher education sector intent upon shaping those decisions. Indeed, it could be fairly argued that support for expansion and social diversification originated within the sector as opposed to being imposed upon it by government. Top-up fees, however, have proven more divisive and different policy networks have sought to persuade government to arrive at decisions favourable to their own particular interests. So those responsible for delivering policy goals have also been actively engaged in policy formation.

Likewise, although there may be an analytical distinction between the strategies formulated by the funding councils to deliver policy goals and the actual implementation of those goals by the HEIs, in reality these phases of the policy-making process also interact. In response to the policy goals of expansion and diversification, the funding councils have constructed targets (so-called benchmark data) and offered incentives to secure their achievement (or, in the euphemistic words of *The Times Higher Education Supplement* they are 'being encouraged' to meet – 11 October, 2002: 3). The University of Sussex's *Widening Participation Strategy*, submitted to HEFCE in July 2001 and subsequently funded with the help of the Council's earmarked resources, is typical of many such schemes. And, in moves that seem designed to deflect such pressure, some universities have taken tentative steps in the direction of positive discrimination (although they would undoubtedly deny the appropriateness of the description). Thus institutional action anticipates the regulatory framework. Regardless of how such behaviour is interpreted, the social profiles of entrants are known, and HEFCE resources are available to universities prepared to set up schemes designed to move the statistics in the 'correct' direction, and to reward with additional teaching income the recruitment of the 'desired' students. Moreover, the universities have little choice but to be actively engaged in this process because, as the 2003 White Paper makes clear, the government expects each HEI to pursue the goal of socially diversifying its undergraduate population – to opt out is not an option (D*f*ES, 2003: 92).

The prescriptive state?

Historically the British universities have been described as independent corporate bodies managing their affairs without external interference and determining their own futures. 'University autonomy' is probably the most commonly used phrase in any description of British higher education. And yet the instigation of the regulatory state in the form of the funding council model of governance demonstrates that there are boundaries to autonomy, which can become especially pressing when there are clear and persistent government policy goals.

The rise of the regulatory state raises the question of how the boundary between regulation and control is to be determined. Whilst it is evident that to date there has been no attempt to require the universities to construct their admissions procedures on the basis of prescribed regulations, it is equally evident that no matter how they conduct their affairs they are nonetheless meant to fulfil politically determined policy goals. In effect the state is defining the end (an access profile that is to move in a particular direction) if not the means for achieving it. But there are clear indications that the present government is steadily bearing down upon the means, and in the process further eroding the boundary between regulation and control.

The White Paper presented in 2003 outlined government proposals to appoint an Access Regulator (D*f*ES, 2003: 75), and the 2004 Higher Education Act contains a clause to create a Director of Fair Access to Higher Education who will head up the proposed Office For Fair Access (OFFA) to be located in, but not fully incorporated into, HEFCE. The precise form these proposals will take has been subject to a review by Steven Schwartz, the Vice-chancellor of the University of Brunel and, although the proposals have yet to be implemented, OFFA is to have two central functions:

1   To persuade institutions to adopt the consensus developed by the Schwartz Review 'on the legitimacy of a range of measures which can be used in assessing applicants and identifying a set of underlying principles that will promote fair and transparent admissions processes at English HEIs' (Admissions to Higher Education Steering Group, September 2003: paragraph 7).
2   To negotiate Access Agreements with institutions that intend to charge variable fees (within the cap of £3,000 per annum, and to monitor how they are functioning in the knowledge that approval to charge variable fees could be withdrawn or financial penalties imposed should there be breaches of the Agreements (D*f*ES, 2003: 75).

In view of the fact that the right to charge variable fees is to be linked to the successful negotiation of Access Agreements, it is difficult not to come to the conclusion that the government is employing a financial leverage to bend the universities to its policy goals. Moreover, whilst the principles formulated by the Schwartz Review may turn out to be entirely reasonable, and broadly acceptable to the universities – after all Schwartz is a vice-chancellor and his findings will be strongly influenced by university opinion – again it is difficult to see what choice HEIs have but to go along with the recommendations. Those who resist, especially if they intend to charge variable fees, will need to be on very firm ground.

The government's tactics on securing its access policy goals pose a significant challenge to the funding council model of governance. The government is not merely defining policy goals (which, given the interactive decision-making process, draws in the higher education policy networks) but is also creating the means by which those goals are to be implemented. It is thus taking over HEFCE's role and, interestingly, the bureaucratic mechanism to implement its goals, that is OFFA, is not going to be fully integrated into the Funding Council. Thus, whilst there is frequent re-iteration of the need for imaginative university leadership and high quality management, the government is creating policy parameters that appear so restrictive as to negate the need for either leadership or quality.

It may be possible to take comfort from the fact that the interactive decision-making process is such that both policy goals and the means by which they are implemented are shaped from below as well as imposed from above. However, this is to be unduly blasé about a process that appears to be steadily moving in one direction. Moreover, the '50 per cent participation target' by 2010 has been far from universally welcomed and, furthermore, grassroots opinion is frequently divided on the key policy issues. Perhaps, more significant, is the fact that some interests are better placed to influence policy outcomes than others. On a range of higher education issues we have seen different parties mobilising their influence to shape policy goals. The funding council model of governance may incorporate a broad consultative process and distribute information far and wide, but this is not the same as saying all policy networks have equal access. What the contemporary politics of access reveals is that not only is government action threatening institutional flexibility but it is also surreptitiously undermining HEFCE's role. Are we moving from the funding council model of governance to direct political and departmental control?

An equally blasé interpretation of current events is to insist that the access guidelines to emerge from the Schwartz Review are likely to be so broad in scope and innocuous in spirit that no university could possibly object to them. Furthermore, the desire to reach amicable agreements on both the formation and the monitoring of Access Agreements is likely to be so pronounced that few, if any, problems are likely to emerge. Both these scenarios appear realistic but they do not, however, conceal the point that both changes would further erode the boundary between control and regulation in the direction of the former. Will they prove to be the thin end of a wedge?

Conclusions

Whilst there may be equivocation regarding the political drive for a '50 per cent participation rate' by 2010 (a shift towards supporting further expansion but without naming a target), the intention that all HEIs should embrace the further social diversification of their undergraduate student populations is as strong as ever. There are a number of evident links between access to higher education and social reproduction theory: the role of higher education in elite socialisation, the social stratification of access according to institutional prestige, and higher education as a social mobility route. While this chapter has at least implicitly genuflected to these themes, it has attempted to locate its analysis in a more explicitly political science context rather than base it on the broader societal implications of widening access and expanding social diversity.

Access policy reflected the characteristics of the mode of governance, as governing modes changed so the state expressed its policy goals in different forms. However, a key argument of this chapter is that the present strategies for fulfilling access policy actually threaten the current funding council model of governance – and thus policy change may be the birth pangs of a new system of government. Access has always been a critical policy issue because of its profound significance for the general character of higher education; thus this chapter enhances that significance. Although it is impossible to predict with certainty how the state and universities are to interact in the future, it is evident that by bringing access to the fore-front of the higher education policy agenda a turbulent situation has emerged. English decisions impact upon Scotland/Wales and vice versa, the proposed imposition of top-up fees threatens the government's stability and has wider electoral resonance, the policy networks scurry back and forth to protect their interests, and the funding council model creaks.

However, these contemporary political skirmishes may be camouflaging critical developments in higher education that are largely external to the political process and yet may have a greater bearing upon how the system develops, including how the issue of access is to be understood. Tradition-ally, the British system of higher education has been marked by a pyramid of prestige (Halsey, 1960–61), but we are now moving into an age of diver-sification and stratification with alternative models of the English univer-sity taking root. Institutional differentiation in access patterns appears to be emerging with respect to: social characteristics (especially age and class background), modes of entry (the traditional 'A' level route versus a variety of non-traditional routes), part-time as opposed to full-time study with obvious implications for pursuing employment whilst studying, resi-dence on campus or living at home, and – more problematically – choice of degree programme (vocational or non-vocational).

The most interesting explanations of low working-class participation in English higher education have focused upon the importance of cultural variables (Archer *et al.*, 2002, 2003). Pursuing a university education is more 'risky' for those with a working-class background: the certainties of present costs (financial, but perhaps also social and cultural) have to be weighed against the possibility of future gains (the apparent financial returns to graduates are not evenly distributed – some are bigger winners or losers than others). Whereas to date the wider post-war expansion of higher education has been only marginally and temporarily affected by government policy (the middle-class demand – which has overwhelmingly fuelled the expansion – now seems to reflect an ingrained cultural norm), it is likely that future working-class demand can be stimulated by purpose-ful state and institutional action. In concrete terms this means state action to award means-tested grants and/or exemptions from the payment of fees, and institutional action to encourage applications and provide support to maintain high retention rates (and also augmenting grants with bursaries). Already we have seen steps in this direction and it is no coincidence that the attempt to introduce top-up fees was accompanied by moves to augment financial support for the students from poorer families.

Undoubtedly this was a purposeful and successful political move designed to secure the passage of the legislation, but it is also a harbinger of the future direction of policy.

The increasing diversification and stratification within higher education can therefore be interpreted as a rational response to established cultural boundaries. Evidently, under pressure from the state, the elite universities may well broaden their social base but it would be naïve to imagine that such moves would have much of an impact upon the overall social profiles of English higher education. If this is to occur, then the changes will have to take place in other parts of the market. The issue then would be how these different segments can be linked to create a genuinely joined-up system, and whether the Californian model offers a viable prototype (Douglass, 2002).

Although this chapter has attempted to place the access debate within a relatively narrow political science context, nonetheless it important not to lose sight of the broader picture in which politics, sociology and economics interact to shape the wider role of the university. Higher education is a critical resource in the reproduction of contemporary capitalist economies, and in terms of access the key consideration is the part universities play in the enhancement of human capital: its transmission of specialised technical competence, its ability to encourage the acquisition of transferable skills and its socialisation of desirable social values. In the context of competitive economies operating within an increasingly globalised market the expansion of a pool of human capital with such qualities is clearly desirable. But it is equally important to recognise that there is a differentiated, stratified labour market. Access may be widened, the workforce may be more skilled and flexible, and some may have enhanced job opportunities but there is also the reality of stratification – something the contemporary political debate in its general trumpeting of the virtues of higher education seems to ignore.

References

Admissions to Higher Education Steering Group, *Consultation on Key Issues Relating to Fair Admissions to Higher Education* (Bristol: HEFCE, September 2003).

Ainley, P., *Degrees of Difference* (London: Lawrence and Wishart, 1994).

Archer, L., C. Leathwood and M. Hutchings, 'Higher education: a risky business' in A. Hayton and A. Paczuska (eds) *Access, Participation and Higher Education: Policy and Practice* (London: Kogan Page, 2002), pp. 106–21.

Archer, L., M. Hutchings and A. Ross, *Higher Education and Social Class: Issues of Exclusion and Inclusion* (London: Routledge/Falmer, 2003).

Archer, M.S., *The Social Origins of Educational Systems* (London: Sage, 1979).

Aston, L. and B. Bekhradnia, *Demand for Graduates: A Review of the Economic Evidence* (Oxford: Higher Education Policy Institute, 2003).

Bekhradina, B., *Widening Participation and Fair Access: An Overview of the Evidence* (Oxford: Higher Education Policy Institute, 2003).

Bleiklie, I., 'Justifying the evaluative state: new public management ideals in higher education', *European Journal of Education*, 33, 3 (1998), pp. 299–316.

Bourdieu, P. and J.-C. Passeron, *La Reproduction* (Paris: Editions de Minuit, 1970).

Committee on Higher Education (Robbins Report), *Report* (London: HMSO, 1965).

Deer, C., *Higher Education in England and France Since the 1980s* (Oxford: Symposium Books, 2002).

Department for Education and Skills, *Higher Education Funding for 2000–01 and 2001–02* (letter sent to Sir Michael Checkland, Chairman of HEFCE, 23 November, 1999).

Department for Education and Skills, *Higher Education Funding for 2001–02 and Beyond* (letter sent to Sir Michael Checkland, Chairman of HEFCE, 29 November, 2000).

Department for Education and Skills, *The Future of Higher Education* (Norwich: HMSO, 2003).

Douglass, J., *The Dynamics of Massification: A Comparative Look at Higher Education Systems in the UK and California* (Oxford: OxCHEPS, September, 2002).

Halsey, A.H., 'A pyramid of prestige', *Universities Quarterly*, 15, 4 (1960–61), pp. 341–5.

Halsey, A.H. and N.G. McCrum, 'The slow but certain arrival of equality at Oxford University', *The Times Higher Education Supplement* (17 November, 2000), pp. 22–3.

Marsh, D., *Comparing Policy Networks* (Buckingham: Open University Press, 1998).

Ministry of Education/Scottish Education Department (Anderson Report), *Grants to Students* (London: HMSO, 1960).

Modood, T., 'The number of ethnic minority students in British higher education: some grounds for optimism', *Oxford Review of Education*, 19, 2 (1993), pp. 167–82.

Morgan-Klein, B. and M. Murphy, 'Access and recruitment: institutional policy in widening participation', in P.R. Trowler (ed.) *Higher Education Policy and Institutional Change* (Buckingham: Society for Research in Higher Education/Open University Press, 2002), pp. 64–78.

National Committee of Inquiry into Higher Education (Dearing Report: Summary Reports and Reports 5 and 6), *Higher Education in the Learning Society* (Norwich: HMSO, 1997).

Owen, G., 'British graduates enjoy highest salary premium', *The Times* (30 October 2002), p. 4.

Rhodes, R., *Understanding Governance: Policy Networks, Governance, Reflexivity and Accountability* (Buckingham: Open University Press, 1997).

Robertson, D., 'A fair, flexible system is an economic necessity', *The Times Higher Education Supplement* (19 July, 2002), p. 12.

Royal Society of Arts, *Aim Higher: Widening Access to Higher Education* (RSA: London, 1989).

Salter, B. and T. Tapper, *The State and Higher Education* (Ilford: Woburn Press, 1994).

Shattock, M., 'Demography and social class: the fluctuating demand for higher education in Britain', *European Journal of Education*, 16 (1981), pp. 381–92.

Tapper, T. and D. Palfreyman, *Oxford and the Decline of the Collegiate Tradition* (Ilford: Woburn Press, 2000).

Thomson, A. and T. Tysome, 'You are all too elitist, says Hodge', *The Times Higher Education Supplement* (28 June, 2002), p. 1.

Trow, M., 'Problems in the transition from elite to mass higher education', *General Report on the Conference on Future Structures of Post-Secondary Education* (Paris: OECD, 1974) pp. 35–101.

University Grants Committee, *University Development, 1952–1957* (London: HMSO, 1958).

University of Sussex, *Widening Participation Strategy* (Falmer: University of Sussex, July 2001).

Wolf, A., *Does Education Matter?* (London: Penguin Books, 2002).

11 A transatlantic persuasion

A comparative look at America's path towards access and equity in higher education[1]

John Douglass

Among the universities of America there is none which has sprung up by itself like Bologna or Paris or El Azhar or Oxford, none founded by an Emperor like Prague, or by a Pope like Glasgow. All have been the creatures of private munificence or denominational zeal or State action. Their history is short indeed compared with that of the universities of Europe. Yet it is full of interest, for it shows a steady growth, it records many experiments, it gives valuable data for comparing the educational results of diverse systems.

(Lord James Bryce, 1891)

Throughout much of the nineteenth century, Americans looked across the Atlantic to the great universities of Europe for inspiration and ideas on institution building. A significant number of Americans gained their training under the Humboltian model. Many were influenced by the notion of broad access to citizens of appropriate talent ventured in both Germany and Scotland. The English college and the practical emphasis of the École Polytechnic in Paris also shaped America's own experiments. Another important influence was the predilections of a young nation built on the realities of a pluralistic society and a national government with few immediate financial resources – beside plenty of land. American political culture was generally fearful of central government control in the aftermath of a revolt against the British crown, deferring to states and local communities to promote education in all its forms. The response was perhaps predictable: where there once were very few institutions of higher learning, each state was generally supportive of a great diversity of institutional types. Many were the offspring of sectarian communities; others were chartered and funded by state governments as a means to educate the farmer and promote local economies.

For many of America's most eminent political leaders, higher education was also essential for the nation's professed democratic experiment. America was essentially a cultural backwater in desperate need of institutions that could create on its own learned individuals, and promote prosperity and culture. For a young nation yearning for legitimacy, and its own breed of civic participants and leaders, promoting the establishment of colleges and the emerging ideal of the university was an absolutely fundamental component for nationhood. For all these reasons and more, the United States embarked remarkably early and, eventually successfully, on the idea of promoting and creating systems of mass higher education.

In part because of America's success, Europe and many other regions of the world are now looking across the Atlantic, and in the case of Asia across the Pacific, to the United States for ideas on how to expand access to higher education in ways that fit their own political and national cultures. Most national patterns of moving towards mass higher education systems are post-Second World War phenomena, characterised by national governments attempting to transform and absorb an existing set of elite and class-oriented universities into a new and larger network of publicly funded higher education institutions.

This chapter focuses on three themes. The first theme offers a brief discussion of the political culture of the United States, the role of higher education as a key aspect of nation building, and the resulting and unique pattern of public and private colleges and universities. A second theme includes an analysis of America's contemporary diversity of institutional types, higher education participation patterns, and a comparative look at the EU with a particular focus on the UK. The United States first envisioned the idea of mass higher education, but arguably it has lost its leadership position in this creative movement. Most members of the EU have made spectacular strides towards robust mass higher education systems – particularly in recent decades – with participation rates comparable to the United States.

The third and final theme focuses on the general patterns found in building mass higher education systems. As these systems mature, issues related to expanding access to 'underserved' populations and institutional authority to set admissions policy have become an increasing focal point of debate. To varying degrees in the US and in other mature HE systems, admissions policy-making has moved from a largely internally driven academic decision to an increasingly external and politically driven process. As higher education has increased in its value as a public good vital to socio-economic mobility, creating an equitable society, and increasing national competitiveness, government and, in the case of the US, the courts have become major influences on admissions policies.

There are significant differences in the organisation of higher education (HE) sources of power and authority in the USA when compared to most of the EU. Even with these differences, however, one sees a pattern of convergence in values and in the type of initiatives intended to broaden access and to increase the participation rate of designated populations.

Notions of mass higher education

What are mass systems of higher education? A paradigm offered by Martin Trow in the early 1970s generated a simple definition based on the percentage of the 'college-aged' population (eighteen- to twenty-one-year-olds) participating in tertiary education. At that time, the idea of a mass higher education remained fixated on this traditional college age cohort. If less than 15 per cent participated, then it was elite; if some 15 to 40 per cent participated, then it was a true mass system; and if participation of the assigned cohort was over 40 per cent, then it was universal in its character – virtually open to anyone (Trow, 1974, 1981). Numerous studies in the 1970s predicted a steady progress from elite, to mass, to universal access, and with participation rates of possibly 80 per cent among the traditional college-aged cohort.

Under Trow's terms, most of the United States developed mass higher education systems by 1940, and most state systems emerged as universal access systems before 1970. A state such as California which aggressively attempted to expand access to higher education created a mass system as early as 1935, and a universal system by 1960. The UK and most other EU countries, in contrast, entered the realm of mass systems only in the 1970s. As late as 1965, EU countries had only about 10 per cent of the 18 to 21 age cohort in tertiary education (all forms).[2]

There are some problems with such figures and comparisons. Americans have always taken an expansive view of what constitutes higher education. Much of the enrolment in the USA has been in post-secondary programmes that many European countries consider more appropriate to secondary education, or that should be defined as vocational training. We will return to these caveats. Yet clearly, America has been bold in its attempt both to foster a great variety of educational institutions and to encourage participation in HE.

A further and more nuanced exploration of the character of mass systems might include other variables related to the perceived demand for higher education and its supply. On the demand side, one could weigh three general variables:

- Social and political expectations of the population.
- Perceived labour needs and other products of higher education (for example, knowledge production and societal and economic benefits of science and technology).
- Broader ideas on the role of higher education in democratic participation, self-enlightenment, opportunity and equity.

The supply side variables are rather simple – essentially the organisational structure that might meet demand: institutional infrastructure; system governance; and funding capabilities and mechanisms. In the case of the United Kingdom, for example, the intent to create a mass system arguably officially began in 1963 with the Robbins Report, which presented the case for a significant expansion of the prevailing university system. Yet this institutional infrastructure took some three decades to build. In 1963, there were only twenty-four universities in the UK, with six 'new' universities being planned. Approximately three-quarters of Britain's contemporary universities and a relatively new non-university sector have emerged over the four decades since the Robbins Report (Scott, 1995).

In a rudimentary manner, the three variables noted offer a framework for analysing the character of mass higher education systems and the match between demand and supply. To some extent, the USA has been progressive in *both* developing demand and creating the appropriate infrastructure to meet this demand. Indeed, an interesting dynamic is how much supply drives demand. Among the supply side characteristics of the US system are: a diversity of institutional types, low fees, financial aid programmes, local or regional access to colleges and universities, as well as a curricular system that enables students to accumulate course credits and allows students to matriculate between institutions in their path to a degree. Supply and some combination of the demand-side variables noted (expectations of the population, labour needs, and the political saliency of HE for promoting democracy and opportunity) are essential prerequisites for mass systems.

Political culture and higher education

America's path towards mass higher education is tied directly to debates in the mid-1800s, and rooted in a general effort to create institutions that could promote both the ideas of a participatory democracy and economic development. In 1862, in the midst of America's Civil War, a Republican-dominated Congress passed legislation presented by Senator Justin Morrill of Vermont that formed one of the great watersheds in America's history. Influenced by European models, particularly in Germany and Britain, the United States had only just begun to create free 'common schools' and secondary schools to educate the masses. In 1862, Morrill's Bill simultaneously launched a movement to create a great array of state universities intended to open their doors to all Americans. The Bill offered federal land, of which the national government had plenty, largely in the American West, to each state to be sold and placed into an endowment for the support of existing or new universities. The amount of land allocated to each state depended on the size of its population. The US constitution placed no direct responsibility on the federal government to establish and regulate education; instead, this was the responsibility of each state government. The federal government could and did, however, provide financial support primarily by dispersing land.

The Morrill Act (also known as the Agricultural College Land Grant Act) offered one of the largest allocations of federal funding to promote higher education in the history of the United States – matched closely only by the post-Sputnik infusion of funding some 100 years later. But there was a stipulation in Morrill's Bill: institutions that received the land and resulting funds needed to be more than simply versions of the great European universities – for which, in reality, America had no immediate hope or desire to replicate. They needed to be practical institutions, teaching 'applied' subjects; and they needed to be open not to an aristocratic elite, but to a broader array of American society. Without excluding 'scientific and classical studies', wrote Morrill, each college or university receiving land scrip needed to include teaching in,

> such branches of learning as are related to agriculture and mechanic arts, in such manner as the legislatures of the State may respectively prescribe, in order to promote the liberal and practical education of the industrial classes in the several pursuits and professions in life.
> (The Agricultural College Land Grant Act, 1862)

The Land Grant Act of 1862 created a demarcation in the path of America's interests and efforts in higher education. Previously, America had been through two phases in establishing colleges and a few institutions that began to call themselves universities. In the colonial period, British authorities chartered only nine colleges among the thirteen colonies. Each college was initiated and sponsored by the dominant sectarian interests in a region, intended largely to serve three general purposes: to train their clergy, to educate the state's more privileged classes and, more generally, to develop civic leaders. These colonial colleges were quasi-entities of the state in that they were created by royal decree and received some funding from colonial governments; but they were also quasi-private. Once chartered they were governed largely independently and remained tied to the sectarian interests that led to their establishment. All would eventually become fully private institutions.

Once independent of England, America's new government struggled over issues of central versus state government control and deferred in most matters to local authority. With religious pluralism a central component of the new nation's purpose, communities defined by their sectarian and ethnic characteristics established a large number of new so-called colleges (often more like secondary academies) along the eastern seaboard and mid-Atlantic states. They were autonomous entities, chartered by state governments as corporations, mostly devoid of any public funding, and all governed by independent lay boards with members drawn from local communities

Before 1862, there were a few significant efforts to create public state universities. A number of prominent statesmen, including Thomas

Jefferson and George Washington, saw a distinct path for America higher education built on the triumphs of European institutions and intellectual thinkers. Many of America's political leaders in the decades after the Revolutionary War envisioned a collection of colleges and universities as central agents of maturation for a young nation born in the glow of the enlightenment. In virtually all efforts at institution building, Europe stood as a powerful influence, good and bad. Europe was a symbol of culture and intellectual development, yet also the despised home of a repressive society built on undue privilege and inequitable power. In the struggle for independence, Americans first understood what they were against, and then more slowly what they were for.

The love–hate relationship with the Old World very much coloured the ideas of prominent American leaders such as Jefferson. In Jefferson's view and that of other national leaders, the Old World systematically used its educational institutions to maintain a corrupt social class system, justified by prevailing notions by the ruling elite of a divine order. Under this corrupt rubric, socio-economic mobility was not to be nurtured, but restrained. Influenced heavily by Europe's own critics such as Rousseau and Locke, American political leaders viewed overt control by the state, whether monarchical or otherwise, and state-sanctioned religion as the chief sources of misery, poverty and moral depravity. The net result in Europe was pent up anger and despair among the masses that, in the case of France, resulted in violent social upheaval.

Influencing the sentiments of Americans was a new sense of optimism and a belief in the human spirit. America's political leaders professed the innate goodness of humankind. America's constitution spoke of 'life, liberty, and the pursuit of happiness'. It offered the idea of the state as a catalyst for a full and meaningful life, not a Hobbsian tool of sustaining a social order. In the American view, education could perpetuate social and class distinctions, or it could break them down; colleges and universities could simply preserve knowledge, or they could be a great catalyst for new ideas and for expanding America's economic and democratic experiment. But how to promote higher education suitable to a new American nation?

Following Jefferson and Washington's failure to convince Congress to establish a national university, Jefferson put his full efforts and resources into creating the University of Virginia – a public institution established by the State of Virginia in 1819 and built on the ideals of a meritocracy. Jefferson articulated the idea that through the establishment of a comprehensive state school system stretching from the primary school to a selective university, America could create a 'natural aristocracy of talent'. While generally supportive of private institutions (he graduated from William and Mary, one of the nine royally chartered colonial colleges), Jefferson thought them incapable of meeting this larger good.

Creating supply

As the USA expanded westward and acquired new territories, state universities were established in Michigan, Wisconsin and Minnesota under the rubric of promoting the public good. The passage of the 1862 Morrill Act, however, created a fully fledged public university movement. The Act led to the establishment of some sixty-eight 'Land Grant' colleges and universities devoted to an education and research model thought suitable for a changing national economy. Some of these institutions were devoted only to agriculture and 'mechanical arts'; most developed into comprehensive universities. Particularly along the eastern seaboard and mid-Atlantic states (for example, Pennsylvania and New York), some land-grant funds went to existing private institutions. But most funds generated by the Morrill Act went to creating new public institutions. Soon many states and more overtly recognised the advantages of promoting higher education and research with practical aspects for local economies. They began to fund existing and new public universities and colleges on their own, and not simply with funds generated from the federal land grants.

The Morrill Act created a turning point, providing a grand vision of a network of publicly funded colleges and universities tied to local economies and needs. At the same time, America also had an existing and growing number of private institutions, almost all with sectarian ties, but a significant number that would eventually move towards a more secular model. The result was a diverse and growing number of HE providers and experimentation in institutional types. But it was also a network of colleges of often meagre quality and extremely low admissions requirements. Reflective of a political culture that rewarded entrepreneurialism, Americans took an expansive view of what exactly constituted a higher education. The enthusiasm for higher education created a supply of institutions and enrolment capacity that often outstripped local and regional demand.

The latent development of secondary schools in the United States, for example, created only a small supply of qualified students. Many private institutions failed and, in reality, were more often academies filling a cultural void, first by training the clergy, and increasingly by educating a small clique of gentleman and gentlewomen. American society was also dominated by an agricultural mindset that placed limited value on higher learning, particularly if it was not practical in orientation. Even state efforts to create agricultural colleges were often confronted by low enrolment. And there were also factors related to the prejudices of American society. For all the talk of the equality of humankind, almost all private institutions and many public institutions, particularly in the American south, barred entrance to African Americans. Most private institutions were open only to men, or set quotas on the number of women allowed to enrol. Until after the Second World War, almost all elite private colleges and universities along the eastern seaboard – Yale, Princeton, Columbia – had quotas to limit the number of Jewish students from immigrant families who sought entrance (Douglass, forthcoming).

Yet in contrast to Europe, American higher education was relatively more accessible to all social groups. The decentralised amalgamation of institutions led to an increasing array of post-secondary institutions that met a particular need or clientele; for instance, a growing number of women's colleges, training institutes and colleges for Afro-Americans, public universities in cities such as New York that served primarily immigrant populations, 'farmers colleges' and polytechnics focused on agricultural education, and a vast number of publicly funded normal schools trained and accredited teachers.

In Lord Bryce's 1890s tour of the USA and in his musing on American culture, he clearly saw great advantage in the nation's dizzying conglomeration of colleges and universities. The small college and the state university 'give the chance of rising in some intellectual walk of life to many' and were making it possible for many Americans to have 'the swiftest progress, and to have the brightest future'. 'The great university of the East, as well as one or two in the West', he surmised, 'are already beginning to rival the ancient universities of Europe' (Bryce, 1981: volume 2, 569).

Promoting demand

Many public universities, to encourage enrolment and their place within American society, particularly in the middle and Far West, were open to women with no quotas. Few charged tuition at their outset, and most maintained low fees. Only in the American south were African Americans or other groups formally excluded by public institutions. As part of a general scheme to promote the flow of students into higher education, many of these state universities had the responsibility of accrediting local public secondary schools to help promote the development of a college preparatory curriculum. In states such as Michigan, Wisconsin and California, students who graduated from an accredited high school with minimal performance measures were assured admission to their state university. In these and a number of other progressive states, lawmakers and educational leaders successfully created what they called a widely accessible 'educational ladder' that stretched from the common school, through the public secondary school, to the state university – a refashioning of Jefferson's ideals.

Yet one more American aberration – colleges and universities in the United States did not settle on the European model of a university course in a specific subject, leading to examination, leading to a degree. Instead the vast majority of American institutions adopted a modular course system leading to a 'major' (or field of emphasis). Students earned units of credit for courses, accumulating these credits over time until they acquired their degree. Reflecting British roots, and in particular the practice of

Scottish universities in the 1800s, the American curricular model also viewed the undergraduate experience as a period for gaining a general education first, and for finding a specialised field second.

In 1821, the University of Virginia, under the direction of Thomas Jefferson, offered the option for students to build, in effect, their own collection of courses leading to a degree. In the late 1800s, institutions such as the University of Michigan, and later Harvard, experimented more broadly with elective courses focused around the major. They each required a set of general education courses thought essential for enculturation, which were usually studied in the first two years of a four-year baccalaureate degree programme. More and more institutions drifted towards the elective model, further increasing the importance of the modular system and the accumulation of credits towards a degree. This framework created tremendous flexibility for the student: a student did not need to choose immediately a field of study upon entrance, and they might intermit for a period, or transfer their units from one institution to another. It would prove a decisive element for promoting access.

By 1900 demand for HE began to rise. Education became the anointed elixir for most of America's perceived ills and for its social and economic well-being. This was a conclusion of many political and business leaders influenced by the growing complexity of American society, including the difficulties of assimilating yet another flood of immigrants. Many educational leaders again looked across the Atlantic for inspiration, and in particular to Germany's education system, to the model of the *Gymnasium*, they attributed both the economic and military might of the nation.

British Prime Minister Tony Blair stated several years ago that he had three priorities during his tenure: Education! Education! Education! Nearly a hundred years earlier, Andrew Carnegie made almost the same statement, reflecting the clamour of a rising caste of industrialists who sought social order and trained labour through the promotion of public and private schools and universities. Carnegie exclaimed, 'Wherever we peer into the first tiny springs of the national life, how this true panacea for all the ills of the body politic bubbles forth – education, education, education.'[3] With hubris garnered by their increasing economic success, Americans prided themselves on their pragmatism. A new wave of institution building and experimentation began during the first decades of the twentieth century – particularly in the public sector. In California, ideas of expanding higher education access, while preserving the select admissions policies of the state's University of California, led to the first publicly funded network of 'junior colleges'. In this institution sprung a vehicle essential for America's brand of mass higher education.

Under legislation passed in 1907, California sanctioned local communities to use tax dollars to create these two-year colleges as extensions of local public high schools. Under a curriculum approved by the University of California faculty, the junior colleges in California offered both vocational courses and a two-year degree programme leading to the Associate of Arts (AA) which qualified a student to enter the university's sole campus at Berkeley. It was an 'open door' college, accepting all and any students for its vocational and adult-learning programmes, and providing a path for students to complete their secondary education, complete the AA, and to then matriculate onto the University of California.

Beginning in 1910, almost two new junior colleges (or what are now re-titled community colleges) were established each year up until the 1960s. Today there are some 114 colleges. The junior college model was quickly adopted by many other states, again particularly in the Mid- and Far-West, which generally lacked a sufficient supply of private institutions. In the Northeast, private institutions still dominated, and indeed their market position and political clout slowed the growth of public HE institutions.

Historical patterns of participation

Beginning in earnest in the 1930s, the junior college grew as a significant route for access to post-secondary education. Many state university campuses also grew dramatically in their enrolment size, and state governments established an increasing array of regional colleges – often solely for training teachers, and over time these expanded to provide first degrees. Even with the growth of public institutions, most students enrolled in private higher education. While significantly higher than any other nation and steadily progressing upward, participation rates in the United States remained relatively low until the immediate post-Second World War era. In 1920, for example, some 8.1 per cent of Americans in the traditional college age cohort of eighteen- to twenty-one-year-olds were in a college or a university. By 1930, that number grew to only 12.19 per cent. A year before the USA entered the Second World War, the percentage increased to 15.3; a decade later, in 1950, the number jumped to 19.27 per cent (Bureau of the US Census, 1957; US Department of Education, 2002).

The participation rate for 1950 does not fully reflect the surge in participation in the post-Second World War era. A large number of returning veterans, many over the age of twenty-one, took advantage of the GI Bill – the first large-scale financial aid programme provided by the federal government which gave grants for veterans to use at either public or private institutions. Again reflecting the assigned role of the federal government, the GI Bill gave grants directly to veterans to use for tuition and fees, and not to institutions. In many public universities between 1946 and 1950 veterans represented as much as 50 per cent of enrolment. No other nation had a similar programme.

The post-war years solidified the consensus that greater access to higher education was a key to America's professed democratic values and for promoting equity – seemingly proof of the superiority of American capitalism over the communist threat. But there was a relatively new element. Increasing access was also viewed as a pivotal ingredient for developing and maintaining the nation's technical and military superiority. In 1947, President Harry Truman established a special commission to look at issues related to higher education. The commission produced a multi-volume report entitled *Higher Education for American Democracy* concluding that 'at least 49 per cent of our population has the mental ability to complete 14 years of schooling', and that '32 per cent ... [had] the ability to complete an advanced liberal or specialised professional education'. What prevented Americans from achieving these college-going rates? The reasons were multiple: economic hardship; racial, religious and geographic barriers; and simply the lack of enrolment capacity in existing institutions. The report argued that every American should be 'enabled and encouraged to carry his education, formal and informal, as far as his native capacities permit' (President's Commission on Higher Education, 1947: Volume 1, 56–61).

Thomas R. McConnell, one of the co-authors of *Higher Education in America*, later noted that there were, 'Critics in whom the aristocratic attitude still lingered and others who feared the report's emphasis on expansion of public higher education would endanger private colleges and universities' (McConnell, 1973: 2). Not all higher education leaders thought mass higher education a good idea. What were the real benefits of a proliferation of second-rate colleges and so-called universities (a title claimed by many institutions in the absence of regulatory controls), with weak to virtually no admissions requirements, enrolling mediocre students?

The year the report was issued, the private sector of the higher education community still enrolled about half of all students in the nation – although the publics were growing fast. Pushed by the GI Bill and local demands, many states began an effort to build new campuses *and* to coordinate the growth of an expanding collection of public colleges and universities. By the 1960s, the public institutions enrolled nearly 80 per cent of all students. Participation rates for the eighteen–twenty-one age cohort climbed dramatically to a fifty state average of 30.1 per cent. However, reflecting the different approaches of the various states, some states had much higher rates of participation. For example, in California, a leader in access to higher education throughout much of the twentieth century, some 37 per cent of the eighteen–twenty-one age cohort attended a post-secondary institution (mostly the ubiquitous junior college). Nearly 55 per cent of students graduating from California's high schools went directly into higher education, while the national average was closer to 45 per cent (Douglass, 2000). Higher education participation rates would continue to grow after 1960, although after 1970 the rate of growth would slow, and in fact stabilise or even decline, if only for a time, in some states.

A key component in America's path towards mass higher education was development of multi-campus public university and college systems. California was the first to pioneer this concept when the University of California established a campus in 1919 in the growing city of Los Angeles. The invention of the junior college diverted much of the demand for higher education, but it could not satisfy it in a state constantly growing in population. By the 1930s, the Los Angeles campus (or what became known as UCLA) shared not only the same governing board and president with Berkeley, but also the same general admissions standards, regulations governing faculty hiring and promotion, and with the same role in graduate education and research. The president of the University of California successfully advocated the idea of 'One University' with potentially multiple campuses, collectively serving the needs of Californians (Douglass, 2000a).

However, the growth of public multi-campus institutions, and efforts at coordinating state systems of HE, developed mainly in the post-Second World War period – and largely to increase educational opportunity and induce cost savings. This advent often forced existing institutions under a single governing board – a board sanctioned by state governments, but respecting relatively high levels of institutional autonomy. 'The freestanding campus with its own board, its one and only president, its identifiable alumni, its faculty and student body, all in a single location, and with no coordinating council above it', stated Eugene Lee and Frank Bowen in 1971 in one of the first studies on the multi-campus systems, 'is now the exception whereas in 1945 it was the rule' (Lee and Bowen, 1971: xii). By 1971, some 40 per cent of all American HE students were in a multi-campus public institution. By the year 2000, three out of four undergraduate students in the United States were enrolled in one of some fifty public multi-campus systems dispersed among thirty-eight states (Gaither, 1999: xix).

Yet it is important to reiterate the great variety of approaches by the various states. In California, some 88 per cent of all students today are enrolled in three distinct public multi-campus systems (the University of California, the California State University, and the California Community Colleges). The vast majority of enrolled students are California residents. In a state like Massachusetts, some 55 per cent are in private institutions and a high percentage are from out of state. However, in both states, one sees a steady and similar expansion in HE participation. Figure 11.1 provides a general indicator of participation relative to population within seven major states over time. There is a relative uniform pattern of increases in participation, particularly for the period from 1918 to approximately 1968. In part this was serviced by the tremendous growth of public state universities and community colleges. Between 1920 and 1970, some 500 community colleges were established in the USA – again, concentrated largely in western states. For example, and again reflecting the dominance of private higher education in some states, New York did not establish a community college until the mid-1950s.

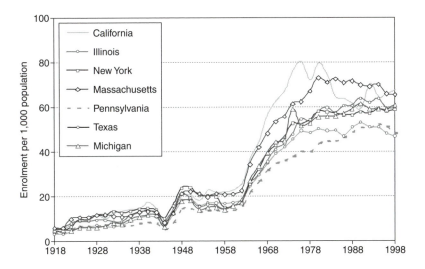

Figure 11.1 Higher education enrolment per 1,000 of population in seven major US states (source: US Census, table and data developed by author).

Contemporary patterns of participation

Arguably the advent of the junior college in the early twentieth century and the gradual development of state systems of public higher education created a turning point that converted the promise of high access into a near reality. In many states, the infrastructure of institutions and a general commitment to broad access were in place well before the Second World War. Hence, the American path was not a conversion of elite institutions into vehicles for mass higher education; rather, we see a more organic development of a great diversity of institutional types, which in essence allowed for the preservation and indeed maturation of a significant cadre of elite college and universities.

However, and as indicated in Figure 11.1, over the last several decades post-secondary participation rates among the American public have been relatively stable, particularly among the traditional age cohort. There is a need to disaggregate: while growth among eighteen- to twenty-one-year-olds is climbing only slowly, more robust growth rates are found among adults. Yet the fact that participation rates among the traditional age cohort have stabilised is an unexpected event. In the 1970s many HE scholars and analysts predicted continued growth in participation rates.

Is there a natural ceiling which will perhaps stabilise at the levels shown in Table 11.1? Or do other factors explain the American experience? For one, there have been significant demographic changes, including large increases in the number of immigrants, which have influenced college-

Table 11.1 US college going rates and young adult enrolment, selected states and national average 2000

	High School to college rate (%)	Young adult enrolment (18 to 21) (%)
North Dakota	63	43
New Jersey	54	39
Massachusetts	54	38
Nebraska	51	40
Wisconsin	46	40
Illinois	49	35
New York	44	35
Pennsylvania	43	36
California	43	38
New Hampshire	43	37
Michigan	41	40
Ohio	39	34
North Carolina	34	32
Texas	32	30
Georgia	31	26
Florida	29	30
Nevada	25	20
US average	39	32

Source: National Center for Public Policy and Higher Education, *Measuring Up 2000: The State-By-State Report Card for Higher Education,* 2000.

going rates. After 1970, US immigration laws became much less stringent. Combined with a surge of illegal immigration this has led to shifts in the demographic composition of the population, particularly in border states such as California and Texas. Some immigrant groups have fewer real and perceived opportunities and expectations of entering a post-secondary institution. Mexican immigrants and their children, for example, have extremely low high school graduation rates relative to the general population. This is reflective in some measure of cultural factors and their often high concentration in low income communities. In border states such as Florida, Texas and California, the low participation rates of the fastest growing minority group – Chicano/Latinos – is a major problem.

Economic downturns and shifts in political priorities are additional factors for explaining the general plateauing of participation rates among the younger age cohort. After years of building mass higher education systems, many states have shifted much of their energy towards other policy problems. Perhaps more importantly, government has entered an era of attempting to control or reduce government services. This shift and a number of deep recessions have contributed to a significant decline in state and federal investment in public higher education. 'State support for public higher education on a per-student basis has dropped steadily' recently lamented David Ward, President of the American Council for Education, 'and, at the federal level, there has been a dramatic shift in the emphasis from grants to loans for promoting college access. As a result, the United States has witnessed an unravelling of the successful higher education financing partnership among government, institutions, and families that has served our nation so well over the last century' (Ward, 2004: 9).

In this economic and political milieu, poverty has increased. In some states, such as California, college-going rates among students who graduate from high school and then enter a post-secondary education have declined over the past decade. In 1970, California boasted a rate of some 55 per cent of students graduating from high school going directly to tertiary education; in the year 2000 the rate was a mere 48 per cent. This has occurred within an economic environment that needs a labour pool with more post-secondary training and higher education.

In contrast, enrolment growth rates in Europe and other parts of the world have been increasing steadily, even spectacularly. Whereas higher education issues are not generally major news items, in many EU countries they garner significant national debate. European norms generally followed two stages in the movement to mass higher education, all in the post-Second World War era. In the first two decades after the War, as Guy Neave states, European governments and the higher education community engaged in a period of 'reconstruction around the time-honoured mission which, beginning with the early 19th century in the shape of the Humboldtian reforms in Prussia and the French creation of the Imperial education system, associated the university with meritocracy, with the modernisation of government, the upholding of the historic professions involved in the administration of law, health and public order' (Neave, 2002: 61).

Another stage followed, first dominated by government efforts to democratise higher education, often (as in the case of Germany) under schemes that sought to make all universities equal – in their claim on government funding, in their claim on students, in their roles in research and perhaps eventually in their prestige. Throughout the 1960s, in the United States and in much of Europe, governments sought a partnership with their respective higher education communities to build new institutions and expand access with the goal of promoting social change.

Beginning in earnest in the 1980s, on both sides of the Atlantic, that alliance between government and higher education eroded and the relationship became more combative. Governments, particularly in the EU where ministries of education wield a level of power with no American counterpart, sought large-scale increases in HE participation rates with relatively few additional resources. The Bologna process increased emphasis on higher education as a tool of economic development and competitiveness, and the persistent concern of most European countries with mitigating class differences have resulted in a surge in participation rates – particularly over the last two decades. To some extent, the higher education community in each country has been a reluctant or ambivalent partner in these government-initiated attempts to increase access. The results, however, are astounding. HE enrolment has grown by over 50 per cent in England over the past two decades, and in France by a staggering 72 per cent.

Indicative of the differences between the US and European HE markets, Figure 11.2 provides data on enrolment increases by major continents. Even with significant population growth in North America (dominated by the US), overall HE enrolment has grown by only 2.6 per cent between 1990 and 1997 – this at a time when immigration has contributed to a 11.4 per cent increase in the number of students in elementary and secondary schools. In sharp contrast, Europe has experienced an increase in HE enrolment of 15.2 per cent over this short seven-year period, while growing at only 3.1 per cent at the non-tertiary level. One sees even greater increases in Africa, Asia, and Central and South America. Such significant percentage increases in these parts of the world, however, also reflect relatively recent and large-scale increases in participation. Few regions of the world match the participation rates in the US and in the EU – although this may change shortly precisely because of government initiatives.

Many EU countries have approached the HE participation rates found in the United States or, in a few cases, have now exceeded US rates. Figure 11.3 provides recent data on HE participation rates in the United States and among a group of five OECD countries at key points in the

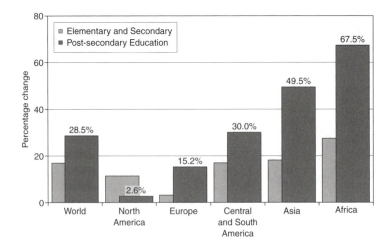

Figure 11.2 Percentage change in student enrolment by area of the world, 1999 (source: Organisation for Economic Cooperation and Development, Education at a Glance, August 2001).

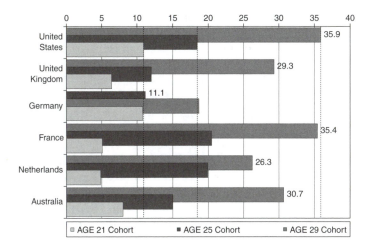

Figure 11.3 US and five comparative OECD countries – percentage change in student enrolment by area of the world, 1990–97 (source: Organisation for Economic Cooperation and Development, Education at a Glance, August 2001; US Department of Education, National Center for Education Statistics, Integrated Post-secondary Education Data System, 2002).

Note
Tertiary is defined as post-secondary in the USA, and in the UK post-sixth form, aged eighteen or older and enrolled in FE or HEI institutions.

career of an individual: at age twenty-one when most students are enrolled in a Bachelor's degree programme; age twenty-five when students are either engaged in a normal Bachelor's programme (a sizeable proportion in states like California), or in vocational training, or in graduate programmes; and at age twenty-nine, when most students are in continuing education programmes either to switch careers or to attain further accreditation and skills.

In the USA, and as noted previously, there have been only marginal increases in the participation rate of the traditional college-age cohort (age 18–21). However, this group constitutes the fastest growing cohort within most of Europe and in Australia. France now essentially equals the USA in participation among this group of its citizens, with a 35.4 per cent participation rate. At the age level of twenty-five, France and the Netherlands exceed US participation rates, and the UK matches them. At the age level of twenty-nine, Germany matches the USA. These participation rates reflect the general structure of each nation's higher education systems – for example, Germany's significant investment in the *Hochschulen* for technical and vocational education, while still maintaining a relatively small university sector.[4]

The USA has a long history of adult education and, as noted, a HE system that allows for a high degree of mobility between institutions. The ability to transfer from one institution to another creates avenues for students to enter, leave and re-enter higher education. More and more American students take advantage of this ability to transfer between institutions. An estimated 30 per cent of all students who enter tertiary education in the USA transfer at one time or another to a different institution in the course of their HE experience. This is a dynamic that, thus far, does not exist to any large degree in the EU or other OECD countries. While students under twenty-two years of age remain the largest single market in US higher education (representing approximately 55 per cent of all HE enrolment), over the last two decades the fastest growth has been among part-time students over the age of thirty years – an indicator of the essential role of lifelong learning in post-modern economies (US Department of Education, 2002). And part-time students in the USA are also becoming more common among those within the traditional college age cohort.

Figures 11.4 and 11.5 provide a summary of the range of HE institutional types in the USA and their market share in terms of the number of institutions and enrolments. Some 61 per cent of all US HE institutions are two-year colleges or technical/vocational institutions. Doctoral institutions that are 'research intensive' represent only about 7 per cent of all the institutions in the USA. Liberal arts colleges, the vast majority of which are private, represent some 14 per cent of all institutions – most of which have no graduate programmes.

While there is a great diversity of institutional types, Figure 11.4 illustrates the dominance of the public sector enrolment, with the majority of students in two-year community colleges and four-year university pro-

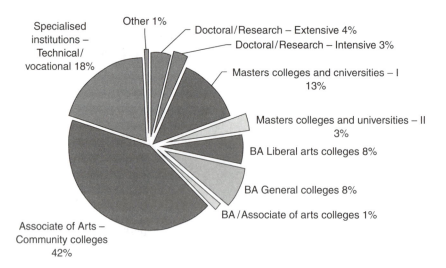

Figure 11.4 Diversity in US HE: institutional types 2002 (source: US Department of Education, National Center for Education Statistics, Integrated Post-secondary Education Data System, 2002).

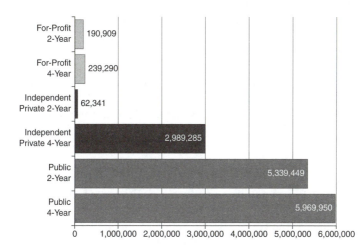

Figure 11.5 US higher education enrolment in degree granting institutions by sector, 1999 (source: US Department of Education, National Center for Education Statistics, Integrated Post-secondary Education Data System, 2002).

grammes, and moreover, approximately 76 per cent of all enrolments are in the public sector. The private or independent sector, including accredited institutions such as Stanford and Harvard and a vast array of small colleges, are focused almost exclusively on the four-year sector and enrols approximately 20 per cent of all students in the USA.

For-profit institutions with accreditation, such as the University of Phoenix, are a growing sector, yet they remain relatively small in overall enrolments when compared to the public and independent sectors. They account for only 4 per cent of all enrolment in degree granting institutions. These institutions are also largely focused on niche markets of vocational and professional programmes that are relatively low cost to operate, and for which moderate to high fees can be charged. Thus far, these providers have not significantly influenced the market for public institutions, in part because the market for educational services is growing rapidly.

There is another small but significant area of the tertiary market in the USA. These are public colleges, universities and a growing number of for-profit institutions that offer non-degree granting programmes. These providers also focus on largely vocational courses and technical training, or professional advancement programmes; for example, required continuing education programmes for accountants and lawyers.

So the USA remains a leader, if a more insecure leader, in providing higher education opportunity, and is still a high access nation. But we need to ask, access to what and with what affect on student completion rates?

Americans take an expansive view of what exactly constitutes post-secondary education. The growth of the junior college as an extension of the high school and its critical role in expanding access to a post-secondary experience typifies the American blurring of the dividing line between secondary and higher education. Shackled to the traditional notion of higher education as a form of higher and specialised learning within a university, EU member nations are only beginning to warm to this broader notion of HE. There are costs to America's approach. For one, while America boasts more than its share of the best research universities in the world, and high-quality teaching colleges (both public and private), it also includes a large number of marginal to low-quality institutions. America's broadly accessible system also suffers from high levels of attrition matched by only a few EU members. For example, France which has made HE access a 'right' under law and, as noted, has significantly increased access at levels similar to the USA, also has relatively high attrition rates.

How accessible should mass higher education systems be? There are costs and benefits to national systems with fewer or no admissions requirements. More selective systems – such as the university sector in the UK – tend to have lower attrition rates. Student graduation rates are extremely high in the UK relative to the USA and other EU countries. In addition, open access systems almost always include low fees for students or are tuition-free. There are few 'opportunity costs'. The positive aspects of high-access systems with minimal or no admissions requirements is that they create important opportunities for students to experiment and potentially to find their academic interests. Americans have long valued this role for HE, reinforced by the idea that this is when students should choose their specialist field of study.

The negative aspect is that high-access/high-attrition systems are generally financially costly. They can also have a deleterious affect on the morale of teaching staff constantly confronted by a significant portion of students who are either incapable of collegiate work or have only marginal interest in pursuing their course of study. In 1970, the Carnegie Commission on Higher Education stated its advocacy for broad access to some form of post-secondary education, but not universal access. It was a potential waste of an individual's time, and a costly and damaging approach for institutions. 'We do not believe that each young person should of necessity attend college', stated the commission. 'Many do not want and will not want to attend, and it cannot be shown that all young persons will benefit sufficiently from attendance to justify their time and expense involved'. Their suggested rule: there should be open access 'for those who want to enter institutions of higher education, are able to make reasonable progress after enrolment, and can benefit from attendance' (Carnegie Commission on Higher Education, 1970: 11). The difficulty, of course, is in judging who does have a reasonable chance of progressing and completing a degree.

Systems with high attrition rates are inherently more costly. But there is an important caveat related to America's higher education system that generally does not exist – thus far – in other national systems. As noted previously, students in the USA have the ability to step out of and back into the higher education system. Students can accumulate course credits. This supports socio-economic mobility and increases the overall efficiency of the system – if degree completion is the ultimate goal of mass higher education. Recent OECD data show that the percentage of students who ultimately receive their Bachelor's degree in the USA is among the highest in OECD countries. Some 33.2 per cent of the age cohort receive their degree at the theoretical age they are suppose to graduate (a four-year period in the USA). Finland and Norway have similar rates of graduation. The UK has the highest, at 36.8 per cent, while France (a high access nation) and Germany (a relatively low access nation) have rates of 24.9 and 16.0 respectively.

Creating opportunity: a convergence of approaches?

America and much of the EU have followed different paths in creating mass HE systems reflective of their political culture. European models remain reflective of their elite origins and the interventionist policies of national governments; American HE constitutes a vast public and private mix, including the advent of multi-campus public college and university systems.

These differences noted, there are important similarities in the goals and, increasingly, in the approaches taken by both US and EU systems to expand access – indeed, one might argue a convergence of goals and values. Over the past forty years, in both the USA and the EU, reforms and institution building have increasingly focused on general issues of providing universal access (not universal attendance) and enrolment of non-traditional populations. As these mass HE systems have matured and become more robust, the political discourse and policy-making has moved to a second stage of development: proceeding from a relatively passive to a more active effort at inclusion.

Reflecting America's political culture, in a large part influenced by the legacy of slavery and the constant influx of immigrant populations, much of the contemporary focus in the USA on HE access has revolved around issues of race and ethnicity. In contrast, mitigating economic class divisions has been and remains the major focal point of equity issues in Europe. In part because socio-economic mobility has been a basic building block of American society – indeed, a romanticised national ethos and exaggerated reality – issues of class, particularly in the post-Second World War era, have not had the same political saliency as in Europe. To a significant degree, American political culture tends to deny the reality of class divisions.

Stage 1 – building capacity and organising HE

In 1972, Sir Eric Ashby stated that HE in the United States was 'not a co-ordinated system but a constellation whose units influence one another but are not subject to any master design' (Ashby, 1973: 278–83). Ashby's observation was only a partial truth. Most states embarked on a significant and important effort to coordinate their constellation of public institutions in the post-Second World War period. Some states, notably California, had a coherent system, with mission differentiation and matriculation agreements dating back to 1907. But most states had a state university and a collection of campuses established over time with sometimes competing missions and few, if any, formal relationships with other institutions. One observer called American HE a 'happy anarchy'. But in the mid-twentieth century this began to change. In 1939, a total of thirty-three states had no state governing or advisory board to help coordinate the growing array of institutions. By 1960, all but two states had some form of a coordinating board. Some thirty-three of America's fifty states had some form of a 'superboard' – a legislatively sanctioned governing body with authority over most, if not all, public universities or colleges in the state (Douglass, 2000: 414–15).

Also in 1960, California developed its so-called 'Master Plan for Higher Education', which outlined a general strategy for preserving the state's pioneering tripartite structure of HE (a multi-campus and statewide University of California, a multi-campus regional set of four-year colleges, and local community colleges). The plan provided a guide for establishing new campuses and planning for enrolment growth. It was remarkably successful. As part of a commission studying how to expand higher education in the UK, Lord Robbins visited California in preparation for the influential 1963 report that would bear his name. During the 1960s alone, some twenty-three states emulated California's effort at creating a statewide plan – although not necessarily the particulars of California's approach towards mass HE.

These efforts at organisational reform and planning also launched new approaches to enrolment management. In California, for example, in 1964 the multi-campus University of California system established a process of 'redirection' to place all eligible students (that is, applicants with a reasonable chance to make progress and graduate) somewhere within the university's eight general campuses if they met prescribed admissions standards. The objective was to match or distribute enrolment demand to public universities and colleges where there was capacity – even if it was not the student's first choice. Similar practices have been adopted in other states. Similarly, the United Kingdom has a 'clearing' mechanism whereby students who have failed to make the grades required for entry into the university of their choice may nonetheless be offered a place at a university which makes lower demands.[5]

Whether in the USA or in the EU, governments funded the establishment of new HE institutions and attempted to encourage or impose statewide priorities and management systems. In America, this included the formation of multi-campus systems and the further development of a wide variety of HE institutional types and options for students. State governments made demands on higher education and did increase their regulatory controls, but essentially maintained the corporate structure of autonomous governing boards managing the operations and growth of public institutions. It was the higher education community, rather than government that spearheaded the movement towards mass higher education. In Britain and throughout most of the EU, government took on a more aggressive and dominant role in management, in part because there was an inadequate infrastructure to pursue mass higher education, and no existing academic culture that fully embraced the idea. The paramount value of equity to some European governments, combined with regulatory controls, dominated national HE policy-making in this initial stage. The primacy of equity, in fact, tended to force uniformity in institutional types (at least in formal government policies). Higher education remained tied to a single idea: a university education. Access to anything less was, indeed, simply a perpetuation of class divisions.

Yet in both the USA and the EU, the dominant initial effort was to create supply and to encourage demand. This included expanding enrolment capacity and providing significant subsidies for public HE institution's that either required no fees from students or, in the case of the USA, kept fees generally very low at public colleges and universities.

Stage 2 – recruiting and encouraging the disadvantaged

The 'build it and they will come' framework created opportunity, but often did not encourage participation by lower income and other socially disadvantaged groups. In the USA, the federal government again emerged as an important influence in shaping American HE. The post-Sputnik era launched a significant role for the federal government to fund research – again, not at the institutional level, but by giving grants for specific faculty-directed research projects. More importantly, in 1965 lawmakers in Washington passed legislation creating the first large-scale federal student aid programme for 'disadvantaged' students. Students from low-income families could receive grants and loans to enter a college or university and pursue a higher education degree.

The American civil rights movement also added a tremendous new consciousness of the problems of both poverty and racism. The Johnson administration signed into law the 1963 Civil Rights Act which, among many other things, formed a basis for President Lyndon Johnson's 1965 call for 'affirmative action' seeking pro-active efforts at inclusion, particularly for African Americans and the low-income population. In a speech in

1965, Johnson stated, 'You do not take a person who for years has been hobbled by chains and liberate him, bring him up to the starting line of a race and then say, You are free to compete with all the others, and still justly believe that you have been completely fair' (cited in Graham, 1990: 174).

Beginning in the 1960s in the USA, both public and many selective private colleges and universities launched a more interventionist approach intended to enrol more 'underserved' groups. This included new programmes for secondary and elementary schools oftentimes operated by HEI's with two general purposes:

1   Improvement of the college-preparatory skills of target populations.
2   Raising the expectations of prospective students and guiding them onto the HE admissions process.

The first Equal Opportunity Programmes established by many universities had these purposes, created in the immediate aftermath of the 1963 Civil Rights Act. By the 1970s, most selective colleges and universities in the USA developed affirmative action policies that extended well beyond outreach programmes into the actual process of admissions. At public as well as private institutions, alternative admissions routes emerged, centred largely on increasing enrolment of specific racial or ethnic groups. In the USA and in the UK, there has been an initial phase characterised by significant political pressure for public HEIs to increase 'under-represented' (US parlance) or 'underserved' (UK parlance) populations, yet leaving universities with substantial autonomy in altering their admissions policies to increase student diversity. This dynamic, however, is slowly changing. The focus on increasing enrolment of 'underserved' students corresponds with the politicisation of admissions issues and a broader debate regarding both the general goals and the processes related to equity. In the UK, for example, one sees an increasing array of new policy regimes established by the Department for Education and Skills and the Higher Education Funding Council for England to link funding with performance in meeting government goals for inclusion (Department for Education and Skills, 2003; Admissions to Higher Education Review, 2003; Parry and Thompson, 2002).

In England, for example, the Labour government has set a goal of increasing the participation rate of eighteen- to thirty-year-olds. This has been accompanied by a variety of incentive programmes tied to funding and a proposal for new regulatory regimes. Currently, the government plans to establish a new Office for Fair Access (OFFA) to create a policy framework for pressuring and demanding that institutions increase their representation of lower income groups. The scheme proposed by the Department for Education and Skills (*DfES*) also threatens to link government-induced targets with ministry funding – although how OFFA will actually function is still not entirely clear. Meanwhile, in the USA, the courts and public referenda are shaping admissions policies and decisions, particularly at highly selective public universities.

A challenge to affirmative action

Pro-active efforts at inclusion mark the latter stages of mature mass HE systems. Yet this progression is not without significant controversy. Americans have been embroiled in a debate for some thirty years on the merits of affirmative action, essentially highlighted by divisions on the meaning of meritocracy, the purpose of public universities, and the proper allocation of what is seen as a highly desired public good. Will a similar pattern occur in the UK and EU?

A number of challenges to affirmative action emerged by the late 1970s in the USA, largely focused on the perceived inequity and damage to individuals of 'reverse discrimination'. An important transition came in 1978. That year the US Supreme Court decided a case involving a white male who applied to a University of California medical school but was not admitted. Alan Bakke brought a lawsuit against the university for reverse discrimination. A number of minority applicants scored lower on the medical exam (the MCATs) than Bakke; yet they were admitted under a quota system established by the medical faculty specifically designed to increase minority enrolment. Setting quotas served as an administratively easy way to increase minority participation.

In a narrow five to four vote, the court ruled that quotas were illegal and a violation of Bakke's individual rights. But more importantly, the court stated that race and ethnicity *could be* considered in admissions decisions, as long as it is only one factor among many used by university officials in reaching their decision. The *Bakke* case provided decidedly mixed signals. For the HE sector, it seemed to affirm the right to use racial preferences in the admissions process. It also fuelled a political and legal movement against affirmative action that began to have significant influence by the 1990s. Reflecting the diverse sources of influence and authority related to the purpose and practices of American HE, a growing number of legal cases, voter initiatives, and state government restrictions on affirmative action seemingly shifted the tide against affirmative action in admissions.

In California, the University of California's lay board, the Board of Regents, became engaged in a debate over the future of affirmative action, skilfully prodded into action by a single member of the board intent on ending racial preferences. In 1995, the board banned the use of race and ethnicity in the process of university admissions, as well as in all contracting and hiring. The board's action was followed by a statewide ballot, Proposition 209, passed in 1996 and amending the state constitution to ban the use of race and ethnicity quotas in all public agencies. The state of Washington followed with a similar voter initiative. Court cases also became more prevalent, alleging reverse discrimination in the public universities of Texas and later Michigan. A federal court considering a case of reverse discrimination at the University of Texas ruled against the use of race as a criterion in university admissions. The *Hopwood* case was appealed and later upheld by a federal district court with jurisdiction over some five states. This was again appealed for consideration by the US Supreme Court. But the court refused to hear the case. The lower court's ruling therefore stood. By the late 1990s, there was a substantial number of lower court decisions restricting the use of affirmative action in admissions, which could have led to a decision by the Supreme Court essentially overturning *Bakke*.

These court cases and initiatives reflected a significant and growing public opposition to the use of affirmative action, in turn leading to new restrictions (or anticipated restrictions) on how universities set and administered admissions. It induced some legislatures to establish new policy schemes intent on expanding access to under-represented groups, but without the tool of race and ethnicity. Both conservatives and liberal lawmakers have sought systematic ways to make public universities even more inclusive. In the states of California, Washington, Texas, and Florida, legislation, propositions, or court orders forbade considering race as a factor in admissions.

In Texas and Florida, state legislatures passed admissions plans that eliminated race as a factor in public college and university admissions. To compensate for possible substantial declines in minority enrolment, they also established a guarantee of admissions to the top 10 per cent in Texas and 20 per cent in Florida of the public high school graduates. In California, a similar 'per cent plan' was developed, but not by the state legislature. The University of California enjoys a high level of autonomy from lawmakers under California's state constitution over its internal management, including setting admissions requirements – a level of autonomy similar to universities in the UK. A decision by the lay board and a subsequent amendment to the state's constitution passed by voters forced the university to rethink how it might approach maintaining or increasing the enrolment of under-represented groups.

California's state university proceeded to develop a number of new 'race neutral' policy changes, including admitting all students from the top 4 per cent of the class of each high school in the state. This percentage plan became known as 'Eligibility in the Local Context' (ELC). This is a new provision that comes on top of the university's historical commitment to admit all eligible students from the top 12.5 per cent of California public high school graduates (a statewide mandate). In addition, the University of California also recently composed a new 'comprehensive review' process for admissions that includes a wide range of socio-economic and new 'academic' criteria for consideration for no more than 50 per cent of all admissions. The other 50 per cent are limited to traditional academic factors: grades and test scores.

The University of California's 'comprehensive review' elevates criteria traditionally used in university admissions such as geographic and eco-nomic representation, while also establishing new factors. With the experience of the *Bakke* case, and criticism regarding past formulas giving significant weight in the admissions process to race and ethnicity, the new process avoids individual scores for each academic and socio-economic factor – the model used just prior to Proposition 209. Instead, the focus is on a 'qualitative' and holistic look at a student's individual merit, likeli-hood for academic success at the university, and contribution to the social purpose of the institution. This is a process one finds more typically at private institutions, which are not compelled to provide as much trans-parency on how they make their admissions decisions (University of Cali-fornia Office of the President, Student Affairs Services, 2003).

In part because of this lack of transparency, 'comprehensive review' has not been without its critics – particularly among those who charge that it is simply a stealth method for racial preferences, or those who champion test scores over all other criteria. While some admissions practices at highly selective institutions may be more publicly defensible than others, there remains the fact that some form of discriminatory decision-making will occur. Berkeley and UCLA, for example, each receive approximately 36,000 to 38,000 applications in recent years to fill a mere 4,000 freshman enrolment positions. The admissions pool is self-selected and includes some twenty thousand students with a straight 'A' average in required courses.

California offers an example in which legal restrictions were placed on an institution regarding affirmative action that then resulted in a rethink-ing of admissions policy that, essentially, maintained the institutional goal of greater diversity. The University of California fashioned its own new policy regime. In contrast, in Florida and Texas, state governments imposed new admission schemes to help mitigate the projected impact on the enrolment rates of minority groups. The general effect of these per cent plans, including the University of California's, has been moderate progress in expanding access to lower-income and low-participating racial and ethnic groups. For example, the loss of racial preferences at UC pro-duced a significant drop in under-represented minority enrolment at the freshman level, from nearly 21 per cent to 15.1 per cent. As supporters of affirmative action bemoan, and critiques point out, this illustrates the uni-versity's previous high dependence on using race as a criterion for admis-sions. As Table 11.2 shows, there has since been a moderate increase in this cohort with the introduction of comprehensive review, but not to the percentage levels reached in 1994.

The venture of American HE into affirmative action, and the political debate surrounding institutional efforts to mitigate inequities in society, reflect a state-centred and dispersed process of policy-making. While there is a general commitment to broadening access, the maturity of essentially 50 different higher education systems, and the multiple sources of author-ity (state government, federal programmes, courts, lay boards, HE state

Table 11.2 Percentage of UC system-wide first-time freshman enrolment and socio-economic characteristics before and after affirmative action: 1994, 1998 and 2002

	1994	*1998*[a]	*2002*[a]
Under-represented minorities	20.7	15.1	17.4
Eligibility in the local context	n.a.	n.a.	20.9
First-generation college	32.2	28.9	31.5
Low family income	23.8	18.7	18.9
From low performing high schools	n.a.	16.6	18.7
California rural schools	5.7	7.5	8.0
California urban students	39.3	37.3	38.4
California suburban students	47.7	47.9	48.1
Participants in university outreach programs	n.a.	9.5	n.a.

Source: University of California Office of the President, 'Undergraduate Access to the University of California After the Elimination of Race-Conscious Policies', 2003.

Note
a Post University Use of Racial Preferences and Proposition 209.

systems, and institutional management) do not lend themselves to a nationwide approach.

Within most states, there currently are no goals equivalent to the British Labour government's proclaimed target of meeting set participation rates between the ages of eighteen and thirty; only general statements of a desire for some form of broad representation of all groups in public HE. In California, for example, the State of California and the University of California have a shared general policy commitment:

> Mindful of its mission as a public institution, the University of California seeks to enrol, on each of its campuses, a student body that, beyond meeting the University's eligibility requirements, demonstrates high academic achievement or exceptional personal talent, and that encompasses the broad diversity of cultural, racial, geographic, and socio-economic backgrounds characteristic of California.
>
> (University of California Board of Regents, 25 May 1988)

Arguably, the general structure of state systems such as California's lend themselves to a greater number of opportunities for a post-secondary education and a greater institutional desire to increase participation of under-represented groups. In either case (set targets of participation or general goals for representation), the objective of government is to induce institutions and systems of HE to expand access. Clearly, the tendency in the United Kingdom is to set a wide range of targets and to use them both as a political statement by the party in power and to push for reforms within the HE sector. Within America's contemporary political culture, issues related to the rights of individuals have taken precedence over larger issues of how to increase access and representation. Neither the national government nor state governments seem overly concerned about the general health and quality of America's HE sector or its ability to include more students.

Merit, access and equity

In the USA and the EU, a significant debate continues on how to approach the issues of merit, access, and equity, which – as argued here – represents the latter stage of a natural progression in the development of mass higher education systems. There are generally three values that frame this concern:

- HE is a vital public good, essential for educating, training, and imparting status and upward mobility to those who can benefit from post-secondary education.
- As such, HE needs to be made available equitably to all segments of society.
- Equity is generally framed in terms of seeking a fairer representation of underserved populations.

Although these values are widely shared, a fundamental and unresolved issue remains – one that, in turn, creates significant tensions and acrimonious debate. It can be boiled down to an either/or question, and many view it in these simplistic terms:

- Is higher education, and specifically public universities, a source for personal development and individual socio-economic mobility? Or
- Is it a source for shaping a more equitable and economically competitive society?

Essentially, public HE serves both functions. The debate revolves around the appropriate balance between these two goals. In the USA, the idea of public universities as tools of social engineering has strong historical roots, translated into a variety of admission practices over time. In Britain, this notion is also gaining in political saliency demonstrated by the current Labour government's increasingly aggressive attempts at widening access and making HE more socially relevant. The government is the instigator for moving from a passive stance (simply creating opportunities for access) to a more pro-active approach: for example, recasting university goals related to admissions, and seeking to influence the admission process to increase underserved representation within the university sector.

Where institutions have open door admissions policies, or nearly so, the tension over balancing the interests of individuals and that of society is largely non-existent. Both the American community colleges and the

Further Education sector in England are open admission institutions welcoming almost all who desire their services – although with somewhat different missions and clientele. In universities with more competitive admissions processes, however, the proper weighting of individual versus social-economic purposes is a source of often heated debate. It now draws the interest of governments and higher education leaders, the general public, and a growing array of interest groups vying for their share of a scarce public resource – whether it is a place at Oxford or at the Berkeley campus of the University of California. Central to the debate are different views regarding what constitutes merit and who should benefit from the most selective HE institutions. This debate has become more heated in recent years in part because the returns for the individual (in terms of higher salaries and social standing) have greatly increased.

Public universities are built on a model of a meritocracy, essentially providing an equal opportunity to attend a university after meeting set academic standards. These standards establish a threshold that supposedly defines what a student needs to accomplish in order to have a reasonable chance of collegiate success – including degree completion. Implicit in this paradigm is the idea that if a growing number of students meet these assessments of merit, the HE sector will grow to accommodate them.

Government and public higher education institutions offer an opportunity, but not an entitlement, to attend HE. Particularly in the UK, and to a lesser extent in the USA, merit has historically been defined by narrow academic criteria. In the UK, written A-level examinations in three or more subjects, with students classified in general categories of achievement on the tests, constitute the coin of the realm. In the USA, an accumulative grade point average (GPA) in required secondary school courses and standardised tests such as the SAT form the core academic criteria. In the debate over who should have access to public universities, and to selective institutions in particular, a significant contingent of advocates believes that standardised tests provide the best indicator of a student's ability to succeed in the university, and that by admitting these students society will be best served. This assumption largely ignores research that shows that grades are still the best indicator of collegiate success, that standardised test scores (both the SAT I and the SAT II, focused on subject matter) are generally marginal indicators of a student's collegiate success, and are highly correlated with social class. A recent and significant study at the University of California, the largest research university system in the USA, showed these results (Geiser and Studley, 2002). Nevertheless, there is a strong feeling, largely among conservatives antagonistic to ideas of socio-economic engineering, that high test scores should, in effect, serve as an entitlement for admission to the most selective public universities.

Others, in particular much of the university community in the USA argue for a merit system that sets minimum academic requirements (a threshold), but that also considers a variety of other factors in admitting a class of students. Under this rubric, individual merit is balanced with the larger social purpose of a public university. These other factors include the circumstances of the applicants and their personal achievements – academic, social, civic, and athletic – and criteria related to representation: geographic, lower income, race and ethnicity. As noted, this more broad interpretation of merit has strong historical roots in the founding and development of American public universities. Admissions practices have long recognised geographic representation and, for instance, can be found in the 1868 charter of the University of California.

In simplistic terms, over the past decade both moderately and highly selective public universities in the USA have been pressured or forced to increase the use of academic merit at the expense of socio-economic criteria. This has come in the aftermath of a significant debate over affirmative action, and the use of racial preferences. In the United Kingdom, we see an institutional culture that remains devoted to the notions of academic merit, but now under pressure to broaden the notion of merit more along American lines. In both nations, larger political agendas and authorities outside of the academy are driving change, each linked to differing and sometimes competing ideas of how to promote social and economic progress. US higher education has already gone down a path related to overt efforts to expand access that the UK is now considering. Current Labour government initiatives clearly have their eye on the practices and events across the Atlantic.

Thoughts on the future of mass HE systems

America's approach to mass HE remains a powerful international model. The nation's investment in HE has created a vast network of institutions which collectively constitutes one of America's most significant market edges in the global economy – because of its general quality, its research productivity, its significant role in developing and sustaining new economic sectors, and its success in educating and developing a professional labour force. Although less tangible, another major benefit of mass higher education systems is their important role for promoting a culture of aspiration. Such systems exude the idea of a society that affords multiple opportunities to overcome economic, racial and ethnic barriers. Robust HE systems are an investment by a nation that is constantly attempting to improve the abilities and success of its citizens.

Yet the American experience illustrates a number of modern conundrums for mature mass higher education systems. Here are a few observations. First, after years of growth in HE participation rates, there comes a point when the overall rate of enrolment growth tapers off or in some cases declines marginally. In the USA, this has happened in a number of states even as the labour market for HE degree recipients continues to grow. Demographic shifts related to immigration and the age of the population, disparities in the quality of secondary schools, and the declining ability or will of national and local governments to fund HE, each contribute to changing patterns of demand for HE. Another variable may be the idea of a natural limit in the number of people in a given population that can benefit from HE. In 1947, President Truman's commission on higher education boldly stated (and with really little analytical basis) that only 32 per cent of the population could complete and benefit from a higher education. Whatever the percentage, there are assumed limits on who may benefit, in part influenced not simply by psychometric assessments of intelligence (a field historically coloured by racism), but by the quality of schools and the environment in which talent is nurtured.

Whatever the reasons for the slow down in participation rates, the major question is no longer how to build mass HE systems, but how to sustain them and, in some cases, how to reshape them to fit changing HE markets and societal needs. Arguably, HE systems that have multiple providers and multiple purposes (as in the USA) have a better ability to make these changes. The HE sectors in EU nations, on the other hand, have been historically less dynamic. While making dramatic strides in promoting access, most EU nations remain tied to binary systems (a university and a vocational or polytechnic sector). A greater diversity of institutions, greater uniformity in degree titles and standards, and the ability to matriculate between institutions (the latter two an objective of the Bologna process) remain the major challenges for higher education in the EU. While many in the international HE community are fearful of globalisation, and specifically the potential encroachment of private and for-profit providers on previously closed national systems of HE, this development will help to diversify the choices of students.

There is another possible area for change. A key component in America's path towards mass higher education – one generally lacking in Europe's progression – is the development of multi-campus college and university systems, often uniting a series of institutions with similar missions under a single governing board. The benefits of such organisation are a greater coordination of resources, self-monitoring of quality, and a sense of collective commitment to the distinct mission of a group of institutions. Another advantage is the political clout garnered by such an arrangement – in the halls of government and potentially among a larger public who can view the collective vibrancy of a group of institutions as of greater import than a single and seemingly lone university or college. One outcome of mass higher education, and the increasing role of HE for socio-economic status and prosperity, is that there is an increasing pool of stakeholders.

Some 45 per cent of all post-secondary HE students in the USA are enrolled in multi-campus institutions – the largest being the California State University system with some twenty-three campuses, which is focused on undergraduate teaching and offering degrees up through the Master's level. The political culture and history of institution building in the EU has prevented any such amalgamation. But one might perhaps consider informal relationships between like institutions (such as the Russell Group in England) or regions that could lead to more formal ties – in admissions practices, matriculation agreements and government-funding requests.

A second observation: within mass and universal access systems supported by government, what is the relative role and autonomy of elite universities? Particularly in Europe, the initial effort was to push for equity in funding, in missions, and access with the general goal of no longer favouring an elite group of institutions, but rather of creating a homogeneous set of public universities. However, many EU members, including the United Kingdom, are now beginning to discuss more openly the value of a more differentiated network of institutions – where some universities might be centres of excellence in both teaching and research, and others more focused on teaching. To compete on the global stage economically, nations with advanced economies desperately need a group of universities that can attract talent and sustain a high level of research productivity. Mass higher education systems are not incompatible with supporting elite universities, as long as there is:

1   A meritocratic and socially responsible system for admissions.
2   Opportunities for students to matriculate to these institutions from what might be termed second- and even third-tier tertiary institutions.

Indeed, the American HE system has been constructed in a manner that has both created and sustained a large number of elite public institutions. Private institutions have done this largely through funding by private benefactors, and by organisational structures that hire, promote, and reward excellence. In the public sector, the benefactor has been the state. The internal organisation and faculty reward structure are similar. But what is different is their place in a larger network of public and to a lesser degree private institutions that essentially allows for their existence. In states such as California, for example, the advent of the public community college was due in part to its ability to broaden access to higher education; but it was also established as a means to protect and enhance the state's most selective public university (Douglass, 2000).

This leads to a third observation. Recognising that mass HE systems are not incompatible with the notion of sustaining or promoting elite universities, there remain difficulties in creating a meritocratic and socially responsible system of admissions to these institutions. Further, there is the question of the proper locus for setting policy – at the institutional level, or by government. In the example of England, there is the prospect of increasing regulatory controls and influence by the national government.

The American example is more ambiguous, and linked not with government initiatives but with the courts and anti-affirmative action political movements. As noted, public universities, such as those in California, Texas, and Michigan, have been sued over their use of racial preferences, and, in the case of the University of California, their lay board voted to end a policy that previous incarnations of the board had endorsed. The momentum of lower court cases in the USA appeared to signal a future ruling by the US Supreme Court that might overturn *Bakke* and the legal ability of public universities outside of California, Texas, Florida and Washington to use racial preferences. The rash of suits, lower court rulings against racial preferences, and the conservative nature of the current Supreme Court membership all indicated as much.

By the summer of 2003, the court appeared ready to make its first ruling on the issue since *Bakke*. In a case very similar to *Bakke*, two students sued the University of Michigan for essentially using racial preferences over traditional academic gauges of merit – grades and, in particular, test scores. The court again ruled in a narrow five to four vote against the University of Michigan's inflated weighting of race in the undergraduate admissions process. But the court also upheld the conclusion of the *Bakke* decision – race and ethnicity could be considered by a public university as one factor among many, but not as a dominant factor.

Therefore, in a refreshing turn of events, the Supreme Court has reiterated the notion that public universities should balance individual academic merit with their larger social purpose. Although there are different political environments in the various US states, and state laws reflect those differences, the Michigan case offers the opportunity for many US HE institutions to revisit their admissions practices. In doing so responsibly, they have an opportunity to re-assert their autonomy.

Finally, a central question for the future of mass higher education systems is the relative role of HE institutions and the academic community versus external influences in shaping the organisation and activities of institutions. National governments have long been major players, indeed instigators, for creating mass higher education. Relatively new external influences, however, are becoming evident: international accords such as Bologna and soon the General Agreement on Trade and Services (GATS), the related spectre of greater international competition, and even intervention by the courts. There is also the potential to broaden access and to cause shifts in domestic markets thanks to the increasing integration of instructional technologies. It seems certain that the diversity of providers will grow and that demand for HE will also expand. How might the academic community exert a more powerful influence on shaping mass systems, in shaping its own destiny? Put another way: higher education is now such a central component to national development and the global economy that it is widely viewed as too important to leave to the academics.

There is no easy answer to this conundrum. Thus far, the general, and perhaps unavoidable, tendency of the higher education community has been to seek independence and greater autonomy for individual institutions. Only governments and their departments of education are seemingly concerned about the collective HE enterprise often acting, as governments do, under a larger political agenda albeit with perhaps marginal knowledge of the actual workings of the academy. Any assertion of a stronger role by university and college leaders will require greater cooperation, some consensus of opinion, concessions that might lead to greater differentiation of missions, and, most importantly, a greater self-awareness of how the collective whole of higher education institutions meets the wider needs of a nation. Barring such a revelation, governments and markets will only grow in their power and influence.

Notes

1 Elements of this chapter reflect my pending book *The Social Contract of Public Universities* (forthcoming Vanderbilt University Press).
2 According to Department for Education and Skills statistics the participation rate of students under twenty years of age in higher education in Great Britain rose from approximately 12 per cent to 17 per cent from 1980 to 1989, and then increased rapidly to 35 per cent by 2001.
3 The steel giant's interest in promoting education resulted in a huge philanthropic programme to build libraries in hundreds of communities, and colleges and university campuses. Libraries were Carnegie's ideal form of perpetuating democracy, and social and economic mobility. Later, he established numerous funds to study and support education, including the Carnegie Foundation for the Advancement of Teaching.
4 It should be noted that comparative data collection on national higher education systems has some problems. Put simply in this case, data in the USA are biased towards counting all tertiary education; data in the UK tend to exclude some forms of post-secondary vocational courses. Yet it is reasonable to assume that these figures are broadly reflective of comparative enrolment patterns.
5 'Clearing' happens after students receive the results of their A-level or other university entrance examinations. It is the process through which unplaced students can seek a place on courses with unfilled places. (Students are unplaced because they did not achieve the results necessary to take up a conditional offer, declined an offer, or did not receive any offer.) About 10 per cent of all accepted applicants are admitted through clearing each year, although the figure varies greatly from university to university. Because of time pressure, the normal selection processes are often contracted, with the result that a student might be admitted on the basis of confirmed results and a telephone interview.

References

Admissions to Higher Education Steering Group, *Consultation on Key Issues Relating to Fair Admissions to Higher Education* (Bristol, HEFCE, September 2003).
Agricultural College Land Grant Act, *U.S. Statutes at Large 12* (1862: 503).
Ashby, E., 'Any person, any study: an essay on American higher education', in L.B. Mayhew (ed.) *The Carnegie Commission on Higher Education* (San Francisco: Josey-Bass Publishers, 1973), pp. 278–83.
Bryce, J., *The American Commonwealth: Volume 2* (London: Macmillan and Co., 1981).
Bureau of the US Census, *Historical Statistics of the United States* (Washington, DC: Bureau of the Census, 1957).

246   *John Douglass*

Carnegie Commission on the Higher Education, *A Chance to Learn: An Action Agenda for Equal Opportunity in Higher Education* (New York: McGraw-Hill Book Company, 1970).

Department for Education and Skills, *Widening Participation in Higher Education* (London: HMSO, 2003).

Douglass, J.A., *The California Idea and American Higher Education* (Stanford: Stanford University Press, 2000).

Douglass, J.A., 'A tale of two universities of California: a tour of strategic issues past and prospective', *Chronicle of the University of California*, 4 (Fall 2000a).

Douglass, J.A., *The Social Contract of Public Universities* (Vanderbilt University Press, forthcoming).

Gaither, G. (ed.), *The Multicampus System: Perspectives on Practice and Prospects* (Sterling, VA: Stylus Publishing, LLC. 1999).

Geiser, S. and R. Studley, 'UC and the SAT: predictive validity and differential impact of the SAT I and SAT II at the University of California', *Educational Assessment*, 8, 8 (2002), pp. 1–26.

Graham, H.D., *The Civil Rights Era: Origins and Development of National Policy, 1960–1972* (Oxford: Oxford University Press, 1990).

Lee, E. and F. Bowen, 'The multicampus university: a study of academic governance', a report prepared for the Carnegie Commission on Higher Education (New York: McGraw-Hill Book Company, 1971).

McConnell, T.R., *From Elite to Mass to Universal Higher Education: The British and American Transformations* (Berkeley: Center for Research and Development in Higher Education, 1973).

Neave, G., 'On looking through the wrong end of the telescope', in De Boer, Huisman, Klemperer *et al.* (eds) *Academia in the 21st Century* (Netherlands: Advisory Council for Science and Technology Policy, 2002).

Parry, G. and A. Thompson, *Closer by Degrees: The Past, Present and Future of Higher Education in Further Education Colleges* (London: Learning and Skills Development Agency, 2002).

President's Commission on Higher Education, *Higher Education for American Democracy, Volume 1* (Washington, DC: Government Printing Office, 1947).

Scott, P., *The Meanings of Mass Higher Education* (London: Open University Press, 1995).

Trow, M., 'Problems in the transition from elite to mass higher education', *General Report on the Conference on Future Structures of Post-Secondary Education* (Paris: OECD, 1974).

Trow, M., 'Comparative perspectives on access' in O. Fulton (ed.) *Access to Higher Education* (Guildford, England: Society for Research into Higher Education, 1981), pp. 89–121.

US Department of Education, National Center for Education Statistics, *Integrated Postsecondary Education Data System* (2002).

University of California, Board of Regents, *University Policy on Undergraduate Admissions*, 25 May 1988.

University of California, Office of the President, Student Affairs Services, *Undergraduate Access to the University of California After the Elimination of Race-Conscious Policies*, (UC Office of the President, 2003).

Ward, D., 'That old familiar feeling – with an important difference', *The Presidency*, 7, (Winter, 2004), 9.

12 Conclusion

The reshaping of mass higher education

Ted Tapper and David Palfreyman

The universality of expansion

This book has incorporated case studies drawn from different traditions of higher education: continental Europe, the United States, Britain and hybrids thereof with subtle variations reflecting both national (for example, Wales and Scotland) and regional (for example, the Nordic countries) traditions within the models. In spite of the evident differences, which have deep historical roots, there is no denying the fact that all the national systems of higher education examined here have become, to use contemporary jargon, mass systems. Whilst it is possible to discern different dates at which the mass threshold was crossed, with contrasting and fluctuating rates of expansion, nonetheless the mass model is now universal. Moreover, although in part this is a result of a definitional sleight of hand, that is, the understanding of higher education has been broadened to bring it closer to the generous American interpretation, the expansion is real rather than a camouflaged fiction.

In spite of the occasional reservation – perhaps most infamously expressed in Kingsley Amis' 'more mean worse' – the expansion has been generally welcomed. The equivocation is about the effects of expansion rather than expansion itself. Thus, resources and strategies are needed to prevent student disaffection and high drop-out rates, to provide tolerable facilities and meaningful learning environments, and to link the experience of higher education in a positive way to the wider society. Above all, mass higher education has to avoid the Italian experience of becoming an acceptable long-term 'parking lot' for middle-class youth; a convenient resting place at which to equivocate further on one's future role in life. Whilst many would support universal exposure to the experience of higher education, especially in the context of a broad public commitment to the idea of lifelong learning, few would advocate the right to remain ensconced indefinitely within the warm and convenient embrace of the university.

Explanatory themes and forms of intervention

Not surprisingly, following closely on the heels of the expanding experience of mass systems of higher education has been the search for explanations. As we have shown, the universality of the experience is enveloped in an explanatory consensus but with different emphases within the particular national contexts. These explanatory variables fall into four flexible and interacting categories: the availability of students, the accessibility of institutions, the political and economic pressures, and a cultural milieu which feeds off the other variables and provides the context within which individuals make choices about their future lifestyles.

Historically within all our national systems students have fallen mainly into the age range 17/18 to 21/22 and so demand has been determined by simple demographic variables with projections required to take into account the changing relative sizes of those social groups more or less likely to participate in higher education. But part of the phenomenon of expansion has been both the expected response to demographic logic and the progressive undermining of that established logic. Perhaps, most critically, the expansion of higher education is part of the growth of education more generally, especially – in continental terms – at the upper secondary stage. Thus, almost regardless of the size of the 17/18 age cohort, over time the number of young people deemed capable of participating in higher education has expanded. Vital to this process has been the growth of qualified university applicants amongst previously under-represented groups, of which women is clearly the most striking example. There may be some concern that women focus upon particular degree programmes and are less inclined to pursue postgraduage studies, but at the undergraduate level women now constitute a majority across national systems in general. In effect we have seen changes that have eroded the established demographic straitjacket.

The American chapter argued that one explanation of the early movement towards a mass system of higher education in the USA was the sheer diversity of provision. In the USA an astounding range of niche markets were catered for, which increased the overall size of the student population. To a limited extent the same phenomenon has occurred more recently in the other countries that form part of our study (for example, the founding of business schools) but, perhaps more significant, have been those changes in institutional character that encourage wider participation. There is the greater diversity of degree programmes, the movement towards credit accumulation, the development of more structured courses and greater flexibility in permitting students to change their course of studies. Whilst such changes may have been designed – as is true of Germany, Italy, France and the Netherlands – to retain students, they also make it possible for a wider range of students to consider participation in the first place.

In part the mass continental systems evolved out of the universal acceptance of the idea that everyone who demonstrated successful completion of upper secondary education was entitled to a university place. The more restrictive British model has retained (and still retains – just!) the idea that universities have a right to select their own students, but has been willing to embrace alternative forms of entrance qualifications to the traditional A-levels whilst greatly expanding part-time higher education. Consequently, institutional change has modified the student social profile with increases, proportionately as well as numerically, in the number of both part-time and older students. Put simply, institutions can change in ways that make themselves more accessible and, consequently, have the potential to modify the demographic straitjacket within which access to higher education has been constrained. In the context of enhanced institutional autonomy, which appears to be at least a general continental trend, it is not inconceivable that individual universities will purposefully takes steps – for example, to strengthen their financial security or their academic standing and status – that will impact significantly upon their social profiles.

However, it would be naïve not to recognise that institutional behaviour only makes sense if it is interpreted within the context of the wider political, economic and cultural environments. That very variety of higher education of which Americans are justifiably proud owes more to the belief in the link between education and a democratic citizenry, allied to the sheer cultural diversity of the USA, than it does to institutional entrepreneurialism. Likewise, the institutional changes, that to a greater or lesser degree, have been experienced by all the higher education systems in this study have been influenced by political inputs often purporting to be acting on behalf of broad societal pressures. On the one hand there are the general political themes, often expressions of a value position, that legitimise state action in favour of increasing and widening access to higher education while, on the other hand, there are the concrete measures designed to put values into practice.

The value positions have been widely shared. An educated citizenry is good for democracy and thus higher education needs both to expand and to be socially inclusive. The general value position is most strongly expressed in Poland as in the post-communist era it struggles to create a system of higher education that is both inclusive and in tune with democratic values. But universally in recent years we have witnessed political exhortation and state action on behalf of the increased participation of a range of social groups: the poor (universally), the working class (the United Kingdom), women (the Netherlands), those living in more isolated rural communities (Scandinavia and Poland), racial and ethnic minorities (the United States) and now those with disabilities (the United Kingdom). The list of targets is potentially inexhaustible with perhaps, especially in the context of 'lifelong learning', the aged to follow! Ironically, Poland finds itself in the position of expanding higher education whilst, partly because of the lack of resources, diminishing the privileged access position enjoyed by those from working-class and peasant backgrounds (social groups supported in other national systems) in the years of communist rule.

And what is politically desirable also, or so we are told, makes good economic sense, for both the effective functioning of the economy and the socio-economic status of the individual. Although the strength of the message will vary from place to place and over time, it is impossible not to be struck by the universal political exhortation in favour of the knowledge society, and the dire economic predictions that will allegedly follow for those nations that fail to recognise the importance of human capital in creating and sustaining growth in the context of what is usually called the global economy. Whilst these claims may be true, the conclusion that they are driven as much by missionary zeal as by a search for understanding complex socio-economic trends is hard to conceal.

However, when it comes to concrete political action, as opposed to the expression of value positions, it is possible to discern a decidedly pragmatic response in the varying patterns of state support for access. Moreover, it is a response that appears to be converging, albeit slowly and haphazardly, across the nation states. There is a deeply rooted historical tradition of limiting access to certain degree programmes (*numerus fixus* programmes to use the Dutch phrase) with a tendency towards downloading responsibility for selection to individual institutions (whilst trying to make selection fairer). The restrictions are a statement about apparent national manpower needs, the recognition of the potentially dire consequences of gross institutional overload, and the sheer magnitude of the likely cost to the state when students are not required to pay full-cost fees. Medics, for example, are very expensive to train, and even more so should they practise abroad or remain unemployed.

Although most national systems have moved towards increasing fee costs in real terms – as part of what can be described as the slow marketisation of higher education – there is still a general tendency to subsidise fees. With the exception of the elite private American universities – and even then only for the well-to-do – generous subsidy remains the norm for most students. Moreover, fee remissions (or perhaps free entry), low-interest loans, various forms of financial support and, even in some cases, grants are on offer to the students from poorer, and in many cases, not so poor families. However, what we may be witnessing is a slow move towards full-cost fees for those deemed able to pay with a means-tested financial aid package for everyone else. At the moment, regardless of what trends there may be, the picture remains diverse: the acceptance of variable fees in Australia and the USA, the move towards variable fees but with an imposed ceiling in England, and modest fee increases in the continental model but still a commitment to general subsidies accompanied by targeted additional financial aid. Whilst this patch quilt may suggest the opposite of a trend and, indeed the opposite of rationality, the constraints of the national cultural and political contexts should not be forgotten. It is impossible to ignore the strength of the European (including British) legacy of state subsidy and the fear of middle-class Australians and Americans of being priced out of higher education, especially its more prestigious echelons. Within such contexts the process of change is inevitably cautious, and invariably driven by short-term political considerations. Even the reality of severe constraints upon state provision, as it evidently the case in Poland, does not automatically generate a change of direction.

Although political intervention in access issues has been an experience common to all the national systems under investigation, the form of that intervention has varied and what impact it has had on levels of participation is disputable. At its most extreme, intervention is direct and targeted, most clearly seen in the examples of *numerous clausus* (the Italian phrase) programmes, with the possibility of the state controlling the selection process and even distributing the chosen few among the institutions of higher education. But such direct, centralised bureaucratic control is the exception rather than the rule with the state preferring to determine overall student numbers and perhaps constructing admissions guidelines, but permitting selection at the institutional level. English institutions of higher education are currently faced with the prospect of working with the Office for Fair Admissions (OFFA) should they wish to charge variable fees. The intention is to permit institutions to charge higher fees, up to the £3,000 cap, in return for 'access agreements' designed to encourage greater diversity in the social composition of the student population. This is a classic example of bureaucratic state regulation of access but, as our chapter on English higher education makes clear, it remains to be seen precisely how heavy-handed an intervention it will prove to be.

Most forms of state intervention have been indirect and can probably best be described as supportive in character. Clearly the most widespread examples are the various financial aid packages with the precise details assuming somewhat different national forms. Although participation at large is widely subsidised, there is also a pronounced tendency for resources to be targeted at particular social groups that historically have been under-represented in higher education. And then there is the general political exhortation in favour of participation with campaigns to make more information available to would-be students, and to encourage applications for particular courses – note the interesting Dutch efforts to persuade students to make wise decisions about course selection and, more especially, to encourage women to enrol in applied science programmes. In part, changes to the Italian system of higher education were influenced by the belief that if students considered more carefully the selection of their degree programmes then drop-out rates would decline.

Although access to higher education in the USA has obviously not been free of political intervention or bureaucratic regulation, undoubtedly the most interesting input has come from the US Supreme Court. The major focus has been the level of participation of African Americans, and the extent to which institutions of higher education can use affirmative actions programmes to enhance that participation. The courts are the arena in which a complex political struggle is being fought and, although affirmative actions have been approved by the courts, the parameters which within institutions can operate appear to have become more restrictive over time. The issue has still not been finally resolved and perhaps the best that can be hoped for is the construction of unstable and temporary periods of judicial consensus until the problem disappears – assuming of course that the problems caused by the legacy of discrimination and relative poverty can ever be resolved.

Much of the current interest in access issues in the United Kingdom has been stimulated by changes in the system of student financial aid – with Scotland moving in a different direction from England and (so far) Wales. The fear is, as it was some years earlier in Australia, that requiring students to bear more of the costs of their higher education (essentially by paying fees that meet a larger percentage of teaching costs) will heighten the entry barrier to those from socially deprived backgrounds – especially when it comes to studying at the most prestigious, and probably most expensive, universities. At least in terms of general participatory rates, although it is too soon to make definitive statements, the early indications from Australia are that this has not occurred.

The situation in the United Kingdom post-2006 (when the new variable fees will be introduced) will undoubtedly be very closely monitored. Besides charting social patterns of access, it will be very interesting to plot the transnational implications of the change. Will English students flock to the Scottish or continental universities in search of cheaper degrees? Will greater demand from well-qualified English students – denied places at the elite English universities as admissions officers calculate OFFA's equations – force some Scottish students out of their more prestigious institutions? And what will be the local reactions? In the context of a relatively open-access model the German universities might welcome British students, but it is not difficult to imagine the political reaction should English students start to squeeze Scottish students out of university places. But both German and Scottish universities have to face the fact that, as a result of the fee increases, English universities may be more favourably resourced institutions offering better research opportunities for faculty and enhanced facilities to students. In this context, would not the current trend in Germany towards creating an elite stratum of universities intensify? Increasingly, therefore, national decisions on access are likely to have a transnational impact.

However, it is important not to lose sight of the fact that the various pressures upon access, as well as their concrete manifestation in the form of incentives, rules and procedures, as well as innovative institutional behaviour, simply provide the context in which individuals make decisions about their futures. For example, if unemployment is high they may decide to pursue higher education in the belief that it is preferable to be a student rather than unemployed. Alternatively, the demand for labour in certain fields – for example, information technology – may be so intense that the offer of a well-paid job could be sufficient to tempt the student to leave university for the workplace. Obviously different kinds of pressures come into play dependent upon the social location of the individual. It appears that the participation of the middle classes (or, at least, the more elevated segments of the middle class) has reached close to saturation point: almost as if partaking of the experience of higher education has become an established cultural norm, a *rite de passage*. For those from families that traditionally have not been accustomed to participate in higher education, the choices could well be more instrumental: the balance between current costs and lost opportunities against potential rewards and enhanced prospects. In some cases opportunities to participate may arise more 'fortuitously': enforced redundancy, purposeful decision to change career, or even children who have reached school age. Such circumstances potentially present individuals with opportunities that previously may have seemed foreclosed. How then will the individual resolve the issue? Again we are in the realm of pragmatic decision-making. Given the universal commitment to diversify social participation in higher education, and the fact that the student population is aging and likely to continue to age, the need for individuals to make pragmatic calculations as to the merits of studying for a degree will increase.

The chapters in this book, although dealing with the same issues, represent different approaches to the analysis of access to higher education. Consequently, although there is general agreement on the importance of the pressures that shape patterns of access, most of the authors (with the analysis of the Nordic countries and the Netherlands as the exceptions) have preferred not to construct models that attempt to explain the interactive process or evaluate the relative importance of its constituent parts. The dominant trend by far has been to outline the range of pressures that have influenced access to higher education within the particular national settings, and to argue that expansion is the result of an interactive process – what Douglass in his chapter on the USA has referred to as the relationship between demand and supply side variables. In parallel fashion, Aamodt and Kyvik have argued that expansion in the Nordic context was driven by a combination of state policy, individual demands and labour market needs. But it is the interactive argument that again prevails: 'our main conclusion is that the interaction between individual demands and political priorities has been the most important driving force behind the increased access'. Kaiser and Vossensteyn in the their chapter on the Netherlands, whilst not arriving at any conclusions as to what precisely has widened access, downplay the *specific* importance of political intervention. Even those campaigns encouraging more engagement by women, 'took place before any active policies were developed in this area'. In terms of the British debate, whilst current expansion is politically supported, it would be difficult to claim either that we arrived at a mass system through a politically planned process or even that political measures were the major determinants of expansion. The one demonstrable conclusion is unfortunately bland: whilst the particular expansionist pressures may be universal, their precise impact is bound by national parameters.

The impact of mass higher education

This is not the context for the presentation of a full treatise on the character of mass higher education. Rather the aim is to draw attention to three important developments that have been closely associated with the rapid expansion of student numbers, all of which, to varying degrees, have been discussed in each of the individual chapters: the impact upon the value systems in which the higher education institutions are embedded, the role of the state in regulating higher education, and the general response of institutional structures and processes to the realities of mass higher education.

With the exception of the United States all the systems of higher education analysed in this book were, until comparatively recently, elite models in terms of levels of access. Higher education was perceived as a precious commodity that only the carefully ordained – academically and, in some cases, socially and culturally – could fully appreciate. The USA with its strong emphasis upon the teaching of useful knowledge (probably best represented by the creation of the land grant colleges) offered a different model. And yet there have been, at least since 1945, strong – and almost universal – commitments to open access to higher education in the sense that there should be no untoward impediments placed in the way of those who wanted a university education and were considered to have the pre-requisite qualifications. Consequently, and more especially in the continental model, the acceptance of open access, underwritten by various forms of financial aid, took root. There was no crisis of values until the negative effects of expansion started to manifest themselves: the cost to the state of an expanding subsidy to the middle classes (a regressive tax in the British debate), the decline in the quality of the experience of higher education as resources dwindled in relation to demand, and the questioning of the value of the end product – what was a mass-produced degree worth? What we have witnessed are fascinating attempts to avoid taking measures which would challenge directly the traditions of open access (for example, by allowing institutions to recruit all students selectively and charge full-cost fees) but, nonetheless, a recognition that the problems have to be tackled. The outcome is a mélange that changes the nature of the product (shorter and 'more relevant' degrees), adopts strategies that will encourage greater student responsibility and aid retention (more guidance, credit accumulation and credit transfer) and shifts – if only marginally – of more of the costs onto students and their families (somewhat higher fees and more targeted financial support).

However, the range of possible responses to the value conflicts generated by mass higher education is considerable. It can be argued that the USA, with its historically rooted pluralism, and complex mixture of private and public provision, was ideally placed to take in its stride the arrival of mass higher education. Institutional diversity permitted a ready absorption of growth, whilst the assumed link between the expansion of educational opportunity and the strengthening of a democratic culture meant that rather than threatening the established value system it reinforced it. Thus the USA, unlike the continental models, has been able to hang onto its understanding of higher education without experiencing the tensions, and making the continuous adjustments, that those national systems have been obliged to undertake.

The French situation is unique because of its ability to combine within one value framework a tradition that encourages open, non-selective entry with a highly competitive and fiercely meritocratic model. Moreover, there are separate institutional representation of these traditions, to be found respectively in the universities and the grandes écoles. It would seem possible therefore for one system to encompass two different traditions running in tandem. In stark contrast Britain seems unable to reconcile itself to either a binary model or diversity. The polytechnics have been become the new universities but academic drift was under way long before the formal amalgamation. Moreover, we are witnessing valiant efforts to sustain a relatively narrow definition of the university in which each institution is supposedly committed to pure research, diversifying access, and aiding local economic and social development. One wonders for how long the centre can hold!

All the national case studies demonstrated political involvement, either directly or indirectly, in shaping access to higher education. But it is interesting to note the move towards greater institutional autonomy in the continental model as the state encourages the universities to adopt measures that will enable them to cope more effectively with the consequences of rapid expansion. Thus the institutions assume more responsibility for determining access to certain degree programmes (the *numerus fixus* programmes) and they have greater flexibility in designing the structure of degrees and determining their course content. In effect there has been a shift towards the institutional autonomy that has existed formally in the United Kingdom and *de facto*, if not *de jure*, in the American state universities.

Ironically the strengthening of the accountability culture has led the British system of higher education to move in precisely the opposite direction. Moreover, in England the current government's desire to increase and widen access to higher education has resulted in more state bureaucratic intervention: the right to charge variable fees will be linked to access agreements designed to broaden student social profiles. Our chapters show parallel commitments in all of the individual national systems and, even in Australia, in the run-up to the next election, issues of equity are beginning to re-appear on the political agenda. However, the extent of the preoccupation, and the measures which the current government feels are needed to enforce change, suggest that it is a peculiarly English disease. France, at least until now, seems prepared to embrace a system that suggests the commitment to sustaining meritocratic values is as important as enhancing equity; while other continental models pride themselves on their relative openness and, although social inclusiveness is not perhaps as complete as it should be, it is not an issue that commands intense political interest and can be dealt with by targeted campaigns and packages of financial support. The peculiarity of the English situation is probably best explained by the dominance of class in interpretations of its culture and its continuing, if declining, significance in shaping national political life.

In the USA the pre-occupation has been with race rather than class but the battles have been fought in the courts rather than more overtly in the political arena. Moreover, although the American system of higher education may once have been elitist in terms of its size and social representation, it was never elitist in terms of its values. Furthermore, there are numerous examples of institutional initiatives to broaden access, which have been challenged in the courts. It is more a question of legal challenges to change rather than institutional inertia and, at least contemporarily, it would be difficult to sustain an image of the leading American universities, an image that is widely shared in Britain, as desperately attempting to retain their social exclusivity. Moreover, a uniform pattern of central state bureaucratic control is far less feasible given the genuine private–public mix and the critical importance of state, as opposed to, federal government responsibilities for higher education.

If the growth of mass higher education has demonstrated a perhaps surprising resilience in the established values systems that envelop the universities and, with perhaps the exception of the United Kingdom, has not led to more intrusive state control of admissions, it has nonetheless had a profound impact upon what can best be described as the character of higher education. The critical feature of mass higher education is its sheer diversity, even in the USA with its historically based pluralistic model a powerful feature of expansion has been the creation of the junior/community colleges with their two-year programmes. Although both the continent and the United States have experienced the rise of the mega-university (sometimes, as in the case of California, situated on more than one campus) expansion has been fuelled by the creation of new institutions and even new institutional layers often purposely committed to teaching different curricula, invariably more vocationally oriented, than was to be found in the traditional university sector. So in Germany we see the expansion of the *Fachhochschulen*, in the Netherlands of the *hogescholen* sector, in Finland of a new polytechnic stratum based on former vocational schools, and in England of the so-called new universities, formerly polytechnics (between 1965 and 1992) and prior to then a patch quilt of colleges, variously titled, offering mainly what was quaintly known as advanced further education.

So mass higher education is not simply 'more of the same' but is qualitatively different from the traditional elite model: a more varied student intake (although not as socially diverse as perhaps it could be); more complex relations between students and institutions (many studying on a part-time basis, living at home and commuting to the university, and sometimes working long hours even if registered as a full-time student); a wider variety of degree programmes with an emphasis on both specifically vocational and/or transferable skills; and a relationship to the job market that has to be seen more as middle-class social reproduction at large as opposed to elite socialisation. Within this mass model are still to be found some examples of the old model – the grandes écoles, the Universities of Oxford, Cambridge, Harvard and Princeton – but they are the exception rather than the rule, and certainly can no longer claim to be models that should be replicated, even emulated. The mass system, therefore, has emerged only because it has proven possible to create new forms of higher education. Indeed, of the national systems examined in this book it is Italy which seems to have suffered most from the rapid expansion of student numbers and, interestingly, it is the system most dominated by the mega-university and to date appears least able to diversify. The implication is that mass higher education brings in its wake diversification, and that it is diversification which most enables it to function meaningfully. But, in spite of diversification, the Italian system of higher education demonstrates conclusively the continuing 'crisis of the university' as underfunded expansion threatens quality. In such circumstances considerations of equity in access are simply buried by the struggle to construct reforms that will hopefully secure meaningful survival.

Whither mass higher education?

Several of our chapters have predicted that their national systems of higher education can be expected to expand further and, although reforms may be necessary, the intention is not to limit intake but rather to increase relevance and throughput. Indeed, the British government is committed to a 50 per cent participation rate of those below the age of thirty by 2010. To predict social trends is a hazardous occupation but there is some tentative evidence to suggest that the great wave of post-war, and more particularly from the mid-1980s to the late 1990s, expansion may be drawing to a close. The most important quantitative evidence comes from the USA, the first nation with a mass system of higher education. Our American chapter points to the slowdown, even decline, in enrolment rates amongst the traditional student-aged population (entering higher education at the age of 17/18 and graduating some four years later), which is compensated for only by an increased enrolment of older students.

Furthermore, the slowdown in enrolment rates, whilst it may be expected inasmuch as it was easier to enhance enrolment when it was low, is a widespread phenomenon suggesting that higher education may be reaching the limits of its 'natural' recruitment base. As has been argued in this chapter, the 'natural' base in the past has been expanded by a combination of rising demand, institutional change, political support and economic pressure but the issue is whether this is a process that can continue indefinitely. Furthermore, it seems logical to expect slower rates of penetration when social groups that traditionally have not entered higher education are sucked into its orbit. It would seem reasonable to predict that for these social groups it would take longer to reach the self-generating expansionist threshold that Wolf (2002) has hypothesised.

What is perhaps more important is not so much whether expansion is going to continue indefinitely, until presumably everyone at one time or another experiences higher education, but whether the issues it generates are capable of resolution. There are four possible scenarios. First, in a system of mass higher education access issues move on and off the agenda depending upon the prevailing balance of political forces; they may be judged more or less significant in relation to other long-term concerns (for example, how higher education is to be financed or its capacity to train appropriate forms of human capital). Second, they never materialise as serious political issues because of the strength of the prevailing belief systems. So, whilst it may be possible to point to the negative consequences of mass access, it is these that have to be dealt with as opposed to reformulating the belief systems and accompanying practices that were responsible for the negative outcomes. Third, access issues are reformulated in a guise that makes it possible to pursue more decisive action. For example, to a greater or lesser extent, HEIs have been perceived as local institutions serving the needs of the region, state or even local community. Within this context it is possible to imagine universities pursuing forms of research, establishing degree (or sub-degree) programmes, and encouraging modes of participation that would be inconceivable within the traditional parameters that govern access. Thus concerns such as equity or relevance are placed on the agenda indirectly but more decisively.

Finally, it is just conceivable that the pressures generated by the expansionist impulse can be responded to constructively. Inevitably the pattern of responses would vary from one national context to the next but it could be expected to consist of an amalgam of the following variables: means-tested fees; various forms of subsidised financial support for most students, with grants for those from the poorest families; a mixture of private and public provision with student support based on personal, state and institutional inputs; institutions that are highly selective and others that have open enrolment; degree programmes with structures and pedagogical practices that encourage varying student relationships to the institution; and a more relaxed attitude to retention rates in a context that permits credit accumulation over time and institutional transfers both up and down the prestige hierarchy. Inevitably there will be debates on the balance between system diversity and system coherence with different national interpretations of what constitutes meaningful higher education. But one thing is certain: mass access cannot be contained by a narrow, well-defined straitjacket of values and institutional practices and structures.

It is tempting to point to the USA as representing the most viable model for a mass system of higher education. Moreover, this conclusion has highlighted aspects of the American experience that have made it possible for higher education in the USA to adjust reasonably smoothly to expansion. However, it has to be accepted that national systems are a product of their own historical circumstances and it remains problematic whether practices that seem to work effectively in one context can be grafted smoothly onto another, perhaps quite different, context. However, the idea of policy transference is fashionable and undoubtedly governments have looked abroad for higher education policy ideas.

What is more significant is the emergence of global pressures including cross-national competition, which will undoubtedly incorporate the emerging 'for-profit' American higher education sector as it markets itself internationally. So, rather than the American system acting as a model for others to follow, it is but one source of ideas as all systems, including the American, adjust to pressures for change. Besides the much-trumpeted idea of economic globalisation there is the more tangible impact of regional pressures. For example, it is evident that some of the continental models (for example, France, Germany and Italy) were forced to recognise weaknesses in their systems of higher education in part because of unfavourable comparisons across the European Union (EU). Did their universities provide effective support for their economies within the context of a more competitive market? Why should able students from affluent middle-class families study at home when universities overseas apparently offered high-quality degree programmes in a more structured and supportive environment? Or will students be attracted to cheaper overseas higher educational programmes, perhaps at universities with 'glamorous' locations?

Although the impact of formal agreements (for example, the Bologna Declaration) have yet to make a significant impact, it is evident that increasingly within the EU social policy will be shaped by a European dimension. It is not that the EU will simply impose its will, but more likely that local reformers will look to the EU to provide them with the resources to implement changes in their national systems. This is particularly important in Poland, as a new EU member, which has to demonstrate its democratic credentials as it seeks tangible financial resources to implement change. The consequence is that access policies, even if they continue to be formulated in a national context, will be required to respond to external pressures, including formal international agreements.

The case studies we have presented show very different intensities and forms of engagement with access policy within the particular national contexts. In Britain, and more particularly England, the political intrusion, although ebbing and flowing in strength, has been persistent with the focus very much upon the question of social equity. The USA has experienced the same intensity of concern but with the focus on race and ethnicity. Moreover, the political battles in the USA have been fought out indirectly, within the context of the courts. Furthermore, in spite of the importance of the issue, it has loomed less large than the parallel debate in the UK given the much earlier expansion of the system and the more ready acceptance of diversity, pluralism and the private–public mix.

Interestingly, it is the smaller states in our study – Scotland, the Nordic countries, and the Netherlands – where, although access issues have penetrated the political agenda, they have not done so with the same intensity as in England. In recent years access policy within the United Kingdom has diverged and Scottish sentiment is strongly of the opinion that this is an issue that has been handled more effectively in Scotland than in England. The Dutch and Nordic countries, although experiencing greater diversification and a somewhat enlarged private input in recent years, have made the transition to mass systems without experiencing undue trauma. They appear to have established agreed strategies for handling the social equity issues. It is impossible not to speculate on the significance of the relatively small populations of these countries, their long-established and stable traditions of higher education accompanied by a high commitment to the value of education, their comparative social homogeneity (at least in terms of class and racial composition), the existence of consensual political traditions and – perhaps above all – their prosperity. The contrast with Poland could hardly be more vivid – a higher educational system decimated by political turmoil over a long period of time, the dominance of external political pressures (it has been much more than a question of accommodating them), and acute economic difficulties. What is remarkable about Poland is the extent of the changes to the overall character of the system of higher education since the fall of communism coupled with the continuing commitment to an expanding, open and free public access model.

The great continental systems of France, Germany and Italy represent probably the most interesting models of continuity and change. On the one hand there is the continuity of access values (with the fascinating dualism of meritocracy and open access in the French model) coupled with the hesitant introduction of newly constructed degree programmes and the increasing student (consumer!) preference for vocational degrees. But in both Germany and Italy there are evident stirrings of elitism, driven as much, if not more, by the state's recognition that mass higher education needs to accommodate research excellence and, in this respect, it is interesting to note that the French grandes écoles have broadened their role to become research institutions in addition to training the nation's leading administrative and political cadre.

So, in each nation state we see interesting interactions between contemporary pressures for change and past traditions. The extent to which that interactive process of change is politically driven, certainly in terms of access to higher education, is a matter for empirical investigation. What is certain, however, is that mass national systems of higher education cannot be isolated from the outside world and that they either negotiate meaningful relationships to the dominant external and internal social forces – whether these are expressed politically or through the market – or they perish. Or, perhaps what is worse, they become increasingly irrelevant.

Index